Your Own Worst Enemy

Your Own Worst Enemy

How to Overcome Career Self-Sabotage

Andrew J. DuBrin

amacom

American Management Association

This publication is designed to provide accurate and authoritative
information in regard to the subject matter covered. It is sold with
the understanding that the publisher is not engaged in rendering
legal, accounting, or other professional service. If legal advice or
other expert assistance is required, the services of a competent
professional person should be sought.

Library of Congress Cataloging-in-Publication Data

DuBrin, Andrew J.
    Your own worst enemy : how to overcome career self-sabotage
    / Andrew J. DuBrin.
        p.   cm.
    Includes bibliographical references and index.
    ISBN 0-8144-5033-4 (hardcover)
    ISBN 0-8144-7861-1 (pbk.)
    1. Career development.   2. Success in business.   I. Title.
HF5381.D814   1992
650.1—dc20   91-30484
                                                       CIP

First AMACOM paperback edition 1993.

Printing number

10   9   8   7   6   5   4   3   2   1

Once
again
to
Carol Bowman,
the Total Woman

Contents

Acknowledgments

*M*y primary thanks on this project go to the hundreds of people who have shared their stories about career self-sabotage with me or my researchers. Many of their case histories are found in this book. Abundant thanks are due my editor at AMACOM, Andrea Pedolsky, for seeing the merit in this project when it was still in the preliminary proposal stage. Ms. Pedolsky offered many valuable suggestions that have helped shape the content, structure, and writing style of this book.

Carol Bowman, the woman in my life, receives my gratitude for her interest in my work and for her contribution to my peace of mind and happiness. Thanks also to my immediate family members and to the other people close to me: Melanie DuBrin, Douglas DuBrin, Drew DuBrin, Molly Clifford, Rosemary DuBrin, Tom Bowman, and Kristine Bowman.

Introduction

$\mathcal{D}$o you have a pattern of doing things like

- Losing your wallet or keys the morning of a big event in your life, thus occupying yourself with your loss rather than concentrating on (and enjoying) the occasion? As a result your performance is substandard.
- Investing extraordinary amounts of mental and physical energy in a new job, then slowly realizing that this job really isn't best for you? As a result you start looking for a new position without having established a good record of accomplishment.
- Criticizing powerful people in your organization in such a way that they become embarrassed, annoyed, and vengeful? As a result, a powerful person vetoes your next nomination for a promotion.
- Conducting your personal life so chaotically that preoccupation with your problems drains energy from your career?

You might be doing one or more of these things because you are caught up in career self-sabotage. A person practicing self-sabotage frequently fails at tasks that he or she has the ability to perform. Or the person does not reach attainable goals. Strangely enough, the self-saboteur creates the very conditions that lead to the setback. To create additional hardship, the self-sabotaging person often fails to take advantage of alternatives that are clearly available (such as refusing debt counseling in the midst of financial chaos).

Self-sabotage thus involves doing things against your best

interests, even though you probably could do otherwise. Several aphorisms—"shooting yourself in the foot" and "being your own worst enemy"—get to the heart of the problem. Sometimes the self-saboteur appears to be driven by an unconscious mental process akin to the death wish suggested by psychoanalysts. In many other instances of self-sabotage, the victims are conscious of their path toward self-defeat. Yet they stand by helplessly watching the carnage. The terms *self-defeating behavior, self-destruction,* and *self-handicapping* all refer to this same hidden barrier to career success.

The purpose of this book is to help serious-minded career people overcome their hidden barriers to success. *Barriers* refers to tendencies toward self-defeating, self-destructive, and self-handicapping actions. You will find many notes of optimism here despite the pessimistic subject matter of the book. I hope to help you overcome your blocked potential by explaining the nature of self-sabotage, analyzing the self-defeating actions of others, and presenting a plan for conquering these hidden barriers.

Perhaps you are a close friend or relative of a career self-saboteur. If so, I think you will gain insight into what is happening and therefore learn how to help the person headed toward career destruction.

Identifying and controlling your hidden barriers to career success is a liberating experience. If you stop working against your own best interests, you will achieve more success and happiness. For example, if you stop getting into arguments with people who are trying to help, you will be much freer to enjoy being productive. Even an MBA from the Kellogg School of Northwestern University or the Harvard Business School cannot realize the potential of his or her knowledge and status if ensnared by a hidden barrier to success. If you are your own worst enemy, you have to rehabilitate yourself before you can accomplish your stated goals.

I am concerned primarily with the person who has embarked upon a promising career but is engaging in behavior that can lead to failure, mediocrity, or unfilled potential. My attention is less focused on the person who has self-destructed right off the career launching pad, or the person who makes one out-of-character mistake. Being convicted of driving while intoxicated once in your career, or dozing off at one planning meeting, is not necessarily career self-sabotage. Much more significant is a *pattern* of creating your own roadblocks to success.

Self-sabotage, self-defeat, self-destruction, or self-handicapping can surface at any career stage. Many students flunk out of college simply because they choose not to hand in written assignments even in courses in which they are doing well. A thirty-six-year-old regional sales manager at a computer company sacrificed her chances for promotion to vice-president by insulting her boss during a staff meeting. At approximately age 52, Senator Gary Hart tossed away his chances for the Democratic presidential nomination by involving himself in an indiscreet extramarital affair.

This book is an offshoot of many years of working with, speaking to, and writing about career professionals. My analysis is that many of us create conditions for derailment by erecting our own barriers to career success. Understanding more about self-defeating behavior, including taking a candid look at your own tendencies in this direction, could provide the breakthrough in your career.

You will find valuable information both in the prescriptions given in this book and in the descriptions of the mistakes, misdeeds, and misfortunes of many well-meaning people. The advice you receive may help you to overcome present tendencies toward self-defeating behavior and prevent future occurrences. For example, you may read a story about somebody who mysteriously ruins many big days in his life and recognize similarities between that person and yourself. After recognizing that you too have such a problem, you may be motivated to accept the advice given for overcoming such a problem.

Chapters 1 through 3 deal with measuring your current tendencies toward career self-sabotage and understanding its major causes. Chapters 4 through 10 describe many different forms of the hidden barriers to career success. Sometimes, however, only a thin line exists between a cause of self-defeating behavior and the behavior itself. For example, having a "loser script" may cause career self-sabotage. Yet acting as a loser is a form of career self-sabotage. Chapter 11 explains how organizations sometimes do things that push people toward career self-sabotage. The final chapter presents a master plan for overcoming hidden barriers to success, thus liberating you to become happier and more successful. The other chapters also contain useful advice.

This book has a rhythm and format that you should anticipate. First I introduce a key idea about self-sabotage and then present an illustrative case history or example. Next, I usually offer an analysis of how people find ways out of such a problem. At various points in the book I ask questions of you to help you think through how a problem might be overcome. Most chapters contain checklists of suggestions to get you started overcoming self-defeating behavior.

The vast majority of case histories presented in this book are originals, supplemented by a few examples of public figures. The original cases are disguised to protect the identities of people who have made mistakes that could be embarrassing if publicly exposed.

1

Gauging Your Hidden Barriers to Success

$\mathscr{T}$he work force is strewn with people who never achieve their career goals and never fulfill their potential. Instead of being relatively happy with their careers, they mutter to themselves and confidants, "Why does something terrible happen to me so often, just when things are going right?" Self-sabotaging people never realize their potential because problems continually arise, which they bring upon themselves. They always find a way to trip themselves up, fall on their own swords, shoot themselves in the foot, or bring about self-imposed misery.

Some of these self-saboteurs may be people whose consumption of alcohol and other drugs blocks them from achieving important goals or are otherwise engaged in a wide variety of self-defeating behaviors. Among them are procrastinators, negative self-talkers, people with an irresistible impulse to insult key people, power abusers, sexual harassers, and those who fear success. Even if you have yet to commit a flagrant act of self-sabotage, you could still be harboring inner tendencies in that direction. Understanding self-defeating behavior may help you prevent it from surfacing.

Let's begin our exploration of self-sabotage—and of what can be done to deal with the problem—with Tim.

Tim received his bachelor's degree in business administration twenty years ago, and today works the night shift as a custodial supervisor for an office maintenance company. He earns much less than he did at the peak of his career. Tim is also much more disgruntled than in the past.

After graduating from college, Tim spent three years in a management training program at General Electric. Unsure as to which business function interested him the most, Tim welcomed the opportunity to be rotated through various departments in his division of GE. After six months of employment, Tim received his first performance review. Although he was rated as meeting expectations, Tim's supervisor noted that he had "a tendency to not follow through on important assignments. For example, he was one week late in assembling figures for a competitive report on dishwashers. Another time, he called in sick the day it was his turn to accompany me on a report to top management."

Tim continued to receive mediocre performance evaluations for two years. His supervisor advised him that GE was not displeased enough with his performance to put him on probation. Nevertheless, it was apparent that he did not have the potential for management responsibilities. Rather than face an indefinite time in an entry-level position, Tim searched for another job. Several months later, he found a position as an assistant buyer for a medium-size manufacturer of consumer appliances. Tim's supervisor assured him that he had made the right career decision. "A fresh start might be just what you need to pull yourself together," he said.

It appeared that Tim's boss was right. Tim's career blossomed at the new company. Within one year he was promoted from assistant to junior buyer. His purchasing responsibilities were small, but what Tim did he did well. Tim relished the idea that he was now being treated as a somebody. Suppliers telephoned him regularly, and complimented his choice of clothing and sense of humor. When Tim was late getting specifications ready for a supplier, the supplier would never complain. It was the vendor's role to please Tim.

Tim felt he now had his career under control. He was adored by his suppliers (as long as he placed orders with them), and they helped him perform various job duties such as preparing reports for his company. Within three years, Tim was promoted from junior buyer to buyer, based on his receiving satisfactory performance appraisals. His employer continued to prosper, and Tim continued to avoid any bouts of dreadful job performance. At the beginning of his eighth year with the company, Tim was promoted to senior buyer, as a reward for his length of service and satisfactory performance.

As a senior buyer, Tim was responsible for negotiating multimillion-dollar contracts. During the day, and while he drifted off to sleep at night, thoughts of power and control would often race through Tim's mind. A smile would emerge, as Tim would think to himself, "Finally, I'm home free. I'm getting the treatment I deserve."

Tim soon thought of more ways to expand his power and control.

Gradually, he placed more demands on suppliers. It began innocently at lunch. Tim would strongly suggest, when a supplier came in for a luncheon meeting initiated by his employer, that the supplier pick up the tab. When Tim visited a supplier, he insisted that the supplier pay for the lunch. Most of the suppliers would have preferred that Tim occasionally pay for lunch, but they did not complain out of fear of losing a customer.

When the year-end holiday season approached, Tim made subtle comments about the season of giving and generosity toward your friends. One fall, Tim noted that a major supplier of his company was located in Cincinnati, the site of the upcoming World Series. Tim telephoned the supplier and explained that he would warmly welcome a pair of tickets to two Series games, along with transportation and lodging. When the supplier's sales representative equivocated, Tim insisted that honoring his wish was simply a cost of doing business.

The sales representative discussed the issue with his manager. She, in turn, called Tim's boss. The sales manager and Tim's boss set up a time when the sales representative would telephone Tim. A sting operation was established by having the security officer from Tim's company tape the conversation. At the completion of the call, the security officer walked into Tim's office and escorted him off the premises. After the company sought advice from legal counsel, Tim was terminated.

For a year Tim sought another position in purchasing, before accepting the fact that his tarnished reputation as a buyer blocked reemployment in his own field. His job-hunting strategy then shifted to accepting whatever employment he could find that would come close to meeting his expenses. A family friend who managed an office-cleaning service decided to give Tim a fresh start as a custodial supervisor. "However," said Tim's new boss, "screw up once and you're history."

Maybe the shock of being fired will help Tim develop the insights he needs to prevent further self-sabotage. As his career developed, his self-defeating behavior had already pushed him down a notch on the occupational ladder. Tim might not have tumbled if he had developed insights into his early-career tendency to defeat his own purposes. The reports he submitted late at General Electric were telltale signals of self-sabotage, at least to an outside observer. If Tim had had insight into the possible implications of not completing his work on time, he might have been alert to other signs of handicapping himself. The pattern of greed he developed as a buyer were full-blown manifestations of self-defeating career behavior.

Part of Tim's problem was that he remained too insular and secretive. Also, he didn't get caught for a long time. If he had discussed what constitutes ethical and appropriate behavior with other buyers, he might have become sensitized to how far gluttony can be pushed. Instead, he developed a private code of buyer ethics.

One might argue that if Tim were rational, logical, and intelligent, he would have known how far to push his luck. The compelling counterargument is that the normal rules of logic and rationality do not apply to self-sabotage, self-defeat, and self-destruction. Emotions and other inner forces can compel us to do things that any detached outside observer with wisdom would tell us were dangerous to our career health.

Examining Your Tendencies Toward Self-Sabotage

Self-sabotage exists in degrees. At one extreme lie people who are so self-destructive that they have very limited careers and wrecked personal lives. People with full-blown self-defeating personalities are chronically dissatisfied, and work diligently to undermine their own achievements. Pure self-defeating people, for example, often moan and groan about how bad life is and how few good breaks they receive. At the same time, they engage in many self-defeating acts, such as publicly criticizing the boss or losing important reports.

In the mid-range of self-sabotaging behavior are people who engage in such activities only periodically. From time to time they mess things up for themselves, for instance, by waging a campaign to shoot down a senior executive's project. At the other extreme are people with almost no negligible tendencies toward defeating their own interests.

The questionnaire is based on the signs and symptoms of self-sabotage. It will give you tentative insight into the degree to which you may be sabotaging yourself[1] and alert you to a range of subtle and not-so-subtle self-defeating behaviors. A given statement on the questionnaire could serve as a signal for you to get some aspect of your behavior under control.

The Self-Sabotage Questionnaire

Directions: Indicate how accurately each of the statements below describes or characterizes you, using the following five-point scale: (0) very inaccurately, (1) inaccurately, (2) midway between inaccurately and accurately, (3) accurately, (4) very accurately. Answer every question. You might consider discussing some of the questions with a family member, close friend, or work associate. Another person's feedback may prove helpful in providing accurate answers to some of the questions.

Score

1. Other people have said that I am my own worst enemy. _____
2. I generally avoid situations in which it appears I will have a good time. _____
3. If I don't do a perfect job, I often feel worthless. _____
4. I am my own harshest critic. _____
5. Most of my time is devoted to other people's goals or problems rather than to my own. _____
6. When engaged in a sport or other competitive activity, I find a way to blow a substantial lead right near the end. _____
7. Past setbacks have blocked me from moving on to new challenges. _____
8. When I make a mistake, I can usually identify another person to blame for my mistake. _____
9. I expect to fail on my most challenging work assignments. _____
10. I spend time with people who belittle me and my thoughts or ideas. _____
11. My tendency to procrastinate is sometimes severe. _____
12. I waste a lot of time. _____
13. When I really want something, I will act impulsively to get it. _____
14. I often feel irritable and moody. _____
15. I often wish I were someone else. _____
16. I have trouble focusing on what is really important to me. _____
17. I have trouble taking criticism, even from friends. _____

18. My fear of seeming stupid often prevents me from asking questions or offering my opinion. _____
19. I trigger other people into getting angry with me, and then I feel hurt, defeat, or humiliated. _____
20. I often find myself saying, "I don't feel up to it." _____
21. I tend to expect the worst in most situations. _____
22. I am self-sacrificing even when nobody asks me to make a sacrifice. _____
23. Many times I have rejected people who treat me well. _____
24. When I have an important project to complete, I usually get sidetracked, and then miss the deadline. _____
25. It is difficult for me to acknowledge that I am having a good time. _____
26. After having enjoyed myself, it is typical of me to feel sad suddenly. _____
27. I usually feel guilty after having had a good time. _____
28. When others offer help, I usually reject it even if I need their help. _____
29. I typically allow barely enough travel time to get to an appointment, then get angry at myself for having to rush. _____
30. I hold on to my friends even when they often insult me. _____
31. I choose work assignments that lead to disappointments even when better options are clearly available. _____
32. I frequently misplace things such as my keys, then get very angry at myself. _____
33. I am concerned that if I take on much more responsibility people will expect too much from me. _____
34. I avoid situations, such as competitive sports, where people can find out how good or bad I really am. _____
35. People describe me as the "office clown." _____
36. My expectations in life are far higher than those of most people. _____
37. I crave frequent recognition and attention. _____
38. I have an insatiable demand for money and power. _____

39. When negotiating with others, I hate to grant any concessions. _____
40. For me to be content I need a big thrill. _____
41. When something terrible happens, such as the serious illness of a loved one, I become immobilized. _____
42. I seek revenge for even the smallest hurts. _____
43. I feel doomed to fail. _____
44. I have a blinding ego. _____
45. When I receive a compliment or other form of recognition, I usually feel I don't deserve it. _____
46. Many times I have tried to make friends with people whom I knew in advance would reject me. _____
47. To be honest, I choose to suffer. _____
48. I regularly enter into conflict with people who try to help me. _____
49. I try to get away with as much as I can on the job. _____
50. I'm a loser. _____

Total Score   _____

Scoring and Interpretation. Add your answers to all the questions to obtain your total score. Your total score provides a rough index of your tendency to be self-sabotaging or self-defeating. The higher your score, the more probable it is that you create conditions to bring about your own setbacks, disappointments, and failures. The lower your score, the less likely it is that you are a self-saboteur. The interpretations offered are not based on answers to specific questions but on the general level of a person's score. Such is the case with most personality questionnaires. More precise guidelines for interpreting your score are as follows:

0–50: You appear to have very few tendencies toward self-sabotage. If this interpretation is supported by your own positive feelings toward your life and yourself, you are in good shape with respect to self-defeating behavior tendencies. However, stay alert to potential self-sabotaging tendencies that could develop at later stages in your career.

51–100: You may have some mild tendencies toward self-sabotage. It could be that you do things occasionally that defeat your own purposes. A person in this category, for example, might write an angry memo to an executive expressing disagreement with a decision made by the executive that adversely affects his or her operation. It would make sense to review the actions you have taken during the past six months to decide if any of them have been self-sabotaging. Invite a confidant to lunch, or for an after-work drink, to obtain his or her opinion as to your tendencies toward self-defeating behavior.

101–150: You show signs of engaging in self-sabotage. You probably have thoughts, and carry out actions, that could be blocking you from achieving important work and personal goals. People whose scores place in this category characteristically engage in negative self-talk that lowers their self-confidence and makes them appear weak and indecisive to others. Statements of this kind include "I can't do it," "I'm not the brightest person," "My education isn't the best," or "I'm no good with numbers."

People in this range frequently experience another problem. They sometimes sabotage their chances of succeeding on a project just to prove that their negative self-assessment is correct. A credit supervisor said she would be turned down for promotion to credit manager because top management thought she was unreliable. When invited out to dinner with the company controller to discuss the promotion, she declined the invitation, stating that she had to work late in the office. She was not offered the promotion, thus proving herself right. Her self-sabotaging behavior, of course, was to turn down the dinner invitation. The woman proved to herself and the company that she was unreliable.

If you scored in this range, you will most likely benefit from a careful study of the suggestions offered in this book. Also ask for feedback on your self-defeating tendencies from one or two confidants.

151–200: You most likely have a strong tendency toward self-sabotage. (Sometimes it is possible to obtain a high score on a test like this because you are going through an unusually stressful period in your life.) It is important for you to study this book carefully, and to look for useful hints for removing your hidden barriers to success. Equally important, you might discuss your tendencies toward undermining your own achievements with a mental health professional.

If you are as self-defeating as your questionnaire score suggests, you have to work hard to avoid thoughts and actions that will do permanent damage to your career. On the positive side, your candor in answering these questions could mean that you are looking for help and want to become less self-defeating.

Reversing Self-Sabotaging Tendencies Before They Become Self-Destructive

Throughout this book, and especially in Chapter 12, I describe methods for overcoming career self-sabotage. Among these tactics are: Stop blaming others for your problems; stop denying the existence of problems; make positive changes in your life; and visualize self-enhancing behavior. The process is not complicated, but it involves the most difficult task of career management. Instead of doing something relatively straightforward such as setting improvement goals, you are required to critically examine your own behavior. As you examine your actions and thoughts, search for early-warning signals of behavior that, if made public, could put your career in a tailspin. Many people either consciously or subconsciously block from their awareness their self-defeating behavior. Consequently, you may need to enlist a confidant to help you scan your behavior for hints of self-sabotage. Ask a former boss, for example, "While I was working for you, did I ever do *anything* that looked as if I were trying to hurt my own career?"

Again, self-insight into self-sabotage is not easy to come by. Many people spend over a year in psychotherapy before accepting the fact that they have been erecting barriers to their career success. You have to assume the mental set that you have a problem and that you are going to do whatever is necessary to deal with that problem. Raul, an advertising agency manager, is the exceptional person who did something constructive about his self-defeating behavior. You too can use his willingness to change a negative behavior pattern as a model. He was insightful enough to call a halt to his self-defeating behavior before he inflicted himself with a serious career wound.

Raul began his career as an assistant copywriter in an advertising agency. He chose advertising because he believed he had a creative contribution to make. Raul's career choice proved to be smart. He advanced rapidly, becoming an account executive by his mid-twenties. He handled increasingly larger accounts, and became an agency supervisor by age 30, with several account executives reporting to him. As Raul sized up the situation, he saw he was on a clear track to being invited into partnership in his firm.

If a partnership was not forthcoming in his own firm, Raul was confident that his track record would enable him to buy into partnership in another firm.

Impeccably dressed, with a confident smile and polished interpersonal skills, Raul appeared to be a gentleman and a winner. He had a problem, nevertheless, that was moving him, step by step, toward self-sabotage. Raul describes what happened:

"It took me a long time to admit it, but I was one of those subtle sexual harassers. I never did anything as crude as making vulgar comments to a woman who worked for our agency or for a client. Nor did I ever attempt to coerce a subordinate into having sex with me, or hang photos of nude women in my office.

"There were a couple of things I did do that could have gotten me into a lot of trouble. I've always had an irresistible impulse to brush up against women. I would make it look like an accident or a simple act of standing close as I worked with a woman on advertising copy or layouts. If she recoiled, I would move away immediately, respecting her rights. But if she stood still, I would leave my arm placed against her a little longer. What I was doing was certainly less brazen than what goes on in the subway thousands of times every rush hour.

"No woman ever criticized me for standing too close, so I continued with my friendly brushings. So long as I was unobtrusive, I didn't think I was harming anybody. Until I met the advertising manager of one of our small accounts. She was one of the most beautiful women I had ever seen, and I began to fantasize.

"On the few occasions I dealt with Laura, I felt uneasy and self-conscious. Face it, I had a schoolboy crush on her. Once or twice in our early planning sessions, Laura made passing mention of her husband. Feelings of jealousy flooded through me. I wondered if Laura would have wanted me if I had met her before she became involved with the man she married.

"I knew I was taking a risk, but I thought I had to make one stab at having an affair with Laura. One afternoon I telephoned her at her office. Laura's assistant said she knew Laura was in the building and that she would page her. This wasn't the scenario I imagined. It would have been better to talk to Laura when she was working alone in her office. Sounding preoccupied and distant, Laura said, 'What can I do for you? I thought we had things under control yesterday.'

"Awkwardly, I explained to Laura that this wasn't a business call. I wanted to know if she would be interested in having dinner with me any evening this week. 'I don't think so' was her curt response.

"I knew then that my fantasy about Laura could never come true.

Naively, I thought it would be business as usual with her company. To my shock, I received a letter two days later from Laura's firm explaining that our agency would not be invited to bid on any future contracts. Furthermore, an associate in Laura's office would now be our contact with the account.

"I brushed off the incident to my boss as one of those unfortunate whimsical changes of mind endemic in our business. I wondered if my boss had more details about Laura's reasons for the changes. I worried that if he did I might be asked to resign. As it worked out, my boss wasn't happy, but we were so busy with other accounts that he let the matter slide.

"The bad judgment I used in inviting Laura to dinner was an important last straw for me. It brought me to the idea that the office is no place to act out my sexual fantasies. What poor judgment I showed in making a move on a married woman who was also my client! The incident also helped bring into focus what was wrong with brushing up against women in the office. I was harassing and intimidating them and possibly creating a bad reputation for myself. I had found a self-indulgent way of jeopardizing my own career. The advertising world has enough people trying to do you in without you helping them along.

"I knew I couldn't make amends for years of harassing women, but at least I tried one apology. Several days later, one of the office assistants came in to help me review some figures. I casually mentioned that I wanted to apologize for invading her territorial space the other day. I told her I realized that I was so absorbed in my work that I momentarily forgot about common courtesy. She smiled and graciously said that she wasn't aware of any problem."

Raul achieved sudden insight into his tendencies toward self-sabotage before too much damage had been done. Raul's firm *did* lose one account under his supervision, and most likely Laura will not recommend Raul's firm to people in her network. If Raul has a deep-rooted problem, he will again find ways to sabotage his career. My analysis is that Raul is healthy enough to control his actions as a consequence of his narrow escape. He did become aware of his long-standing problem and felt some remorse.

Because warding off career self-sabotage begins with a candid self-assessment, I recommend that you scan the self-sabotage scale again and ponder carefully which behaviors and thoughts might be trouble spots for you. Corrective action might be required if even one of the statements on the Self-Sabotage Questionnaire pinpoints a problem area. One such statement appears as item number 1: "Other people have said that I am my own worst enemy." The spontaneous judgments of others, if often repeated, usually provide reliable feedback. It would be worth exploring what people mean when they say you are your own worst enemy. Investigate and see if you need to make some immediate changes.

Another key question is number 8: "When I make a mistake, I can usually identify another person to blame for my mistake." People who refuse to accept some responsibility for their mistakes fall into disfavor with others. They are often bypassed for promotion because they are perceived as being somewhat paranoid.

Knowing how and why so many people put nails in their own coffins can be helpful in overcoming your own hidden barriers to career success. This is the reason why the particular case histories you will be reading in the chapters ahead were chosen. Understanding the reasons why others have tripped up can help prevent you from falling down in the same way.

Assume, for example, that you read a case about a professional person whose career advancement was damaged by behaving immaturely (by telling inappropriate, gross jokes at meetings, for example). You might be triggered into keeping a lid on your own tendencies toward immaturity during working hours. A key theme of this book is that with proper insight and motivation people can learn to overcome and prevent self-defeating behavior.

In addition to explaining why people have engaged in self-defeating behavior, there are many examples of how people have overcome their problems. Understanding how others overcome self-sabotage can give you positive models for doing the same thing.

2

Self-Sabotaging Life Scripts

*E*arly in life our parents and other influential forces, including our peers and the popular culture, program our brains to act out certain life plans. These life plans are known as scripts. Our script determines what we do in many key situations in life. People fortunate enough to have winner scripts consistently emerge victorious. When a tough assignment needs doing, they get the job done. They salvage major accounts about to leave for a competitor; they introduce a successful product during a recession; they figure out how to run software that befuddles everybody else in the office; and they score a goal at the buzzer.

Unfortunately, others have scripts that program them toward damaging their careers and falling short of their potential. Paradoxically, much of this damage occurs just when things seem to be going well. Understanding these negative scripts is very important because the scripts are often a major contributor to self-sabotage. If you are sabotaging your career, it could be because of your script. Reading this chapter will help you understand how a self-sabotaging script can be changed.

Thousands of different scripts exist, all variations on positive and negative, winner and loser, themes. Here I describe eight self-sabotaging scripts found frequently in the workplace. All these scripts are reversible. Even if you do not believe that people are really programmed toward self-sabotage, you will recognize these scripts as behavior patterns that do more harm than good.

LOSER SCRIPTS

Make-Believe

1. Choking
2. The Short Attention Span
3. The Commitment Breaker
4. The Solo Performer
5. The Jealous Person
6. The Irresistible Impulse

Running Away From Problems

7. Friendship at All Costs
8. Biting the Hand That Feeds You

The Loser

The Loser is the master self-sabotaging script. All other self-defeating scripts are but variations and tributaries. Surprisingly, people with loser scripts are found at all occupational levels. If they have limited talent, energy, and formal education, they remain at the bottom rung of the occupational ladder. If they are more talented, energetic, and better educated, they may even rise to professional and managerial positions. But somehow, they screw up at their potential moment of greatness.

As explained by Dudley Bennett, a specialist in the study of scripts, there are two kinds of loser scripts.[1] In the first kind, losers indulge themselves in *make-believe*. They may dwell on the past, cling to old ways of doing things, feel sorry for themselves, and lament, "If I only had. . . ." Losers of this type spend their lives looking to be rescued or wishing for a magical solution to their problems. Many lottery players are acting out this type of loser script.

If we are in the category of the first type of loser, we may imagine a doomsday future and live with dread expectations. We worry about the negative consequences of everything, such as earthquakes, stock market crashes, recessions, and business failures. (Losers are often accurate predictors of negative events, but are poor predictors of good times.) We are so involved in imaginings of the past or future that we miss out on the realities of the present.

The second type of loser script centers around receiving applause and winning the approval of the majority or of key people. This type strives hard to achieve in order to overcome feelings of inadequacy. As Bennett says, "Congratulations from the powerful, rich, high in status, or elite are particularly gratifying because parental figures have always been the source of good things. Those delicious big strokes come from big folks."[2]

Both these loser scripts foster career self-sabotage, although the negative effect of the second is less obvious. Both scripts are substitutes for creating a real sense of self-worth. People who are content with themselves are able to accept the present. They are also able to feel positive about themselves without constant adulation from others.

Make-Believe

Choking

Acting out the loser script takes many forms. A good starting point in understanding loser scripts is to look at "choking." In athletics, as well as in the workplace, some people perform below their proven ability when the pressure is high. Part of the problem is that they become very tense and self-conscious when they know that big stakes are involved. Such was the situation with Teena, a professional photographer.

Teena had a mediocre childhood, with not much warmth and support from her parents. She recalls vividly having come home from school one day to announce triumphantly that she had been chosen as the yearbook photographer. Her father was too preoccupied watching television to do more than simply acknowledge her accomplishment. Teena then looked to her mother for a receptive audience. Teena's mother said that being appointed photographer was nice, but asked why she didn't try to become the yearbook editor.

Teena enjoyed her work as a yearbook photographer but had several uncomfortable experiences in shooting her assignments. Once she spent the afternoon shooting pictures of several clubs only to discover later that she had not loaded film into her 35mm camera. With much embarrassment, she contacted the clubs and explained that because of her forgetfulness she would have to retake the photos. Another time she ruined some action shots of a football game while developing them in the darkroom. As a substitute for the action shots, the yearbook had to use some uninspired shots of the stadium.

After graduating from high school, Teena studied commercial photography at a vocational institute. She then found employment as an associate in a photo store, but continued to look for a position as a photographer. Two years later, Teena found part-time work as an assistant photographer. Business at her employer's studio expanded rapidly, and Teena was offered a full-time position. At first, her employer was reluctant to offer Teena the job because she had knocked over the lights twice when they were on assignment. Teena assured her boss that such performances would not be repeated because tripping over the lights was highly unusual for her.

Teena performed satisfactorily for the next couple of years, including shooting many senior-year portraits. With her boss's confidence in her abilities restored, Teena was assigned a wedding to shoot. She was the main photographer, assisted by a part-time trainee. Teena tossed nervously in bed the night before the day of the wedding, but after reviewing her list of everything that needed to be taken to the wedding, she became confident that everything was properly planned and returned to bed to sleep peacefully.

Teena worked through the wedding shoot with much more confidence than she would have predicted. As she and her assistant were packing to return to the studio, Teena shrieked in disbelief, "I did it again. I screwed up. The whole assignment is ruined." "Why is it ruined?" asked the assistant. "I set the meter at the wrong film speed. We'll have nothing but junk. Forget it, I was never meant to be a photographer."

As it worked out, the photos were not completely ruined. With careful developing most of the negatives were salvaged, but the photos had a dull, flat look. The customers were unhappy, and the owner gave them a substantial discount off the agreed-upon price. Teena was so discouraged that she asked her boss never again to give her an independent assignment. She choked on her best opportunity to prove to herself and others that she was a competent photographer. Her only error was not adjusting the knob on her light meter to match the new high-speed film she was using. A ten-second adjustment would have saved the shoot. Teena had reviewed everything but this one tiny detail.

Teena might be able to bounce back from this one-time incident and gradually regain the confidence of her boss. But until she learns to overcome choking—her way of acting out the loser script—she will lose again and again. She needs to begin by emotionally understanding that she does choke, and then to practice not choking as often as possible. Teena must visualize peak performances in her mind beforehand, and then allow herself to convert them into reality. She is advised to imagine herself on an important shoot, taking care of every important detail and doing a masterful job.

If your tendency is to choke when a peak performance is required, you too could be struggling with a loser script. Review your past experiences under pressure so as to decide whether you do in fact have a tendency to choke. If this is the case, begin to imagine yourself not choking during a command performance.

The Short Attention Span

A clever way of remaining a loser is never to stick with a project or job long enough to be a winner. Having a short attention span is also a good cop-out. The person who doesn't stick around long enough to truly test his or her capabilities can think silently, "I know I could do it (whatever the *it* is) if I just didn't get bored so easily." Rob is an exemplar of this self-sabotaging script.

Fifty-two-year-old Rob has held a succession of jobs in the insurance field over the past thirty years. In each new position, Rob goes through a cycle in which he starts out working extremely hard, rises to the top, slacks off, then is either terminated or voluntarily seeks a new position.

Twenty-one years ago, Rob joined a large independent insurance agency and established himself as the leading producer. He was promoted to sales manager, and then became executive vice-president. Initially Rob devoted a great deal of time to his role as executive vice-president. Then he began working three-day weeks from June through October, taking Mondays and Fridays off as vacation days. On the days he was in the office, Rob took care of many personal errands. With so much time diverted from work, Rob was unable to meet most of his objectives. After Rob coasted for two years, the owners of the agency forced him to resign.

Rob then found employment with another large independent agency. After two years of whirlwind performance, Rob was appointed as vice-president of the multi-state branch operations of the firm. He worked extremely hard for twelve months and produced excellent results. After encountering some problems, such as a high number of claims, Rob began to slack off. He began taking long weekends, running personal errands, and shortening his work days. Rather than firing Rob, the agency offered him a position as an insurance sales representative.

Rob began his sales position with a burst of activity, but his sales soon fell below quota. He was terminated for unacceptable performance, and is now planning to borrow money to purchase his own agency. He pleads with his potential creditors. "This time things will be different. It will be my own show. I'll stick with it."[3]

Rob contends that this time things will be different. In contrast to the past, he will sustain a high level of energy and commitment in his next position. But things won't be different unless Rob analyzes whether he is acting out a loser or a winner script. Until people confront this basic issue, they have a minimal chance of shucking a loser script. If Rob thinks he has inherited a loser script, he can decide not to live by it any longer. A script can be changed by deciding consciously to make the change.

Perhaps you too can benefit from examining your script. So far, does it more closely resemble a winner or a loser script? If you are playing out a loser script, make a commitment to yourself to change scripts.

The Commitment Breaker

A friend of mine told me he was heartbroken and perplexed. He had finally found the woman of his dreams. Within four months they became engaged, and within six months unengaged. She broke off the engagement, and returned the ring. The woman told him not to take it personally because she had broken four previous wedding engagements. My friend learned about The Commitment Breaker script the hard way. The same script can lead to career self-sabotage.

The executive job hopper exemplifies the commitment breaker. Often these people rationalize breaking written contracts or unwritten agreements by contending that they are executives-of-fortune. They are professional managers, available to the highest bidder, to whomever offers the biggest money and the greatest job challenge. A reputation for high-level success is necessary to becoming an executive job hopper. People with much less talent and visibility who make a rapid series of job changes are simply perceived as occupationally unstable. Usually they are forced to take jobs at much lower levels than they desire.

A paradox about The Commitment Breaker script is that it can be disguised as a winner script for many years. A case in point *could* be Rick Pitino, the popular, articulate, and personable basketball coach of the Kentucky Wildcats since the 1990–1991 season. At age 32, Pitino had already been a successful coach at five schools. Among his accomplishments were reversing losing records of both a college team and a professional team. Pitino decided to leave as coach of the New York Knicks to coach at the University of Kentucky. He had three years remaining on his contract with the Knicks, who complied with his request to break the contract. One reason that such contracts can be broken is that a disgruntled coach is unlikely to perform at his best.

Pitino rightfully considered the Kentucky job one of the biggest plums in college athletics. Although Kentucky traditionally has had one of the country's outstanding basketball teams, the program faltered after it was penalized for many violations by the National Collegiate Athletic Association. Pitino has made an excellent start at Kentucky, and we wish him the very best. But should he leave Kentucky early, we suspect Pitino's broken commitment script will sabotage his career. If Pitino can reverse this script, he stands a good chance of becoming a legendary basketball coach.

Are you a commitment breaker? You could be if you answer affirmatively to most of these questions:

1. Have you been engaged to three or more people?
2. Have you voluntarily left three or more jobs in a five-year time span?
3. Do you have a drawer full of major projects you planned to undertake but never got around to doing?

4. Have you canceled more than three life insurance policies?
5. Have you attended more than three schools in the pursuit of one degree?

If your pattern is one of breaking commitments, start the long comeback process. Stick with your present commitments until they reach a logical conclusion. An example would be leaving your job only after you have made a major contribution and after your successor has been identified.

The Solo Performer

Poor team play, described in Chapter 5, can bring about career self-sabotage. It can also be part of The Solo Performer script that represents a deeper-rooted reason for self-defeat. Solo performers are so programmed to work independently that they fail in team efforts. A seasoned entrepreneur describes a self-sabotaging solo performer:

Dave is a twenty-five-year veteran sales representative in the furniture industry. He is an affable, well-educated, and responsible person with a quick mind and excellent sales skills. I first met him fifteen years ago when we shared adjacent booths at a small regional furniture show. We kept in touch over the following couple of years.

Approximately two years later, I was working as a sales manager when I received a call from Dave inquiring about any sales openings we might have. When we met he told me of his disillusionment with promises made him in his current position that never materialized. At the time we had no positions available. A few weeks later, though, I contacted Dave regarding a position on the West Coast. He expressed strong interest despite the relocation involved. The human resources people checked out his background to their satisfaction. Shortly thereafter, Dave joined the company as a sales rep in the Pacific Northwest.

Dave was welcomed by the dealers in the area, several of whom contacted me about the good job he was doing. Previously this territory was doing very poorly. In Dave's hands it began to pick up handsomely. The regional manager was delighted with the sales results. He was also pleased about not having to travel to the Pacific Northwest territory himself. Although the territory continued to show positive sales results, the manager became concerned about Dave's poor attention to planning and paperwork. Dave's chronic complaining about the demands being placed on him by the company also concerned the manager. Because his overall performance was still good, we decided to stay in closer touch with Dave and give him some support and encouragement in the areas of concern.

Upon contacting Dave myself, I mentioned the need for providing more management information from the field. Dave's response was negative, almost hostile. He used my phone call as an opening to complain bitterly about his manager and myself. He had no specific suggestions other than stating that he did not have time for such "nonsense." The regional manager and I passed it off as a guy having a bad day.

Because he was becoming more belligerent, we invited Dave to meet with a human resources specialist. Several conversations were held with Dave regarding the real source of his problems. We suggested that the company would pay for professional counseling, but Dave quickly rejected the offer. Through these conversations and feedback from others, we discovered a pattern of Dave doing a fine job of selling, but only wanting to work on his own terms. We discovered that he had probably been terminated by all four of his previous employers. In each case it had to do not with his selling but with his difficulty in working with management.

We then gave Dave an opportunity to work more on his own terms. Still he became increasingly difficult to deal with, and we eventually had to fire him. Dave soon found another sales position within the furniture industry as a regional manager. He reported to an old friend of his who was a division manager in a large corporation. Within three years, Dave was once again terminated for his unwillingness to work smoothly with management.

While Dave is currently employed in a sales position, people who know him well expect a similar scenario to be replayed. People who know Dave believe the only explanation for his self-destructive behavior is his tendency to blame all his problems in life on his job. Despite his ability to be quite charming, he has never been able to sustain a relationship with a woman. Neither can he hold on to sales management responsibility.

Because he has outstanding sales ability, he is invariably successful in the short term. Yet he can't hold on to a personal relationship or work well with other people in the company. His extreme self-confidence as a sales representative causes him to assume that his other problems are the fault of circumstances beyond his control. Even when confronted by these inconsistencies, he blames outside forces, such as management wrongdoing. Those who know Dave doubt that he will ever change his pattern, but they are also confident that his exceptional sales skills will keep him employed, although unhappy.[4]

The explanation just offered for Dave's problems is valid as far as it goes. He does blame outside circumstances for his troubles. But at a deeper level, Dave is playing out The Solo Performer script. He rebels when he has to get closely involved with management and submit to their demands, such as for marketing information from the field. Dave also has difficulty with the team aspect of a relationship with a woman. He prefers to control the relationship by making the major decisions and circumventing the give-and-take characteristic of modern couples.

According to author John Wareham, a line of self-inquiry that might help Dave overcome his losing script is to ask himself, "What happens to people like me?"[5] If honest, he might visualize an embittered and burned-out sales rep facing the same old battles with management year after year. Equally disturbing might be the visualization of never having a long-term relationship with a woman. Such disturbing scenarios might help Dave change his script.

To check out the possible self-sabotaging element in your script, ask yourself, "What happens to a person like me?" If you envision a dreary scenario, it is time to begin working on a more winning script.

The Jealous Person

Everyone experiences envy and jealousy at some point in their lives. Both emotions involve being resentful of another's success and advantages. Jealousy, however, involves a stronger emotion, thus creating more potential for self-defeating behavior. An occasional bout of jealousy is natural, particularly when a rival receives a big promotion. The Jealous Person script involves a lifelong pattern of becoming so jealous that it creates career and personal setbacks. Steve, a middle manager in a gas and electric company, lived out the Jealous Person script to his disadvantage.

When Steve was 25, one of his closest friends became involved with a woman Steve had dated several times previously. Steve was infatuated with the woman, but she had no interest in sustaining a relationship with him. When the woman in question moved in with Steve's friend, Steve went through an emotional upheaval. Confused and hurt, he refused to play golf with his friend any longer, and barely acknowledged his presence when they met.

To help overcome his feelings of jealousy, Steve courted and won the affection of the first woman who expressed any interest in him. One year later they were married. Shortly after the marriage began, Steve realized that he neither loved nor particularly liked his wife. The couple have remained married, while Steve continues to be jealous of men who have girlfriends or wives they care for deeply.

Steve's progress at the utility company has been modest despite his desire to advance and to have more status than his peers. One of his former managers offers this explanation for Steve's modest progress: "The poor guy goes bananas when anybody gets something he thought he deserved. One time he wasn't chosen for a task force to study the program for subsidizing the utility bills of the disadvantaged. He kept pestering me to find out why he wasn't chosen, and what could be done about the situation. Steve also went over my head to talk to my boss. The incident backfired because top management took a very dim view of his maneuvering.

"Steve had the same kind of problem when he was bypassed for promotion. His face would wince in pain when somebody with equal or less experience received a promotion. One time he threatened to quit if the company didn't appreciate his contribution. I told Steve to do what he thought best because we were well staffed with managers. I thought his childish attitude detracted from his effectiveness as a manager."

Wareham suggests one approach to dismantling his Jealous Person script that Steve might take would be to realistically assess his "comfort level."[6] What is there about his background that dictates that to be happy he must have a flaming romance, be appointed to key task forces, or have a better-than-average middle manager position? Early-life influences shape people's perceptions of what they need to be comfortable. Maybe self-analysis will help Steve realize that his parents and relatives settled for much less in life than he requires. Although many people expect to achieve at a higher level than their parents, many baby boomers are willing to settle for less.

If Steve doesn't reassess his comfort level (or accelerate his accomplishment level), his jealousy will continue to be self-defeating. What about you? Is your comfort level so high that it propels you into becoming jealous of too many people? If your answer is yes, challenge your comfort level and bring it down a notch.

The Irresistible Impulse

Falling prey to an irresistible impulse just once, such as playing the lottery with petty-cash funds, can sabotage one's career. Living out a life script of submitting to such impulses dramatically increases the chances for self-sabotage. Evelyn, whose career reached an early plateau, thinks she has finally overcome her Irresistible Impulse script. She presents a few of the revealing details:

"Ever since childhood I was wild. I was the proverbial tomboy. Growing up in the city, I ran with a crazy crowd. I was the biggest risk taker of them all. We would climb up fire escapes and water towers. We would hitch rides on the backs of trucks. The group dared me to smoke a joint in the high school assembly hall and I did it. I dressed up in rags and panhandled on the subways. Anything for kicks.

"Dropping out of high school didn't exactly help my career. One year of working in a garment factory in Brooklyn convinced me to make something of my life. I studied for and got a GED (General Equivalency Diploma) on the first shot. Then I enrolled in a computer science course at a community college. All the time I was still operating a sewing machine for a living.

"My craziness almost got me thrown out of community college. I had an assignment to write a paper on how food affects your health. I went to the library to do my research. It was overwhelming. The guides the librarian showed me listed hundreds of books and articles on my topic. The assignment was giving me a headache. Then I found a *Reader's Digest* article that was perfect. Since the *Digest* is written in plain English, I decided to copy the article word for word. I threw in a few spelling mistakes so it didn't look like plagiarism. Little did I know my instructor read every article she could find on my topic. Besides that she kept back copies of *Reader's Digest* in her apartment.

"My article sounded familiar. So my instructor searched and found it in one of her old *Digests*. She nailed me with an F. She told me to meet her at her office after class. I gave her a story about my struggle in life. She decided to let me off the hook, if I would do another paper. This time I did an honest job.

"After getting my associate's degree I found a job working with computers in an engineering department. I spent most of my time grinding out some numbers. About 90 percent of my day was spent in my cubicle, at my computer. A friend of mine told me about a computerized blackjack game.

He said it was quite entertaining, and could be played on the job. It was strictly against the rules to play computer games at my company. But I had to do something to break up my routine a little.

"Jerry, my boss, walked by my cubicle one afternoon, and overheard me say "hit me." I explained that I was trying out the blackjack software just to relieve the boredom. Jerry at least listened to me. But he had to give me a verbal warning for playing a computer game. He told me the warning would not go on my records, nor would it affect my chances for advancement. But if I were caught again, it would go on my permanent employee record.

"I thought that if I could play the game a few minutes a day and keep my mouth shut, I wouldn't be caught again. Two weeks later, at four in the afternoon, when my work was slow, I dealt myself a few hands. Jerry walked over to my cubicle. Zap. He made a written record of the violation, and told me that If I were caught again I would be fired.

"I can't get anywhere in my company now. If I quit, I would probably get a lousy reference. I'm still in my cubicle, and I don't know what I'll do next. Life is very dull right now."

Evelyn deserves credit for accepting the fact that being impulsive has gotten her into trouble both in the past and present. A danger signal, however, is that Evelyn is now frustrated. While frustrated, people often return to true form and act out another scene from their script. If Evelyn can resist the irresistible impulse, and patiently rebuild her reputation, she may be able to incorporate a winner script into her life.

You may be suffering from the irresistible impulse problem if you do such things as—

- Grab pastry or beverages from a serving table outside the room of a conference to which you have not been invited.
- Borrow equipment for personal use from the office.
- Poke into files when you have no need to investigate.
- Gain access to computerized information by breaking down the code.
- Snoop into a friend's wallet while she is in another room.

Running Away From Problems

Running Away From Problems is one of the most damaging loser scripts because success requires confronting problems. Almost everybody faces some career adversity. Successful people are usually able to overcome these setbacks and move forward to tackle new challenges.

People whose lives are directed by the Running Away script typically run away from big and small problems both on and off the job. Have you noticed, for example, how some people stuff in a closet an electronic gadget they cannot readily learn to operate? The problem solvers stick with the gadget until they learn how to operate it, or get help. Often they take the same approach to job problems. A middle-aged man named Sean exemplifies the pattern of Running Away From Problems.

Sean currently teaches part-time at a business school. His work history includes stints as an electronics technician in the Navy, as a police officer, a retail store manager, a quality assurance manager, and a computer project manager.

In all these jobs, Sean was either fired or quit because he failed to handle a difficult situation. When problems arose between himself and his supervisor at the retail store concerning handling customer complaints, Sean quit. When the computer project he was managing was behind schedule and over budget, Sean did not show up for work for three days. As a result, he was terminated. In both situations Sean blamed circumstances beyond his control as being responsible for his behavior. He blamed the store manager for being impossible to work with. He blamed the vendor of the software and hardware for trying to undermine his authority.

Right now Sean is facing a tough problem at work. The department head at the business school hired him because of his diverse business background, knowing that he did not have a college degree. When the director of the school learned about this deficiency, she informed Sean that all teachers must be college graduates. Her compromise was to allow Sean to continue teaching as long as he was pursuing his degree.

Sean looked into the degree program at Empire State College, which gives course credit for work experience and offers individual rather than classroom instruction. Sean anticipated already having the equivalent of an associate's degree because of his work experience and miscellaneous course work. The admissions counselor, however, ruled that Sean's credentials fell far short of two years of college credit.

Because Sean works only part-time, his finances are limited. However, there are ways he could finance his schooling. He could obtain another part-time job, or he could borrow money from his aging parents. Sean refuses to accept these means or any other alternative, and has given up on continuing his education. As a result, he will not be offered any more teaching assignments at his school.[7]

Sean's checkered work history is typical of the problem fleer. His occupational drift downward has already begun. His next stop is probably further down the occupational ladder. Middle-aged, unemployed, and without formal credentials for the type of work he prefers, Sean faces a bleak future. If he could somehow accept the reality of his script, it would not be too late for him to change. However, confronting his script is yet another problem he flees. Ask a confidant whether in his or her opinion you tend to flee from problems. If the answer is affirmative, make a prodigious effort to face your next problem head-on.

Friendship at All Costs

On the surface, wanting friends badly might seem like a winner script. Many people enjoy working with those who are constantly smiling, give great discounts, buy the coffee, and give gifts to co-workers and support staff. What's wrong with wanting to be liked, loved, and adored? Plenty, under some circumstances. The Friendship at All Costs script can interfere with good business judgment, thus creating adversity for the person wanting to be liked. The party who is the object of the affection usually benefits. Mary, an interior decorator, is a person who follows the Friendship at All Costs script.

Mary grew up as an only child, abused by her mother and ignored by her father. She had few playmates in her neighborhood, so she eagerly sought friendship. Desperate for companionship, she tried to win it by giving gifts and compliments to people she knew. During her many years as a full-time homemaker Mary devoted time to pleasing neighbors through such means as baking cakes and cookies for them and by volunteering to run some of their errands. She also worked very hard to meet the demands placed on her by her children.

Mary began her interior decorating business when the youngest of her children reached 18. She was encouraged to become an interior decorator by her family. With her husband's financial backing, she was able to launch "Interiors by Mary." Although Mary did not have formal training in interior design (she had majored in elementary education), her natural talent was impressive. Her work was featured in an article in the Sunday morning edition of the local newspaper. A photo essay showed before and after pictures of rooms she had decorated. Mary quickly acquired a healthy number of leads, and Interiors by Mary had a promising future.

The promise of a good business future never materialized. The personal relationships Mary developed with clients and prospective clients interfered with her willingness to charge them for her services. In a typical situation, Mary would visit a potential client's home for a consultation. After surveying the house, Mary would give the client prospect her specific ideas for redecorating. If Mary had been more general in her recommendations, she might have been hired. Instead, the prospective client used Mary's ideas to do her own redecorating.

Mary's poor business judgment finally resulted in the loss of moral support from her family. A homeowner named Eve hired Mary to redecorate her penthouse, and granted her almost free rein. Mary would buy something on the spot, with her own money, if she thought it was appropriate for Eve's apartment. Mary assumed Eve would later reimburse her. However, because they had developed a close friendship, Mary was reluctant to bill Eve for the purchase. Consequently, many out-of-pocket items for Eve's home were paid for by Mary.

Mary did not even bother sending Eve a bill for the household items she purchased. In Mary's mind, she was doing a favor for a friend more than performing services for a client. This feeling existed even though Mary and Eve knew each other only through the client/decorator relationship. Mary's husband and children were angered by her buying gifts for a client. They thought Mary was being exploited, and they were annoyed that her attempts to befriend Eve were more important to her than the survival of the business.

Mary's relationship with Eve exemplified how she handled several other clients. After stumbling around for six more months, Mary was forced to close the business for lack of funds.[8]

How could Mary have been helped? Mary will never be able to run a business efficiently or be a manager unless she overcomes her strong need to be liked by others. Mary can't change the rejecting way she was treated by her parents, or her friendship-starved childhood. All that is in the past. Perhaps by joining a support group Mary could increase her self-esteem and self-acceptance. By so doing she might find that she no longer required friendship at all costs. Instead Mary might be able to develop mutually beneficial business relationships that were cordial but not personal.

How important are friendships to you? Do you repeatedly sacrifice good business judgment in order to maintain a friendship with another person?

Biting the Hand That Feeds You

Striking back at the source of your financial or emotional support is not unusual. Many people rebel against an employer, a parent, or a spouse. Being dependent on another person naturally gives rise to this type of conflict. What is more unusual are people who continually bite the hand that feeds them. Most such people lack insight into how they are sabotaging their careers. One such person who overcame this problem was Tammy. She is a talented and charming person who defies occupational pigeon-holing.

Tammy began her career as a product demonstrator in a department store. First it was small kitchen appliances, then cosmetics, then toys. Tammy's charm, wit, and good looks not only attracted customers to her demonstration table but brought in large numbers. After one year of good service, the store manager offered Tammy a $1.25-an-hour salary increase, and told her that she had a great future in retailing. Nevertheless, he suggested that Tammy be more prompt in arriving for work.

Tammy became infuriated. She told the manager that a $1.25 increase was much below what she was worth, and that criticizing her lack of promptness was insulting. Tammy also said that product demonstrations were beneath her dignity. She never showed up for work again, except to receive the one week's salary owed her.

Tammy decided to give modeling a try. The first agency she contacted agreed to represent her. The agency immediately found Tammy assignments as a clothing model at trade shows and department stores. Her charm and poise made Tammy popular with the trade show officials and stores that hired her. The agency was able to keep Tammy booked frequently. After eighteen months of steady bookings, Tammy demanded a bigger percentage from the agency. She told the agency head that she was being exploited by the large cut taken by the agency on bookings. Tammy also demanded to know why she wasn't getting any photo modeling assignments. The manager explained that although Tammy was very attractive, her face wasn't thin enough, and she was too short for most fashion photo assignments.

Tammy had three more confrontations with the manager over the same issue. One day she stormed into the office and said to him: "You've been deliberately cutting me off from bookings this past two weeks. I've had it. Don't ever call me again. I'm through with this agency."

Tammy then tried a succession of jobs: door-to-door cosmetics sales representative, restaurant hostess, office receptionist, and reservations assistant at a hotel. Each time the pattern was the same: Tammy was hired on the basis of her charm and exceptional verbal skills, and performed up to expectations. She would then find some reason to fight with her boss, and quit. Finally, the pattern changed. Tammy explains what happened.

"Here I was a thirty-three-year-old bundle of talent, having really gone nowhere. My latest job was in the service department of a Cadillac dealer. I processed the invoices after service was completed, and explained the bills to customers. The job required a lot of tact because sometimes the bills were much higher than the customers expected. Shortly after I took that job, I married Jeff, a man in his late forties. He worked as a heavy equipment driver for a construction company. After I was working at the dealer about eight months, Jeff had a heart attack. The doctors said he wouldn't be able to return to work for at least a year.

"About two months after Jeff's heart attack, I almost got into another one of my arguments. My boss said that I handled customers well but I was glossing over explanations of charges. He said that some people were complaining to regional headquarters about being overcharged. My boss said that meant customers did not fully understand what they were being charged for.

"I was ready to start my counterattack. All of a sudden I bit my tongue and listened. I was relying too much on charm, and not explaining facts carefully enough to customers. What triggered me into listening instead of spitting fire was that Jeff needed my income. He was drawing disability pay but it wasn't even enough to cover his expenses. Picking fights with my employer and walking out in a huff made no sense anymore. No longer could I be the self-centered little queen. Destroying my career was bad enough when I was on my own. Doing it when somebody needs you is insanity."

Changing Your Script

Tammy changed her script when being needed triggered her into realizing that self-sabotage no longer made sense. For most others with self-sabotaging scripts, change may take more work. In order to change a self-sabotaging script two key steps are required. You first have to examine your script, and then exercise conscious control to make the change. Professional counseling, support groups, and encouragement from friends and family are all helpful. But the responsibility for changing a loser script remains with the person who has been losing.

Examining Your Script

A short dose of self-analysis often yields fast insights into the nature of one's scripts. To achieve these insights, ask yourself the following ten questions used by John Wareham as part of his method for overcoming losing scripts:

1. *What does your family tree tell you?* Your parents gave you most of your scripts, and their parents gave them theirs. By studying your family tree, you can quickly spot your key personality characteristics, and the outline of your destiny. For example, did your father show great promise but always get into trouble at work just when it was time to be promoted?

2. *What is your comfort level?* The income and status levels attained by your family are likely to represent the socioeconomic level you strive to attain and maintain. You may be running on a treadmill to attain something you don't want. In retaliation, you may be trying to trip yourself up to get off that treadmill.

3. *Are you a "winner" or a "loser"?* Which type of script did you inherit from your parents? If you think you inherited a loser script, make the decision not to live by it any longer.

4. *How do you feel on your birthday?* The answer to this question can provide insight into hidden feelings that shaped your early life, and continue to shape it today. Are you the youngest child who was always compared unfavorably to your oldest sibling? Did your parents have so many high expectations for your success that you hate competing? Are you trying to fail to get even with your parents?

5. *How did the world look to you as a child?* The good and the bad things that have happened to us in childhood often influence our adult behavior. If you ran away from problems as a child, it is

understandable that you do the same today. Wareham admonishes: "Identifying childhood's demons is the *only* way to exorcise them."

6. *What were the recurring roles you carried out in early life?* Were you the helper, the rescuer, the tough person, the clown, the loser? If you are still carrying out one of these roles and it is unacceptable to you, it is time to change.

7. *What did you have to do to get your parents' attention?* Did you have to make them laugh, cry, get angry? Did you have to be sick or injured to be noticed? Did you have to conform to be liked? Which one of these things are you still doing today? Is it working?

8. *How have cultural influences shaped your script?* In your subculture was "beating the system" and "screwing others" the path to acceptance? Is that what you are still doing today?

9. *What happens to people like you?* What does your intuition tell you your fate will be unless you change your approach to life? Do people like you wind up leading a fulfilling and rewarding life? Or do they peak early, and live out the balance of their careers in a purgatory of mediocre jobs? If your intuition indicates that your career script is negative, it is time for remedial action.

10. *What will be an appropriate biographical sketch of you when your life is completed?* Will an objective observer say that you were a nice person who never made waves, and was never noticed? Will you be described as a callous, unforgiving person who provided no comfort to anybody else? Or will you be described as some type of winner? If you don't like your biographical sketch, you will have to change your script.[9]

Exercising Conscious Control

Scripts are formed by a series of decisions made early in life. To change a script, it is therefore necessary to make redecisions. If you change your thinking, your feelings, or your behavior, you are in essence changing your script decisions. This is no easy task, but after you have examined your script much of the important work is already done.

To exercise conscious control over your script, you have to exert the rational, problem-solving part of your brain. Feelings and intuition are not cast aside, but they become secondary players to the mature and responsible (or adult) part of your brain. Evelyn, the technician who played computer blackjack on company time, can learn to censor her own behavior. She might say silently, "I've had enough close brushes with permanently ruining my career. The next time I have the impulse to play a little trick on someone with authority over me, I'll grab hold of myself. I'll make a trip to the copying machine just to cool down. Or I'll call a friend and explain that I've just narrowly escaped committing self-sabotage. Then I'll congratulate myself. I'll put a capital *W* in my daily planner. It will signify that today I've played out a winner script."

3

Inner Forces Creating Self-Sabotage

"*Why* me? Why do I always ruin a good thing for myself? Why can't I get what I want?" The person who made these cries of anguish speaks for all self-saboteurs in the work force. A major hurdle in preventing or overcoming career self-sabotage is to become aware of the inner forces propelling you toward creating your own career setbacks. As you read the cases here, carefully examine self-defeating behavior as it relates to your career. In this chapter, I describe twelve of the most common inner traps that goad people to self-sabotage.

Self-Defeating Personality

The simplest explanation for career self-sabotage is that some people suffer from a personality that fosters defeat. According to psychologists Thomas A. Widiger and Allen J. Frances, people with a self-defeating personality pattern have three distinguishing characteristics: (1) They repeatedly fail at tasks they have the ability to perform; (2) they repeatedly place themselves in abusive and destructive situations to which they respond helplessly; (3) they typically refuse to take advantage of escape routes, even when these are readily available.[1]

People with self-defeating personalities often fail as managers because they wittingly or unwittingly find a way to lower productivity and morale. By so doing they bring about the self-

---

The Twelve Most Common Inner Traps

1. *Self-defeating personality.* Some people have a personality predisposed to self-sabotage.
2. *Narcissism.* An exaggerated sense of your importance can get you into trouble.
3. *Emotional immaturity.* Seeking attention in an immature way can hurt your career.
4. *Self-defeating beliefs.* Expecting to fail brings about failure.
5. *Unrealistic expectations.* Expecting too much brings about failure.
6. *Compensation for feelings of inadequacy.* Feeling bad about yourself can propel you into doing things that harm your career.
7. *Revenge.* Seeking revenge can backfire.
8. *Attention seeking.* Wanting to be noticed at all costs can be self-defeating.
9. *Thrill seeking.* Craving constant excitement and thrills may defeat your own purposes.
10. *Imposter complex.* Believing that you are a hoax can be stressful.
11. *Paranoia.* Being suspicious of so many people diverts your energy from more creative tasks.
12. *Mid-life crisis.* Being discontent with your accomplishments can lead to counterproductive patterns of behavior.

---

imposed misery that feeds their disorder. Observe carefully the self-defeating elements in this scenario:

After many years as a sales representative, Jim Avery was promoted to a management position in a small branch office of a multinational corporation. The promotion was largely the result of the active lobbying of a senior manager in the corporation who had become a father figure to Jim. As a sales representative, Jim was moderately successful, largely because of his frantic activity in pushing a good product. His work always came before his health and his home life. Jim had been divorced twice and suffered from heart disease. Although he had a hearty, backslapping type of approach, some of his customers disliked his pushiness and impatience. For instance, he would call customers needlessly two or three times between regular sales visits, largely because of an unfounded worry that he might lose a customer in the interim.

The new opportunity was Jim's first position with managerial responsibility, and he brought to it what appeared to be enthusiasm and energy but what was really high anxiety. Things went smoothly enough for him at first, except for chronic turnover problems among his small secretarial staff. When questioned about this, Jim would claim that he could not keep experienced support personnel in his area at the salary level that he was allowed to pay. His employees would begin their new jobs with apparent competence and enthusiasm, but he claimed that they soon became resentful at having to do so much work for so little money. He fired one after another of them for abusing their sick time, becoming lax in their duties, developing poor work attitudes, and being insubordinate.

After three years of badgering the home office, Jim finally received a larger budget for his secretarial staff. Unfortunately, the first secretary hired at the new salary level followed the same downhill pattern as the others. She finally quit before being fired, blowing the whistle on her boss on the way out.

It seems that Jim was driving his secretaries to distraction with his insecurity, which showed up as anxiety and dependency. Given the wider array of responsibilities in his new position, he had lost the ability to focus on the business at hand, to plan for the office, and to organize himself and his work. His staff had to manage his calendar, reminding him of appointments and making excuses for him when he missed them. They would spend frantic days at the end of each month taking care of reports that he had failed to keep current.

Jim was also emotionally dependent on his staff. At first they responded soothingly and reassuringly to his constant anxiety-laden chatter; their protective and nurturing behavior, however, eventually gave way to resentment and hostility. They seemed to be running the office, yet their salaries were pitiful.

Jim's insecurity and dependency caused only minor problems when he was a sales representative. When he became a manager, however, these traits became more pronounced. To make matters worse, he no longer had the on-site support of his mentor. The organization overlooked the staffing turmoil because production, though erratic, was slowly increasing at the branch office. In addition, Jim's mentor protected him at staff meetings.

After Jim's third year in his new position, production began to fall at the branch office. Still no one looked too closely at Jim because his mentor continued to protect him. Finally, after a mass resignation of his secretarial staff that brought the office to a standstill, Jim's behavior was investigated.

As a result, he was brought back to the home office and given a minor administrative position.

The extent of the damage became clear only when the replacement manager tried to repair it. Jim Avery had offended so many people in the business community that it took two years before the office returned to the level it had been before Jim took over.[2]

So far, Jim's self-defeating actions have resulted in a squandered opportunity and a demotion, not a complete career collapse. Similarly, many other self-defeating personalities stay employed, although they don't work up to their full potential. Jim Avery showed some of the more subtle signs of a person with a self-defeating personality disorder. His neglect of his health and personal life may not have been mandated by his position. Instead, he chose to take an unbalanced approach to work and personal responsibilities. Many sales representatives are able to integrate the demands of work and family life.

An excessive firing of employees is a risky course of action for any manager. It is all the more risky when the people are fired for whimsical reasons. Jim fired workers for failing to meet ambiguous expectations. A more sensible option for him would have been to first clarify work objectives with his employees. Jim's intense emotional dependency on his mentor and staff is another tipoff to his personality problem, as is his falling behind on reports (though many people procrastinate who have only mild tendencies toward self-sabotage).

How could Jim have been helped? In fairness to him, the organization must share some of the blame. Jim's personality was ill-suited to managerial work, and he lacked the appropriate experience. A higher-ranking manager in his chain of command should have assessed Jim's needs for development as a manager. He was left to sink or swim, and the organization did not intervene soon enough while he was sinking.

If Jim had had insight into the nature of self-defeating behavior, he might have recognized that his dependency was a trouble spot. Some of this insight can be achieved through what you are being asked to do here—carefully examine self-defeating behavior as it relates to your career. Jim was overly dependent on alcohol, his mentor, and his staff. He needed the protection and nurturing of his employees. Yet following the script of a self-defeating personality, he treated his staff so harshly that it resulted in his losing their support.

Narcissism

People who engage in excessive self-admiration are usually headed toward career self-sabotage. Typically the narcissist wants adoration and love from others. People become narcissists, according to Freudian theory, because they did not receive enough love and nurturing early in life. They therefore crave affection. The narcissistic worker becomes self-centered in the pursuit of these unmet infantile needs. As a manager, a narcissist will typically be overagreeable. When confronted by the anger or disapproval of a subordinate, a "yes-manager" will submit to most requests in order to be liked and adored.

As explained by researcher Seth Allcorn, we all want to be liked and admired by others. Yes-managers crave this so much, however, that to avoid alienating others they submit rather than stand firm.[3] Saying yes when the answer should be no is an expression of narcissism because the manager submits to the demands of others in order to be adored.

A yes-manager may be seen by some as good, caring, and responsive to their needs. Others, especially superiors, may perceive the same manager as unable to make tough decisions and too willing to sacrifice organizational objectives to avoid being rejected.

Shirley, a manager of inventory control, sympathized with her team members when they complained of all the regulations that had to be followed in order to implement a just-in-time inventory system. "You know how those bureaucrats are in the front office," she said in response to complaints from below.

When Shirley's boss asked why the new inventory control system was taking so long to implement, Shirley answered, "It's those free spirits working for me. They resist rules and regulations with a passion. But not to worry, they are slowly coming around." Shirley was deliberately two-faced in her attempt to be admired and appreciated by her subordinates and superiors, alike. Her waffling was prompted by an inner desire to avoid either group's withdrawing its love and affection.

If you are waffling or overly agreeable, it could be a sign that you have fallen into the narcissism trap. Learn to recognize that few people can hold a responsible job and not be disliked by someone. Practice taking a stand on an important work issue. Observe the consequences. Most likely they will not be as severe as you imagined.

The need to feel loved is closely associated with a need to feel important and powerful. A narcissist may conduct work in a manner that attracts undeserved attention, and may even resort to devaluing others as a way of looking better. In this way the yes-manager soon becomes an organizational problem. Basing a decision on how well it pleases another person rather than on the merits of the case is also a problem.

Although narcissism stems from early childhood, its impact can be controlled with self-discipline. If you are candid enough to admit that you crave love, affection, and adoration on the job, do not expect total satisfaction of these needs. Instead, try to satisfy them in a few limited situations. Find one or two co-workers, customers, or suppliers who are looking to provide such emotional support and warmth to a work associate.

Confine your obvious attempts at winning admiration to those one or two people. In addition, find constructive ways of obtaining the adulation of others by, for example, winning a productivity award. Another way is to do the best possible job for anybody who uses your work output. Providing extraordinary service to a customer, client, or person from another department can result in your receiving a measure of adoration.

Emotional Immaturity

Fun and humor on the job have been elevated to a higher status than ever before. Many companies hire humor consultants to advise them on how to effectively use humor and fun to increase productivity and morale, and to reduce conflict and stress. Effective use of humor in the workplace is therefore an asset, enhancing a person's human relations skills. Office clowns, however, use humor more to obtain the attention they crave than to improve organizational effectiveness. They crave this attention because of their emotional immaturity. Some people do laugh with the office clown, but carrying out this role is a form of career sabotage. Few office clowns work their way into the executive suite.

Early in life Mark was an underachiever and unhappy. He fared poorly in his studies and in athletics, and was unable to penetrate any clique of interest to him. Mark's solution to his loneliness was to become the class clown. It was Mark who responded with quips to questions posed by the teacher. It was also Mark who tested the limits to which he could use profanity and vulgar expressions before being disciplined by the teacher.

Mark completed a two-year college program, improved his grades over those he had attained in high school, and then attended a four-year college. He majored in accounting, primarily because he could not think of anything else that interested him. While in college, and while holding down part-time and temporary work, Mark continued to gain attention through clowning. At graduation ceremonies, he wore fishing boots that drew a laugh from the audience as he walked across the stage.

Mark's relationships with women were limited because he rarely progressed beyond three weeks of dating any one person. After several weeks of knowing Mark, most women tired of his pranks and quips. He sent one woman he was dating into hysterics when he showed up at her door with a nylon stocking tightly drawn over his face, and a hunting knife in his right hand.

As graduation approached, Mark conducted a job search. He behaved in a manner sober enough to locate a position as a budget analyst with a furniture manufacturer, a position he held for five years. Withon one month of his first full-time professional position, Mark established himself as the office clown. He was the one who would jump out of a supply closet, insert a nude centerfold into an annual report in the office lobby, and wear a rubber mask of Richard Nixon to the office.

A vacancy occurred for an assistant manager position in Mark's department. Despite Mark's reputation as a joker, his manager thought Mark's experience and technical skills justified at least interviewing him for the position. When asked, "Why do you want this position?" Mark quipped, "It beats working." End of interview. End of Mark being considered for advanced responsibility.

Mark's emotional immaturity has already sabotaged his career and personal life. If he wants to prevent further damage,

Mark needs to pursue two courses of action. At the surface level, he must learn to present himself in a more professional way. He can still use humor, but in a more mature and refined manner.

At a deeper level, Mark must question why he needs to be a clown. He must ask himself the brutal question, "What else can I do for attention at this stage in my life aside from acting like a fool?" Mark might strive for the attention and respect of his co-workers by presenting a dazzling analysis of costs on a project. He could also use his creativity to make a witty and clever comment, rather than saying something outrageous and tasteless.

If you are attempting to obtain attention and recognition in an immature manner, shift gears and look for a more constructive way to satisfy those needs. Instead of joking about a problem facing your company, propose a creative solution.

Self-Defeating Beliefs

A 1987 article that appeared in *The Wall Street Journal* claims that a widespread cause of self-sabotage is having erroneous beliefs that create the conditions of failure. These self-defeating beliefs are more specific than self-fulfilling prophecies, which deal generally with our expectations as to whether we or others will succeed or fail. Job hunting is one area in which self-defeating beliefs contribute directly to sabotage.[4]

Some people sabotage their job campaigns before even starting. They think to themselves: "I lack the right experience," "I'm not sharp enough," "I'm too old," "I'm too young," "I don't have charisma," "I didn't graduate from an elite school," and so forth. If you attempt a job search with one of these self-defeating beliefs, you will eliminate yourself from half your potential interviews and will be perceived negatively in the balance.

The antidote is to challenge your beliefs. What is your evidence for believing that your qualifications are inferior? Search for reasons why a prospective employer would want you, even with your supposed limitations. Even if some of your beliefs are valid, such as that you lack the right experience for a particular job, you can still qualify for the job. Emphasize fundamental attributes such as problem-solving ability, interpersonal skills, and varied experience that would be a plus for you in any position.

Negative thoughts about one's capacity to learn new skills can also be self-defeating, and they can block new opportunities. An office assistant said that she was upset because she would never be able to become an executive assistant in her company. Asked how she had arrived at that conclusion, she said, "I could never learn to do an electronic spreadsheet." Asked further if she had ever tried to learn how to do a spreadsheet, she said, "No, because I know I would fail." Finally, she was urged to take home a Lotus 1-2-3 manual for the weekend, and take her time learning a few basic commands.

The office assistant returned to the office Monday morning in a triumphant mood, having made considerable progress in learning Lotus. The reality of her ability to learn something about spreadsheets on her own helped dispel her negative beliefs. A year later she was promoted to an executive assistant.

A strange twist to self-defeating beliefs is that positive beliefs—not just negative ones—can also contribute to career sabotage. Incorrect perceptions of one's skills as being superior can lead to substandard performance. If enough of these poor performances accumulate, career sabotage is in the offing. Managers with inflated self-assessments of their knowledge may fail to request assistance. Similarly, their failure to properly use needed assistance on a given problem can result in even larger problems.[5]

A prominent example is the decision-making errors made by NASA officials leading up to the explosion of the space shuttle *Challenger* and the deaths of seven crew members. The expertise for the proper decision was available but ignored. (In addition to inflated estimates of their knowledge, NASA managers felt pressured to get a launch accomplished on time.) Several engineers on the project strongly recommended against a launch attempt in abnormally cold weather, especially because they had reason for believing the O-rings would not function properly in those conditions.

The three examples of self-defeating beliefs just given point to one of the most important principles for preventing career self-sabotage. Sharpen the accuracy of your perceptions by obtaining valid feedback at checkpoints of your own choosing. Ask an experienced human resources professional, "Am I as poorly qualified for my contemplated job search as I think I am?" Review your thinking on a project with a knowledgeable person in your field, and ask, "Is my logic as tight as I think it is? What facts should I pursue that have not already entered into my decision making?"

Unrealistic Expectations

Many people's goals, aspirations, and expectations are so high that they predispose themselves to unhappiness and defeat. Suppose a woman who enters the work force as a personnel assistant establishes the goal of becoming the vice-president of human resources for a major business corporation. She is so set on becoming a vice-president that she defines failure as not reaching that goal by the time she is 40. Because her chances of achieving her goal are perhaps one in a thousand, this woman will most likely experience defeat of her own choosing. If her aspirations were less grandiose, such as becoming the human resources manager of a medium-size company, her chances for "winning" would be substantially higher.

There is a subtle difference between having unrealistic expectations and having goals that stretch our capabilities. It is good to stretch one's capabilities, but it is hurtful to be crushed if the very-difficult-to-attain is not forthcoming. Map out a realistic approach to reaching your ideal goals, but be prepared to achieve less.

Aspirations for a high income can directly precipitate self-destructive behavior. A case in point is Gordie.

At a young age, Gordie wanted to be self-employed and wealthy. He chose self-employment as the road to riches because he preferred not to continue his formal education beyond high school. Gordie had become proficient at repairing and refinishing automobiles, and decided to turn his avocation into a vocation.

Lacking the capital to start his own business, Gordie sold his friend Rick on the idea of their becoming partners in an automotive collision shop. The two of them opened G&R Collision, specializing in the painting and restoration of automobiles. Using all the money they could scrape up, Gordie and Rick leased a space and bought enough equipment to get the business into operation.

Gordie and Rick lost money the first two years and had to borrow to keep the business going. Gordie believed that his hopes and dreams of making good money had vanished. In contrast, Rick was confident that the business would succeed. Based on the high quality of their work, repeat business and referrals were starting to materialize. During the third year, the business broke even.

Gordie meanwhile became frustrated with working so hard at a business that provided him only a modest income. A chance discussion with a flashy customer got Gordie started in purchasing drugs from the customer and reselling them to other customers. The revenues from drug sales quickly outpaced the revenues from painting and restorations. Gordie was not making the kind of money he had hoped for when he opened the collision shop. He sold his half of the business so that he could deal drugs full time, using the contacts he made at the shop as a customer base.

Gordie's days of high earnings did not last long. He was convicted of drug dealing, and is now serving ten years in prison. Ironically, Rick kept the business and it is now highly profitable. The drug trafficking actually helped business by giving the collision shop something of a mystique.[6]

Gordie's behavior went beyond career self-sabotage to self-destruction. He may well find some type of work in the body shop upon release from prison, but his earnings will probably never come close to satisfying his original aspirations. The tragedy is that Gordie's impatience prompted him to discard his most likely chance for sustained career success—operating a business in which he had a comparative advantage.

If Gordie had secured valid information about how long it takes most proprietorships to generate a large cash flow, he might have lowered his aspirations for immediate financial success. Instead, he allowed his unrealistic aspirations to prompt him to choose a path of career self-destruction.

Compensation for Feelings of Inadequacy

People who feel inadequate sometimes seek ways of making themselves feel adequate that prove to be self-defeating. A feeling of inadequacy might therefore be considered yet another self-defeating belief. However, it is widespread enough to warrant special mention. Feelings of inadequacy lead people to think they cannot compete equally with others because they are handicapped.

Feelings of inadequacy may sometimes drive people to play office politics in an obsequious manner that is self-defeating in the long run. Such is the case with Fred.

A middle manager in a large corporation, Fred is worried that he is not a big enough contributor to be considered valuable. He thinks he could be squeezed out in the next company retrenchment. Fred's reasoning is not totally unfounded. He is far from being considered a fast tracker. Instead, his superiors and co-workers rate him as an average performer. He makes few major mistakes, but he does not come forth with major contributions either.

Fred has a lifelong pattern of worrying about whether he is performing well. As a youngster, while playing Little League baseball, he would often glance at the coach for a sign of approval that he had made the right play. In college, Fred frequently asked his professors if he might submit a preliminary draft of a paper to determine if he had understood the assignment correctly.

Fred's job insecurities are best revealed through his use of body language in contacts with his boss and higher-ranking managers. During a staff meeting, Fred nods approval and smiles whenever his boss speaks. To Fred, the boss is always right. A co-worker commented that Fred nods more vigorously and smiles wider in proportion to the importance and power of the person speaking. In contrast, he usually remains expressionless when a peer or lower-ranking employee speaks.

Fred's immediate boss, soon annoyed with his insincere smiles and nods, asked Fred why he nodded with approval at almost everything a manager said. Fred's smile turned to a worrisome expression. He explained: "I don't think I give approval to everything. But it certainly is a good policy to agree with management. If your own subordinates don't agree with you, who will? I'm here to back you up, not tear you down. And one way I can prove that is by showing my appreciation for your words of wisdom. When you or your manager says something that I think is unsound, you'll hear from me. Do you understand my reasoning?"

In truth, Fred never would express disagreement with a boss. He is too insecure to be anything but a yes-person. Fred's form of office politics has become almost a reflex action. When he spots a person of higher rank, his brain sends a message to his body to express approval. Until Fred becomes a more confident person, he will probably continue to practice his naive form of office politics.

In the long run, his attempts at ingratiation will be self-defeating. His unwillingness to approve co-workers' ideas is in sharp contrast to his approval of the words of those above him. Because of this Janus-like tactic, Fred is on the way to losing the confidence of his co-workers—a fatal mistake in any team effort. Somehow Fred has to assess his strengths, appreciate them, and stop behaving so inadequately. A good starting point for someone suffering from feelings of inadequacy is to prepare a list of personal assets. This basic tactic often has surprising results. It gets people to begin thinking positively about themselves.

Revenge

"Don't get mad, get even" is the advice for people who are wronged. The problem with this advice is that getting even is a form of revenge, driven by anger. Because revenge usually has the same emotional intensity as envy and jealousy, it can be self-defeating. Witness the actions of Caryn:

Caryn was the senior secretary to the regional vice-president of an insurance company, a position she had for six years. In Caryn's contacts with other regional offices she discovered that her counterparts had been promoted to administrative assistants. Caryn wanted to be an administrative assistant because the position would give her more status, salary, and vacation time. She approached Dana, her boss, and requested a promotion to administrative assistant.

Dana liked the idea, and asked Caryn to draft a job description that would increase her level of responsibilities, including work on special assignments. Dana reviewed the description with Caryn, contacted central personnel, and secured the reclassification. Despite the reclassification, Caryn could not understand why Dana was placing more demands on her time and requesting that she accomplish more things independently. Dana in turn could not understand why Caryn was blocking his requests because it was she who had asked for the promotion.

Caryn would openly complain, "What good is it to be an administrative assistant, and get more vacation time? Every time I turn around, Dana has some new project for me. I never get to take the vacation time I have." Caryn soon began bad-mouthing Dana. She would answer his calls and say such things as, "I don't know where Dana is. He never tells me anything anymore."

Caryn's disgruntlement continued, and she stopped providing Dana with the information she was supposed to. Twice when Dana asked her to set up a meeting at a designated time, she neglected to inform the people who were supposed to attend. When Dana returned after waiting futilely for the others, Caryn denied telling Dana that she had set up the meeting.

On one occasion Caryn scheduled several people to meet with Dana, but did not tell him about it until the last minute, when a group suddenly appeared at his office. Caryn insisted to Dana, "I told you this meeting was scheduled. Don't you listen to me anymore?" Her rhetorical question was asked in front of the guests who had arrived for the meeting.

Caryn insisted that all information sent to Dana had to be reviewed by her first. Even items stamped CONFIDENTIAL were plucked from Dana's in-box and reviewed. Caryn would then openly pass judgment on the contents. Once she told a manager reporting to Dana that a promotion for one of her people would most certainly be approved by Dana. Yet Dana had not yet read the request.

One day the company president called Dana, and Caryn took the opportunity to describe Dana's inability to run his operation. Upon speaking to Dana, the president said, "Muzzle her or fire her. I don't care which." Later that day, Dana confronted Caryn: "Ever since your promotion, your performance and attitude have deteriorated. Worse yet, your loyalty to me and the organization has vanished. You wanted a promotion to administrative assistant. You wanted all the advantages that went along with the position.

"Two things you didn't take into account. First, in order to attain that level, we expected a higher caliber of work. Not only did you not give us that, your performance deteriorated. Second, your constant harping about my work amounts to insubordination. I am recommending that you be demoted to an entry-level position in the word-processing center. After one year of good performance, you may reapply for the position of senior secretary."

Caryn's attempt to harm the company and her boss for their treatment of her was obviously self-defeating. Blinded by thoughts of revenge for the greater demands being placed on her, Caryn became derelict in her responsibilities. Caryn should have approached Dana openly (they had worked together for six years) and explained the sources of her discontent. If necessary, she could quietly have reverted to the less demanding position she had held previously and worked hard to receive an above-average salary increase.

As with so many people caught up in a strong emotion, Caryn did not listen to her co-workers. Upon hearing of her discontent, they suggested that she discuss the issue with her boss. Her response was laced with self-sabotage: "He wanted me promoted. It's up to him to make it work."[7]

If you are caught in a situation in which your job expectations are profoundly frustrated, take constructive rather than self-defeating action. Confront the problem with the source of your frustration instead of seeking revenge through insubordination. Recognize also that you may have to take major responsibility for resolving the problem even though your boss shares some of the blame. In the case just reviewed, for instance, Dana was also at fault for virtually ignoring Caryn's actions until she voiced a complaint to the president. Dana's insensitivity would have been self-defeating if the president had taken Caryn's complaints seriously.

Attention Seeking

Frank is addicted to attention. He needs a good deal of it to ward off negative feelings such as loneliness, depression, and anxiety. As with many other attention addicts, the ways in which he seeks attention may lead to career self-sabotage. Since childhood, he has consciously and unconsciously developed methods for gaining attention. When he receives enough attention, he feels relaxed and confident for a while, but as soon as the high wears off he craves more attention.

Frank would prefer to receive positive attention, but for him even negative attention is better than being ignored. He really doesn't care what people are thinking and saying about him so long as they are thinking and saying something. Frank can provoke three types of attention at work, and each type presents its own set of problems.

Frank requires positive attention. He needs to feel that people think he is competent, if not outstanding. In order to elicit positive attention from his peers, Frank brags about his accomplishments even it means stretching the truth. He dramatizes his contributions to successful projects and downplays the contributions of his co-workers. He typically speaks loudly so that others are forced to hear him. And he hopes they will conclude that he is intelligent and witty. Frank likes to be one up on people. When someone makes a humorous comment, he attempts to add an even funnier twist. When someone contributes an innovative idea, Frank attempts to surpass the other person's creativity.

When positive attention is not available, he will seek supportive attention. He presents himself to co-workers as someone who is suffering and needs immediate attention. He may talk about family problems, health problems, or concerns about job burnout.

At other times Frank must settle for negative attention. He prompts negative attention by such means as arriving late to meetings, interrupting the conversations of others by talking loudly on the phone, or making intrusive comments such as, "Why isn't anybody smiling? Are we going out of business?" Other tactics for eliciting negative attention include disagreeing with a plan of action when consensus is almost at hand, failing to understand a point that everyone else grasps, and initiating conflict when everyone else is communicating peacefully.

Frank needs to understand that his intense need for attention is creating an effect the very opposite of the one he desires. Frank's fantasy is that, when he leaves a room, people will make comments such as, "What a great guy Frank is." In fact they are more likely to say, "I detest that guy," and "Why doesn't somebody do something about that character?"[8]

Frank must understand that people who have high self-esteem can function well without continual assurance from others that they are wonderful. People who are not self-saboteurs learn to depend on themselves for some of the attention they need. Although every successful person wants some attention from others, the healthier ones know they are competent and are therefore not so dependent on others for positive feedback.

I can imagine readers thinking, "Yes, Frank needs to understand what he is doing wrong, just as a gambling addict needs to understand that waging bets is ruining his or her life." The recovery process presented here works like this. Assume that you are an attention seeker of Frank's magnitude. You read this and think to yourself, "Frank's problem could possibly fit me." You solicit feedback from a knowledgeable person, such as a trusted co-worker or a former boss. The feedback you receive is that you are indeed an attention seeker. You attempt to monitor your behavior using your own resources. If the problem is not solved, you seek professional counseling.

The problem with seeking attention in inappropriate ways can usually be overcome through a combination of feedback and self-monitoring of behavior. Many forms of self-sabotage can be handled similarly.

Thrill Seeking

Certain high-profile people, in business as well as in other endeavors, are high-risk takers and adventurers. They seek excitement and stimulation whenever they can find or create it. The excitement of making deals is often more important than the money involved. Donald Trump is but one of many professional deal makers who claims to be driven more by the thrill of the chase than by the money his deals generate. When his deals fail, he is understandably emotionally deflated.

Excessive thrill seeking can sabotage one's career, because the craving for thrills may overtake good business judgment. Trump is the best publicized example of a deal maker whose obsessive pursuit of excitement created cash-flow problems for his financial empire. Self-defeating thrill seeking also takes place at more modest levels.

Bill developed a reputation as a computer hacker. At college he was constantly playing around with the system software and would experiment with computers during most of his spare time. Between his junior and senior year, Bill obtained an internship at a major government contracting firm. His internship was to last six months.

During the first several months of his internship Bill performed so well that his supervisor decided to grant him password privileges. Bill was explicitly told, however, that the company was a government contractor, and that he was to stay clear of anything that was not directly in his domain of work.

As part of a security check, management became aware that security had been compromised on a highly sensitive project. Tracing back through the system log files (which had been altered to conceal who had been manipulating the file system), the company determined that Bill was the source of the security leak. When confronted by management, Bill initially denied any involvement with the security breach. When shown the convincing evidence against him, Bill admitted to the violation.

Bill was immediately dismissed from the company. In lieu of pressing charges against him, the company coordinated its disciplinary efforts with Bill's school. Because Bill was an intern, and not a permanent employee, his school handled the discipline. The decision was made to suspend Bill from school for eighteen months. His reputation is now severely tarnished, and Bill wonders whether he will be able to find employment in computer science in the future.[9]

Bill's tampering with the government computer files was driven by the thrills he receives from hacking. No monetary gain was possible because the files were not tied in with bank accounts or other funds. The antidote for Bill and other hackers, financial deal makers, and miscellaneous corporate thrill seekers is to question whether chasing thrills is more important than getting honest work accomplished. If the answer is no, thrill seeking on the job can be supplemented by pursuing thrills off the job. With ample outside thrills, there is less need for thrill seeking on the job.

Off-the-job thrills should be chosen carefully to avoid physical self-destruction. Hang gliding, auto racing, and ski jumping may not qualify as satisfactory sublimations. Safer sports, safe sex, and legal gambling (with outer limits set) are highly recommended for thrill seekers. The antidote suggested here is not universally applicable. Some corporate thrill seekers are already pursuing high-intensity thrills off the job, including personal relationships and community work. All they can hope for is to learn how to monitor their thrill seeking to minimize the chances of self-sabotage.

Unfortunately the remedial action just prescribed may not help all thrill seekers. Some people seek thrills to fight off depression. Only by revving up the pace of their lives can they feel happy. In these cases they may need counseling and/or antidepressant medication to lead a happy life without constant thrills.

Imposter Complex

"I really don't deserve all the accolades I'm receiving. I'm not nearly as competent as most people believe. If my incompetence is ever discovered, it will all be over for me." Such is the thinking of large numbers of competent people in diverse fields who suffer from an imposter complex. These people, according to Pauline Clance in *The Imposter Phenomenon,* secretly believe that they have been overestimated, and that at any moment the truth about them will be revealed. The imposter complex can be regarded as another type of self-defeating belief. An estimated 70 percent of all successful individuals suffer from this complex.[10]

The vast majority of people with an imposter complex are consistently high achievers on the job, and therefore are not sabotaging their careers. For a small minority of these people, however, fears about being an imposter trigger psychosomatic disorders and emotional trauma. Personal relationships are the first to suffer, followed by some decline in work performance.

In a few instances, the imposter complex can lead to self-defeating job behavior. The person with a strongly developed imposter complex might feel so guilty about being a "fraud" that he or she will engage in self-sabotage as a means of self-punishment. An executive might make irrational decisions as a way of proving that he does not deserve the position.

People often overcome the imposter complex through psychotherapy, self-help groups, and understanding friends. Therapist Janice Castro also suggests to her patients with an imposter complex that they remember a cogent observation by W. Somerset Maugham: "Only a mediocre person is always at his (or her) best."[11]

If you experience the imposter complex it is time for personal thought control. Work hard to overcome the self-defeating idea that you are not worthy of your successes. Answering these questions will help you put your thinking in perspective:

- Who does deserve success?
- Are other successful people any more deserving than I?
- Don't most successful people get a few good breaks along the way?
- Since I didn't award myself the symbols of success, such as high income, nice title, and so forth, why shouldn't I let others judge whether or not I deserve my success?

- Nobody else achieved my successes for me, so shouldn't I take most of the credit for them?

Paranoia

Being paranoid often fosters career self-sabotage. The energy invested in checking out people's motives and wondering if co-workers are trying to do you in detracts from a creative, positive approach to the job. Furthermore, a paranoid manager is usually a poor leader because group members realize they are not trusted.

Paranoia aptly illustrates how self-fulfilling prophecies can contribute to career self-sabotage. Paranoid individuals think co-workers are out to destroy them. Based on this erroneous belief, they act defensively and secretly around colleagues. Because of their strange behavior, co-workers do shun contact with them and fail to cooperate. Not surprisingly, the paranoid person's performance evaluation suffers. He or she is judged to be a poor team worker. Thus the paranoid person's suspicions are confirmed.

To prevent career self-sabotage, paranoid people need frequent reality checks on their perceptions. Such checks are difficult to obtain because paranoid thinking prevents these people from trusting most associates enough to confide in them. However, if the paranoia is not too deeply entrenched, such reality checks are possible.

Paul, a management consultant, felt that the two other members of his unit distrusted and disliked him. Worried about his ability to perform under these circumstances, Paul discussed the issue with his boss.

The boss said he would gently inquire into how the other consultants in the unit felt about Paul. The feedback obtained by the boss was quite helpful to Paul. The boss said, "My sense is that the other people in the group want to get to know you better. They think you have a lot of talent, but they wish you were not so withdrawn from them." Paul took the initiative to communicate more openly with the other consultants and in this way overcame his suspiciousness.

If you think others are treating you unfairly, or are out to trip you up, run a reality check. Talking over your concerns with

your boss, a human resources professional, or an outside consultant could help place things in proper perspective.

Mid-Life Crisis

Although in recent years most people have been more concerned about career survival than about mid-life crisis, it can still
be a real problem. The crisis occurs when there is a gap between
what you hoped would happen to your life and what has actually
occurred. People who experience a mid-life crisis have a feeling of
discontent and unhappiness about their jobs and careers. They
feel trapped, and believe that they lack a significant challenge.

People who aren't content with their achievements in their
careers or personal lives at mid-life can become sullen, unpredictable, and self-sabotaging. A former colleague describes the behavior of David, a product manager, in response to his mid-life crisis:

People who knew David gradually realized that he was in trouble. It all
seemed to begin with his being passed over for a director position. He
always talked the company game and acted as if he were the candidate in
line for marketing vice-president. David went on a two-week vacation after
the announcement that somebody else was getting the job he wanted. To
everyone's surprise, he returned a changed man.

First of all, his clothing was completely changed. He had dressed in a
conversative, businesslike manner before. Now he dressed flamboyantly,
with an Italian flair. It looked as if he had bought a hairpiece. David was
beginning to drink heavily, but he was not drunk outright at work. He saved
his heavy drinking for after hours and parties.

David became a dreadful waster of both his own and other people's
time. He was forever urging someone to "escape this madness for a few
minutes and have a cup of coffee." A few people in the department would
close their doors when David approached. They did this because he
interpreted an open door as an invitation to enter that office and stay for
twenty minutes, chatting about nothing directly related to work.

David finally left the company when he inherited some money. He
bought a small fishing tackle store in Maine, which did poorly. His wife
and children made the trip with him to Maine, but soon returned home.

David allowed his dissatisfactions with his career and personal life to drag him down. He was too sullen to realize that

being discouraged with life is not a reason to engage in behavior that only intensifies the problem. Many other people successfully rebound from a mid-life crisis. Often they accomplish it by bringing about constructive changes in their lives. A new work assignment, a new hobby, a new joint interest with one's partner, a careful scrutiny of the good things one has accomplished— all these can help prevent mid-life concerns from being self-defeating.

If you think you might be experiencing a mid-career crisis, choose from among these action steps to prevent your problem from becoming self-defeating:

1. *Take the problem seriously.* Until you admit that your lethargy, apathy, and indifference constitute a problem calling for action, the process of recovery will be blocked. Be honest with yourself.
2. *Practice relaxation techniques.* The mid-life crisis involves substantial stress, making it important to use a stress-reduction technique on a regular basis. Among the most effective relaxation techniques are moderate exercise, ample rest, and meditation.
3. *Switch assignments.* Quick, partial relief from the mid-career crisis can be obtained from switching work assignments. Even being assigned to a temporary task force or project can boost your morale.
4. *Develop realistic expectations.* A basic cause of the mid-life crisis is expecting too much from your career. As opportunities for rapid promotion continue to shrink, more people will have to settle for less dramatic career growth. Learn to derive happiness from growth within your job.
5. *Improve your personal life.* An improvement in your personal life won't cure a mid-life crisis, but it could make the problem more bearable. Improvement could come from revitalizing your relationship with your partner, finding a partner if you don't have one, or making new, interesting friends.
6. *Try new activities.* The more well-rounded your life is, the more protected you are against the mid-life crisis. New

activities might include hobbies, sports, serving your community, or patronizing different restaurants.

7. *Find a new career or a new job.* For many sufferers of the mid-career crisis, the only real solution is drastic, such as placing yourself in a new job or career. Of course, the new job or career has to contain more excitement than the present one.

8. *Maintain a growing edge.* Maintaining a lifelong positive attitude toward self-development and self-improvement can help prevent a mid-life crisis as well as other forms of career self-sabotage. If you prevent yourself from going stale, you keep a fresh perspective that will help you to avoid becoming sullen, bitter, and counterproductive.

In summary, be aware of inner forces propelling you toward creating your own career setbacks. Among the traps described were being a self-defeating personality, narcissism, holding self-defeating beliefs, seeking revenge, thrill seeking, and paranoia. Avoiding or overcoming any of these traps requires careful self-analysis and following some of the suggestions offered here.

4

Clear-Cut Forms of Self-Sabotage

"*W*hy is George doing this to himself?" thought George's boss. "Why is he late with this proposal? A potential big customer is practically begging us to become its supplier. Is George trying to put us out of business? Is he trying to make my life miserable? Or is George trying to get himself fired?"

The third alternative considered by George's boss is probably the correct one. By being late with a proposal, George is doing severe damage to his reputation as a professional sales consultant. George may not be aware of his motives. Many people have to be shaken into recognizing that they are actively contributing to their career demise.

There are a number of actions, attitudes, and beliefs that are readily detectable as forms of self-sabotage. Confronting yourself, co-workers, friends, or family members with these behaviors could plant a seed for constructive change. These self-initiated, self-defeating actions, attitudes, and beliefs can often be reversed.

Procrastination

Procrastination is the leading form of self-sabotage. Many people procrastinate so much at the start of their careers that they never develop much of a career to destroy. The worst offenders flunk out of college because of exams never studied for and papers never written or completed only after the deadlines have passed.

People with less crippling forms of procrastination, such as George, do launch their careers. But later on they procrastinate so much that they lose out on big opportunities or incur the wrath of their bosses.

Almost everybody procrastinates some of the time. Therefore, all procrastination is not self-defeating. My concern here is with people who delay action for no good reason and consequently put themselves at a serious competitive disadvantage.

Why People Procrastinate

People delay doing important things, such as getting their documentation ready for a performance review, because they want to screw up. Whether they realize it or not, they are trying to self-destruct. Procrastination is career suicide in slow motion. Procrastinating on one assignment will not do you in, because people will tolerate such a common foible. Yet a series of deadlines missed or projects never completed will ultimately ruin your career.

Fear of being criticized or evaluated negatively by others can also lead to procrastination. If you delay submitting your input to the budget, you delay having somebody criticize the accuracy of your work. If a researcher keeps polishing a research study instead of submitting it to a journal, the researcher can delay facing the rejection notice that is the routine response to about 80 percent of submissions in most fields.

Paradoxically, people also procrastinate because they fear success. Underlying their fear of success is that it will be accompanied by some disastrous effect, such as isolation or abandonment. An accountant who attended a workshop on time management confessed to the group that she really wanted to avoid being as successful as her father. He became a chief financial officer of a large corporation. As a top executive, he lost contact with many of his friends. Few people offered him emotional support any longer, probably thinking he did not need their help.

Others fear success because of the added responsibility that success may bring. These people talk about their grand ambitions, but in reality find substantial responsibility to be overwhelming. A quick way to avoid success is to procrastinate.

Alan, a human resources manager, was recruited by an executive search consultant for consideration as a vice president of human resources. Alan claimed that this was the great opportunity of his career. After a series of extensive interviews, the client made Alan the first choice for the position. Alan kept postponing accepting the offer until the client finally offered the position to the second-choice candidate. Although Alan grumbled that the client was too impetuous, he was actually relieved to know that he would not be taking on so much additional responsibility.

A straightforward reason for procrastinating is to avoid uncomfortable, overwhelming, or tedious tasks. A person who itemizes deductions might delay preparing his or her tax return for all these reasons. Although wanting to avoid uncomfortable, overwhelming, or tedious tasks may seem normal, putting off such tasks can still take a heavy career toll. A tax consultant wound up in considerable legal trouble because she never got around to filing her own federal and state tax returns for three consecutive years. She boasted, "It will only take me two days to file my taxes when I've run out of extensions."

Finally, people often procrastinate as a way of rebelling against being controlled. Procrastination used in this way is a means of defying unwanted authority.[1] Rather than submit to authority, the person thinks, "Nobody is going to tell me when I should get a presentation completed. I'll do it when I'm good and ready."

Overcoming Procrastination

Overcoming procrastination begins the moment you recognize that your work goals are not being achieved. Feedback from your boss often takes care of this point. The second thing to do in overcoming self-sabotaging procrastination is to raise your level of awareness of the problem. When you are not accomplishing enough to meet your work goals, ask yourself if the problem could be that you are procrastinating over some crucial tasks. Be brutally honest with yourself. If you are undecided as to whether you are procrastinating, solicit the opinion of somebody else who is familiar with your work.

Many people have reduced the extent of their procrastination by calculating its cost. For example, what if you lose out on a promotion to another division because you do not have your résumé updated in time? The cost of your procrastination would include not only the difference in salary between your present job and the promotion you wanted (at least consciously) but also the loss of potential job satisfaction.

Another antidote to procrastination is to force yourself to attack the uncomfortable, overwhelming, or tedious task. Forcing yourself is useful in proving that the task is not as bad as you initially perceived it to be.[2] Assume that you have accepted a new position but have not yet resigned from your present one because the act of resigning makes you uncomfortable. Set a specific time to call your boss to schedule an appointment. Force yourself further to show up for the resignation meeting. After you break the ice with the statement, "I have something important to tell you," the task will be much easier.

A standard way of reducing procrastination is to divide a project that seems overwhelming into small segments that are easier to cope with. If your job calls for inspecting twenty locations within thirty days, begin by making dates to inspect the two closest to home. Planning the job before executing it also helps ease the pain. In this situation you would plan an itinerary before starting the inspections.

The thought of meeting a distant deadline is anxiety-provoking for many procrastinators, Neil Fiore explains, because they envision having to do the whole job at once.[3] If this is part of your problem, think in terms of starting rather than of finishing tasks. As with cutting a task down into manageable chunks, the project facing you will appear less formidable. Starting becomes much easier when you begin with a first step such as taking out a new manila folder.

Deception and Lying

Kim worked as a dealer representative for a major animal feed supplier. Her job was to encourage dealers and wholesalers to purchase animal feed from her company. Kim traveled extensively in order to cover her two-state territory. After three years of good performance, Kim was under consideration for promotion to district manager, a position in which she would supervise five sales representatives and receive an override on their sales.

An impatient and aggressive driver, Kim received three speeding tickets in one year. She pleaded guilty but asked for leniency because her livelihood was dependent on driving. Fearful of losing her job, Kim chose not to tell her boss that her license had been suspended. She continued filling out her sales and other required weekly reports, as if she were physically covering her territory. Kim's deception went unnoticed during the entire month of her suspension.

Kim received her promotion and became the new manager of the Southern Tier region. A new employee was assigned to her old position. He found out from one of the dealers that Kim had not visited him during April and casually mentioned this to Kim's boss during a visit to the regional office. Enraged at the deception, Kim's boss fired her. Kim was unable to find new employment in the close-knit industry of animal feed. After several frustrating months of job hunting, she finally found employment as a sales associate in a shopping mall.[4]

What could Kim have done to prevent her act of self-sabotage? Part of the problem was that Kim's reasoning under pressure was as impulsive as her driving. She failed to carefully lay out the alternative solutions to her problem and then to choose the most constructive one.

Kim might have telephoned her boss and openly explained that she would be unable to make *in-person* visits to her dealers for one month because of her suspension. However, she would cover all her accounts by phone during the thirty-day period. Another alternative would have been to hire a retired or unemployed person to chauffeur her for the month. The latter alternative need not even have been reported to management. Instead of patiently taking a rational approach to decision making, Kim impulsively chose the self-sabotaging course.

Few people tell the absolute truth in all work situations. Most people interpret facts in such a way as to protect their self-esteem and make themselves look good. Assume that your productivity has increased one percent, and your boss asks how the productivity-improvement project is going. It is an acceptable interpretation of the facts to say, "Productivity has improved." An "acceptable" lie has these characteristics:

- You don't take full credit for somebody else's work or ideas.
- How you present the facts is a matter of subjective interpretation.
- You wouldn't be embarrassed if your interpretation of the event were made public.
- Neither any individual nor the organization is harmed by your interpretation of the truth.
- Your statement does not violate company policy, professional codes of ethics, or the law. (For example, you cannot deny the existence of carcinogens in the workplace when you know they are present.)

Stealing and Pilfering

"Thou shalt not steal" works its way into most company policy manuals. But unlike many other policy violations, this one subjects the person caught stealing or pilfering to immediate discharge. Stealing is thus a popular choice among those determined on career sabotage. Michelle is a case in point.

Within six months of graduating from high school, Michelle became a certified cosmetologist. She obtained her first job as a shampoo technician, then took employment as a cosmetic salesperson in a department store.

Michelle's charm and tact, combined with her love of cosmetics, enabled her to be promoted to cosmetics manager within one year. Michelle's boss was impressed with her outstanding job performance and her desire to learn more about cosmetics. She therefore gave Michelle the opportunity to attend a three-week Revlon training program in New York City.

Two weeks after Michelle learned that she was going to the Revlon training program, she began to steal. It began with small thefts such as sales promotion items intended for customers. Next, Michelle began to pocket actual merchandise. With the help of another store associate, Michelle moved on to larger and more expensive items, including jewelry from a nearby department.

As a result of inventory audits, and careful observation, the store's management suspected that the two women were stealing merchandise. One night as Michelle headed toward the door, a security guard asked her if she had taken anything. Michelle insisted she had not. The guard asked to search her belongings. Dumbfounded, Michelle handed her handbag to the guard. He found a fully tagged, gold herringbone bracelet inside the bag. The store manager was called to the scene, and Michelle was fired immediately. The manager also threatened to call the police and have her arrested. However, he decided to let Michelle go with the understanding that she would be permanently barred from working at any store within the chain.

The after-effects for Michelle were severe. She was without a job, and lost the respect of family and friends. Ultimately, Michelle became a part-time custodial worker earning slightly above the minimum wage.[5]

In speaking to a vocational rehabilitation counselor, Michelle developed insight into why she had stolen. She had become frightened by the prospects of the new demands being placed on her. She felt the pressure when she was promoted to a departmental manager. Being chosen for Revlon training meant that the company was targeting her for even more responsibility in the future.

Michelle feared assuming more responsibility. As a result, she made the inappropriate and self-sabotaging decision to steal to ensure that she would not be asked to handle more responsibility. By walking out of the store with tagged merchandise, Michelle greatly increased her chances of being caught and fired. If only Michelle had talked about her concerns with a friend, superior, or counselor when she first became ambivalent about the additional responsibility, she might have reduced some of her anxiety and become motivated to find a more sensible method of dealing with the new demands.

How can Michelle's unfortunate situation help you? If you are tempted to do something as self-sabotaging and dangerous as stealing, talk it over with a trusted confidant. Or write a letter to yourself about your temptation. Most likely, you will find a more constructive way of handling your ambivalence toward taking on new responsibilities.

Projecting an Unprofessional Image

Virtually everyone intent on being successful is aware of the importance of projecting a professional image by means of dressing and grooming themselves appropriately. Fewer people are aware of the importance of the more subtle ways of projecting a professional image. Projecting an unprofessional image in these more subtle ways can be as self-sabotaging as wearing a striped jacket and plaid pants simultaneously. Let's look at two behavior patterns that project an unprofessional image.

Being Frivolous About Serious Situations

Humor in the workplace is highly valued. Yet it is self-defeating to consistently make frivolous comments about situations of grave concern to top management.

Constantine, a quality control supervisor, was concerned about the many defects his department found in the small motors made by his company. He developed a few routines about how the company paid only lip service to quality. For example, he did an impression of the manufacturing superintendent making a speech about quality while a motor he was demonstrating caught fire.

Constantine's frivolity finally led to self-sabotage. When he had an audience in his work area, Constantine would often answer the phone, "Hello, Constantine's Junk Yard. How many scrap motors would you like?" One time Constantine answered the phone with his junk-yard greeting when the vice-president of manufacturing called. Within two weeks Constantine was demoted to quality control engineer. He found out too late that the vice-president found nothing humorous about product being converted to scrap.

Constantine should have been on the alert a lot earlier for signs that his frivolity was not being well received. He might have asked a co-worker, "Do you think people are taking my kidding the right way? Or am I going over the edge?" Make the same reality check on your own use of humor in the office.

Excessive Youth Talk

Language gradually changes over time. Phrases and expressions that may have created a negative impression in the past become acceptable to a later generation. For example, "You guys in marketing" to refer to marketing personnel of both sexes is now at least on the borderline of respectability. But too much talk characteristic of teenagers—called youth talk—can be self-defeating because it diminishes the image of professionalism. Expressions to be avoided include: "He goes," "She goes" ("goes" meaning "says"), "he says," "she says" (both meaning "said"), "I'm like" (meaning "I was thinking"), and "you know" (vocalized pause).

Youth talk is particularly self-defeating within organizations whose cultures favor a refined, professional image for higher-level positions. But even where language codes are less restrictive, such as for entry-level positions or jobs outside of customer contact, youth talk can have a negative impact. A case in point is Susan.

A food service supervisor in a bank, Susan had majored in food administration in college and was intent on climbing the ladder in her field. Her youth talk helped Susan establish rapport with entry-level workers in the company cafeteria. When her boss quit, she recommended Susan as her replacement. However, the cafeteria manager turned down Susan's promotion. His justification was that Susan's manner of speaking was an embarrassment to the bank, and as food service manager she would be speaking directly to many bank officials and key customers.

Susan's speech patterns are so ingrained that she may need speech therapy to learn how to speak in a professional manner. She should take the loss of the promotion as a signal to brush up her professional image before she sinks herself again.

Just in case youth talk could be self-defeating for you, tape your voice. Then play back the results and listen carefully for excessive youth talk. Have a friend, spouse, or domestic partner listen along with you. Make whatever modifications in your speech patterns that appear to be necessary.

Anger and Cynicism

A quick path to self-sabotage is to feel and show anger toward co-workers, superiors, subordinates, or customers. One probable outcome is that the other person will retaliate. Your co-worker will not give you the cooperation you need to get your job done. Your boss will reciprocate with a small or no pay increase, a bad assignment, or a blocked promotion. Subordinates may drag their heels when you need something done and bad-mouth you to your boss. And your customers will take their business elsewhere.

Cynicism and anger are related because cynics are angry. They believe other people are motivated by selfishness and self-interest, and distrust most things management does for workers. Cynics put down holiday parties as a "cheap way for management to squeeze more productivity out of people." And they look upon profit-sharing programs as "a clever way of keeping out a labor union." Cynics are usually perceptive and intelligent, but their anger makes others feel uncomfortable, and fails to inspire. Many people can tolerate a cynic as a co-worker, but they don't want one for a boss. Cynicism thus becomes self-defeating for purposes of career advancement.

Anger can be kept under control if you keep the following guidelines in mind:

1. *Anger hampers concentration and diminishes performance on demanding tasks.* While focusing on what angers you, you give only cursory attention to the most important task at hand. Although anger may get your adrenalin pumping, your efforts lose focus and precision. This is why it is important to calm down before doing creative work. Less mentally demanding tasks can often be handled well when you are angry. Use the energy derived from your anger to clean out your files or conduct a routine inventory.

2. *Expressing anger over an event to a third-party who did not make you angry helps prevent a self-defeating display of rage to the wrong person—such as your boss.* You might say to a close friend, "I'm angry that I was passed over for promotion. I wanted the job and I think I deserve it." Your friend's reaction may help you to calm down.

3. *When angry with another person, first express those feelings to yourself and then share the less destructive feelings with the person in question.* The old saw of counting to ten when angry has merit.

Or write down all your angry feelings and then sort out the useful ideas in your list. Suppose the CEO has imposed a hiring restriction that will leave your department understaffed. Compose a letter to yourself explaining how angry you are at the CEO. Then make an appointment with a member of top management to express your legitimate concerns and rational feelings about the hiring freeze.

4. *Do not carry grudges.* Long-term grudges generate negative stress and can divert productive energy. In addition to recognizing that you are carrying a grudge, choose from among these suggestions that appeared in the October 1985 issue of *USA Weekend*:

- Confront the person you have a grudge against in a way that minimizes the consequences. Be objective and tactful rather than explosive.
- Look at the situation from the other person's perspective. A valid reason may exist for his or her behavior (such as the CEO imposing a hiring freeze).
- Weigh the seriousness of the offense that gave rise to your grudge. It may not be that serious.
- Consider your options. List even the farfetched ones to help you vent your anger.
- Work on accepting the situation. Let go of the anger, and move on to the more positive events in life.[6]

Absenteeism and Lateness

The leading cause of employees being disciplined—absenteeism and lateness—is simultaneously a major form of career self-sabotage. Some tolerant managers are more concerned with the productivity of workers while they are on the premises than with how much of the time they are actually there. Career counselor Tom Jackson once commented: "The last person to leave the building at night is the custodian. That gives you a good idea of the importance of being physically present." Despite the liberal attitude toward absenteeism and lateness held by some, the vast majority of managers look askance at employees with poor attendance and lateness records.

Maintaining good attendance and punctuality is more important than ever today because worldwide competition has forced many private organizations into a permanent belt-tightening mode. Governmental organizations are also under constant pressure to control costs. The person who is habitually absent or late is therefore at risk of termination. Of particular concern here is the managerial or professional worker who finds ingenious ways to avoid being on company premises. Such was the situation with Jacques.

Jacques was the director of research and development (R&D) for a French manufacturer of peripheral equipment for computers. Among the French company's products were printers and cables for interconnecting computers. Jacques described his management style as "providing intellectual inspiration rather than hands-on leadership." In practice, this meant that his two key managers and their staff were pretty much on their own except when Jacques conferred with them on major decisions. Jacques prided himself on his ability to create a permissive atmosphere that fostered creativity.

Jacques's leadership style afforded him considerable personal freedom. He capitalized on opportunities to attend professional conferences in France and other countries. His assistant spent much of her time making travel arrangements for Jacques's information-gathering journeys. Prompted by the controller, the president one day questioned Jacques about the amount of time and money he was investing in travel. Jacques offered this defense:

"One of my primary roles here is to act as a sensor. I have to scan the external environment to see what might be useful for us. I can then relate those new ideas to our technology. If I don't interact with the outside world, our R&D perspective will be too narrow. We might also fall prey to the N.I.H. factor. If something is 'not invented here,' we will reject it. I see myself as helping us guard against a too insular viewpoint."

Jacques was comfortable with his assessment that his trips to conferences were legitimate. Nevertheless, he decided to cut back on some of his expensive travel because it was being challenged by the controller and the president. As an alternative, Jacques sought other ways of finding intellectual stimulation away from the company laboratory. He arranged long lunches with computer science professionals from universities and competitive companies. He attended computer industry trade shows in Paris, and visited former colleagues at their new places of work.

One day a new laser printer was introduced by a competitor. Managers and professionals at Jacques's company huddled together to speculate on how this new product might adversely affect their business. The company atmosphere was so charged with a negative type of excitement that the president called for a 2 P.M. meeting of top management that same day. The president and all the other members of the management team, except Jacques, were present. Marcel, the product and development engineering manager who reported to Jacques, attended in his place. Asked why he was attending instead of Jacques, Marcel explained that Jacques was at Oxford University for the day conferring with a computer science professor.

Marcel stood in so admirably for Jacques that the president regarded Marcel as a potential replacement for Jacques. Several months later, Marcel was promoted to the R&D directorship and Jacques was placed on special assignment, reporting to the president. The president explained that he was being replaced because the company need an R&D director with a greater on-site presence. Jacques's new position was so vacuous that it looked as if the president was inviting him to quit. Jacques now faced the prospect of having to search for a new position as a director of R&D. Not only was there a dearth of such positions available, but Jacques would now have to explain why he had been placed on special assignment.

Jacques' setback fell short of full-scale self-sabotage. The many contacts he had made during his "environmental scanning" trips facilitated his finding a new position with only a one-step demotion. He became the new product development manager for one division of a conglomerate with operations throughout Europe and the United States. Jacques feels lucky to still have a managerial position, and now carefully rations his absences from the office.

Jacques could have avoided his career setback by more carefully scanning his internal environment. By studying the culture of his company more thoroughly he would have noticed that managing from a distance was not its style. The hands-on style he eschewed was valued by the president. Jacques did not take a careful look at the choices he had to make. On the one hand, Jacques wanted the high income and perks offered by an R&D director's position. On the other, he wanted the freedom to participate in external professional activities whenever he liked. It was unrealistic to think that he could hold onto the R&D position and still have all the professional freedom he craved.

Aside from its reminder about absenteeism, Jacques's case illustrates that the failure to confront tough choices can be self-defeating. Fortunately for Jacques, he was set back rather than sabotaged. In order to satisfy a major goal, such as achieving an executive position, you may have to sacrifice some personal freedom.

Clinging to Self-Righteous Values

Successful executives are supposed to cling tenaciously to a set of values that guide them and their organizations toward the ethical choice in tempting situations. Few would argue that ethics are not important. But inflexibly holding on to your values can be self-defeating if you find yourself convinced that you are right and everybody else is wrong.

An illuminating pattern of self-sabotage driven by self-righteousness is illustrated by Henry's situation.

Henry held a series of junior high and high school teaching jobs within the state system over a twenty-five-year career. Several schools parted company with Henry by not renewing his contract. Although he finally received tenure, he was dismissed from one position following a four-year legal struggle. Henry was found to be unfit to teach because of his continual conflicts with students and their parents.

Henry insisted that the goals set for students, from the standpoint of both academics and discipline, were too low. The administration insisted that Henry "cool it," but Henry clung tenaciously to his values. He accused the administration of hypocrisy and his colleagues of pandering to students and their parents in order to hold on to their jobs. Henry spent all of his inheritance and savings on legal fees in an attempt to hold on to his job—to no avail.

Financially and emotionally drained, Henry worked for several years selling used cars, substitute teaching, and waiting tables. Tired and ashamed of being underemployed, Henry returned to the classroom as a junior high school language teacher in another town. Toward the end of the academic year, he wrote a letter to an old friend reviewing his new job experience. In his words:

"My teaching experience in the local school system has not been fruitful at all. I lack the patience and temperament to cope with junior high school. So overwhelmed am I in an avalanche of bureaucracy that I will not renew my contract for the coming school year.

"My frayed nerves could never endure another one-year stint of water torture. It is virtually impossible to maintain any semblance of academic or disciplinary standards. I refuse to compromise my values for the sake of preserving a job I really don't need or want. I don't mean to sound cavalier. Driving a twelve-year old car doesn't bother me. Nor do I mind wearing clothes that are not fashionable. What I do mind is sacrificing my values."

Henry's self-righteousness had put him at odds with administrators, colleagues, students, and their parents. On the verge of being permanently blacklisted from ever getting back into the classroom, Henry was urged by the recipient of his letter to go through one of the most important exercises for overcoming self-defeating behavior. He typed out, to the best of his recollection, all the major altercations he had with administrators in his various teaching jobs. Instructed to look for a common thread to these upsetting experiences, Henry himself found that his standards were too high, perhaps unrealistic, for today's world.

Henry entered the classroom once again, this time at a parochial high school in another small town. Attempting to control his self-righteousness, he fashioned a comeback. Henry wrote a more optimistic note on a holiday card to the same friend:

"Small-town life agrees with me. I left the public school system for Notre Dame, the only Catholic high school remaining between the two major cities located in this area. Never again will I set foot in a junior high school. Although I suffered a substantial pay cut, I am infinitely happier teaching older students. Going to work each day is a "high" for me. This is indeed the most pleasant situation that I have ever experienced as a teacher."

Undoubtedly this is Henry's most pleasant experience as a teacher. Because his behavior is no longer so self-sabotaging, he can now breathe easier. Being more tolerant of others' values has granted Henry the relief of not encountering such a hostile work environment.

Should you find that over a period of time you have entered into frequent clashes of opinions with others, follow the constructive actions Henry finally took. Prepare a written account of your run-ins, and look for a common thread. Perhaps you too have experienced a clash of values. Maybe you could modify your positions in order to prevent further career self-sabotage.

Insensitivity to People

The most consistent observation about career success is that interpersonal skills are vital. Managers and professionals who bully and intimidate others, who are hostile, mean, and rude, or insensitive in other ways are usually headed toward a career setback.

Evidence collected by an institute for the study of leadership demonstrates the negative consequences of insensitivity, specifically how it can block the careers of up-and-coming managers. In a study of top executives, psychologists Morgan McCall and Michael Lombardo compared "derailed" executives with those who had progressed to senior management positions. The leading category of fatal flaws was insensitivity to others, characterized by an abrasive, intimidating, bullying style.[7] When feedback accumulated that the aspirant to senior management treated people extremely poorly, he or she was removed from the promotable list.

Exceptions do exist, of course. Not all insensitive and disliked people suffer severe career setbacks. The late Charles Revson of Revlon was a legendary tyrant. Then it sometimes takes a long time before people can get their revenge on a bully. John Sununu, chief of staff under George Bush, is noted for his imperiousness and intolerance. Introduced at the National Press Club as the "White House Chafe of Staff," he responded that he planned to continue his calculated insults and temper tantrums toward Congress. Later, when Sununu was under attack for having used government aircraft and money for personal trips, several White House associates were quick to volunteer damaging evidence.

Despite the exceptions, insensitivity to people *is* self-sabotaging when one is dependent upon others to accomplish work. Barry's case shows why.

Barry, a senior vice-president of a large commercial printing concern, was only one step away from becoming president of the company. His almost obsessional knowledge of the printing industry, his financial acumen, and his aggressiveness had enabled Barry to become an officer in the company.

Barry's preferred style of leadership was to delegate fact finding and then to have the team member bring a complete report back to him. If the president or another member of top management questioned any aspect of the report, Barry would blame the person who had prepared the report. After meeting with top management, he would castigate that team member. At his angriest, Barry would even threaten to ruin the career of the person whose report had been questioned.

When a report was well received by the CEO or other members of top management, Barry would share credit with the group member on a 90:10 basis. Barry naturally voted himself 90 percent of the credit. The people who reported to Barry resented receiving so little credit for their efforts, but so much of the blame. One day Laura, a financial analyst, mentioned tactfully that she would like to receive more credit for her contribution to top management briefings. Barry accused her of being a "recognition hound" and a "wretched team player."

As a result of his generosity in assigning blame, and his stinginess in assigning credit, Barry engendered the resentment of many people below him. Barry's unpopularity peaked when he brought Laura to a top management meeting to placate her desire for more recognition. At the meeting, Barry introduced Laura, and said he had brought her along so that she could receive full credit for crunching a few numbers for the report. Although humiliated, Laura stayed for the meeting to help interpret some of the figures she had assembled.

Laura decided to seek appropriate revenge. She shared her experience with a few other accountants and financial analysts. Together they composed a letter to the board of directors explaining why they thought Barry was too unpolished to become president of their company. The letter prompted the board to conduct a thorough review of Barry's qualifications for the presidency. Six months later, the current president resigned, and a new president was appointed from the outside.

Barry attributed his being bypassed to office politics. He assumed that people were trying to block him from becoming president because they favored the outside candidate. What Barry failed to accept was that his abrasiveness and credit stealing had converted the professionals on his staff into adversaries. Barry's insult to Laura was the last straw. It motivated his own staff to mount a campaign against his becoming president.

Barry's chances of becoming president could have been salvaged. Why did a senior executive being groomed for the presidency not attend a seminar on leadership styles and learn about how he came across to others? Why didn't he ask for feedback from other members of the management team on how well he was performing as a leader? With appropriate feedback and a commitment to make necessary adjustments, Barry could have achieved his goal.

Barry's real problem then was that he had no awareness of the idea of career self-sabotage. He therefore did not monitor his own behavior or ask for feedback from others.

Even when things are going well for you, it is helpful to ask yourself every few months:

- Is there anything I'm doing that is working against my best interests?
- Are people recoiling from me in any way?
- Am I continually fighting the same old battles?

If your answers are affirmative to these or similar questions, investigate further and take whatever action is needed. Do precisely the things Barry failed to do.

Crossing Swords With Powerful People

In Barry's case, the senior vice-president's staff did cross swords with a powerful person, but they did so collectively and via a quiet, behind-the-back maneuver. Ordinarily, it is self-sabotaging to step on Superman's cape directly. Before attempting an angry confrontation with a powerful person, it is crucial to have formed an alliance with an even more powerful person. Before having a sharp disagreement with your boss over a major issue, first obtain the sympathy of your boss's boss for your position. Jim violated this principle and accordingly suffered the consequences.

Jim was a district manager for a large insurance company, a position he had held for many years. A new regional vice-president was appointed one year. The next year, Jim's district office experienced some difficulties. The insurance market had softened, and a new state insurance law requiring a sixty-day notice of a 10 percent or greater premium increase was instituted. The change in the law caused the underwriting department to fall behind in quoting new business.

In April, the new vice-president wrote a critical appraisal of Jim. He described the district as being out of control and the underwriting department as being poorly managed. According to the vice-president's analysis, the district was writing only one out of five policies that it quoted. He told the district manager to improve this ratio by carefully evaluating the type of policies they were selling and those they were not.

Jim wrote the vice-president a lengthy rebuttal to the negative appraisal of his district. He said that he had been in charge of the district office for almost thirty years and that his methods of control were best suited to the situation. Jim pointed out that external market conditions had caused the underwriting problem and that he could not control them. Jim also said that the district underwriting manager (who reported to Jim) was incompetent and should be replaced immediately.

The vice-president was angered by Jim's letter. He told him that the situation called for action plans, not excuses. The vice-president also said that the underwriting manager was the best in the business, and that Jim should work closely with him. Jim became further enraged by the vice-president's stern response to his rebuttal. He called the vice-president's boss in the home office to complain about how he was being treated. At the same time, he wrote a lengthy, critical memo to his underwriting manager. In the memo he issued sixteen orders and threatened to have the underwriting manager fired if all were not carried out. When the underwriting manager showed the memo to the regional vice-president, the VP initiated actions to pressure Jim into early retirement.[8]

Jim's behavior was self-defeating because he did not want early retirement. His pension was approximately 60 percent of what he would have received had he worked for the company until age 65. After several months of searching, Jim finally had to settle for a part-time position as claims examiner.

Jim's conflict with the regional vice-president need not have been self-sabotaging. Before crossing swords, Jim should have stopped to analyze the power discrepancy between himself and the vice-president. This harsh, anger-ventilating memo was a poor way of resolving conflict between himself and a person with much more formal authority.

Jim might have initiated a meeting with the vice-president to encourage him to look at some additional factors in evaluating the status of the district office. Jim could have brought facts to the meeting to document his side of the story. If the gentle confrontation did not work, Jim might have gingerly approached the president of the company to see if an appeal of the evaluation was possible.

Instead, Jim chose a self-sabotaging alternative. By crossing swords with a more powerful person and venting his anger, Jim wounded his own ego and his career. Jim hurt himself, but his mistakes might benefit you. Beware of sending a fire-spitting memo to a person of higher rank. It could be self-sabotaging. A good alternative is to write the memo but not send it. Then discuss your problem with the key person involved, tactfully and diplomatically.

5

Subtle Forms of Self-Sabotage

$\int$ome of the most adroit self-saboteurs bring failure upon themselves with subtlety and finesse. The process is similar to how day turns into night, and blond hair turns white. Many of their self-sabotaging actions and attitudes seem positive at first, but gradually they assume a downward drift. The person moves one step at a time from high performance through mediocrity to substandard performance. Career sabotage follows after a long bout of substandard performance.

Awareness of these subtle forms of self-sabotage is a starting point in preventing them from moving your career in a downward spiral. You can also use this information to reverse a pattern of self-sabotage already in motion, or to help a subordinate, friend, or spouse.

Power Obsession

An affinity for power is part of the emotional makeup of top executives and deal makers. Without a strong power need, a person is unlikely to invest all the physical and mental energy necessary for success. Nevertheless, an obsession with power is often (certainly not *always*) self-defeating because the power chaser focuses too much on acquiring power. While the chase is on, two important factors are often neglected: the quality of work being performed to acquire power, and building relationships with people.

Another problem with a power obsession is that such behavior alienates many people. If you begin to falter, they will do what they can to facilitate your descent. An example is when Donald Trump's financial empire began to erode. Large numbers of people smirked, "It couldn't happen to a more deserving person."

An obsession with power has led many executives into unsound business deals. An executive who fits into this pattern is William H. Bricker. According to a 1987 article in *Business Week*, Bricker resigned as CEO of Diamond Shamrock to allay concerns that he had become a big part of the problem at his company. Under his direction a once profitable chemical company evolved into a debt-ridden conglomerate with huge, consistent losses.

Bill Bricker had moved rapidly up the corporate ranks to become chief executive at Diamond Shamrock at age 44. His first big assignment was to manage the chemical business. He later served as an apprentice to the president, Raymond F. Evans. Bricker was well-liked by Evans who admired his canny instincts and his sense of team play. Moving up one rung on the ladder made a big difference. Evans explained that "Bricker changed 180 degrees when he became CEO. He just became a different guy. I guess his ego got him."

Bricker became obsessed with the idea of building a big-league energy company. By the time Bricker resigned, Diamond had the trappings of high status. The power symbols included a 12,000 acre-ranch on the Texas prairie, a $1-million box at Dallas Cowboy home games, and a fleet of airplanes for Bricker and other directors. Pheasant hunts were part of customer entertainment at the Texas ranch. Diamond regularly flew in a professional shoot manager from Ireland to organize the hunts. Under Bricker's direction, Diamond took unusual risks for its size. Exploration in a dry hole in Alaska's Beaufort Sea cost approximately $800 million. An analyst said, "Bricker was betting the ranch and lost it."[1]

Bricker's quest for power brought his company to the brink of financial ruin, and set back his career substantially. Events could have worked out more positively for Bricker had he listened to the warning signals around him. Bricker reasoned at one point that the outlook for energy prices indicated that Diamond should plunge into the production of oil, gas, and coal. His company directors opposed acquiring a coal-producing company, but Bricker persisted. Evans, the former president, said, "I had the feeling that he wasn't going to listen to anyone." Many company executives concluded that it was futile to oppose Bricker and the glitzy new culture he was creating at Diamond.[2]

Bricker moved stubbornly forward in his quest to be CEO of a powerful company, surrounded by excess and ostentation. He apparently never stopped to ask, "Is the criticism I'm receiving from the board valid? Am I going over the edge in trying to act like a soap opera stereotype of an energy baron?"

If you have reached a position in which power abuse is a temptation, audit your own possible tendencies toward greed, gluttony, and avarice. Ask yourself:

- How much would a reasonable person in my position flaunt his or her power?
- Would the board of directors approve of the perks I have allotted myself?
- Is the compensation I demand appropriate to my accomplishments, or is it a question of satisfying my ego?
- Would my use of power make a sordid case history in a text about business ethics?
- Is the way I am using my power bound to make others angry and resentful?

If your answers to these questions are mostly affirmative, people are probably already plotting to depose you. Soften your approach and use your power in a less self-serving way. Make a less ostentatious show of power, and display some humility.

Negative Self-Talk

Putting yourself down by making negative self-statements has the cumulative effect of setting low goals for yourself. A negative statement here and there is not sabotaging. Eventually, however, low expectations become self-fulfilling. Asked about negative self-talk in his line of work, police lieutenant Larry Weber said:

"I see it all the time. We have officers who keep saying they will never pass the promotion exam. They put themselves down so badly it comes true. By the time they take the test, they are convinced they are going to fail. When it comes time to take the civil service test, they can't think straight. It works out that they have talked themselves into failing."

To avoid self-sabotage, the police officers who make these negative self-statements must learn to talk positively to themselves. Many people in other lines of work face the same problem. The antidote to self-sabotage through negative self-talk is to engage in positive self-talk. According to the system developed by Jay T. Knippen and Thad B. Green, the first step in using positive self-talk is to objectively state the problem that is casting doubt on one's self-worth.[3] The key word here is *objectively*. Terry, who is fearful of a report-writing assignment, might say, "I've been asked to write a report for the company, and I'm not a good writer."

The next step is to objectively interpret what the problem *does not* mean. Terry might say, "Not being a skilled writer doesn't mean that I can't figure out a way to write a good report, or that I'm an ineffective employee."

Next, objectively state what the situation *does* mean. In doing this, avoid put-down labels such as "incompetent," "stupid," "dumb," "jerk," or "airhead." All these terms are forms of negative self-talk. Terry should state what it does mean: "I have a problem with one small aspect of this job—preparing professional-level reports. This means I need to improve my report-writing skills."

The fourth step is to objectively account for the cause of the problem. Terry would say, "I'm really worried about writing a good report because I have very little experience in writing along these lines."

The fifth step is to identify some positive ways of preventing the situation from arising again. Terry might say, "I'll refer to a book on business communications and review the chapter on report writing," or "I'll enroll in a course or seminar on business report writing."

The final step is to use *positive self-talk*. Terry imagines his boss saying, "This report is really good. I'm proud of my decision to select you to prepare this important report."

Positive self-talk helps overcome self-defeating tendencies in several ways. It builds self-confidence and self-esteem because it programs the mind with positive messages.[4] Making frequent positive messages or affirmations about the self creates a more confident person.

Positive self-talk is also useful in overcoming self-imposed limitations. Such limitations are those we create for ourselves, usually on the basis of very little objective evidence. One example is a person not applying for a desirable position because he or she declares, "The company is probably looking for somebody with more experience (or for somebody younger, or more technical, or from a large company)." The candidate thus disqualifies himself or herself, even though none of these restrictions have been mentioned by the prospective employer.

Fear of Success

Fear of success, as mentioned earlier, can lead to procrastination. The same fear can lead to other forms of self-sabotage, including snatching defeat from the jaws of victory. One such success fearer was found at a university.

A student who was evaluated as doing poorly in her Ph.D. program got the top grade on the qualifying exams. She then proceeded to lose all copies of her dissertation. A thief snatched the elegant briefcase in which she had put them from her unlocked car. The student was shocked that anyone could have been so cruel as to steal something of such great importance to her and of such negligible value to anyone else. She simply did not see that by her carelessness she had virtually invited the theft of the briefcase, which from the thief's point of view happened to be stuffed with useless paper.[5]

The fear of repeating past successes is a more subtle form of the fear of success. People who earn big bonuses and commissions after an outstanding year are sometimes trapped by this curious form of self-sabotage. They find ways of destroying their chances of being as successful as they were in the past. In this way they avoid worry about having to give top performances continually. A financial planner experienced this problem.

Karl had gradually built up his business over a five-year period, earning $225,000 in 1986. To celebrate, he took a vacation at the end of the year, then never seemed to return mentally from this vacation. After achieving his goal, he doubted he could repeat his outstanding performance. Karl prospected less and made fewer new contacts and calls. Through September of 1987 he earned approximately $130,000. After the stock market crash in October, his commissions declined precipitously. His final earnings for 1987 were $139,000.

Clients called to express worry and concern about their investments. Karl reassured his clients. He told them he had advocated conservative investments, thus protecting them against severe losses so long as they could ride out the market. Karl rarely made any buy or sell recommendations to his clients, thus restricting his commissions. He became increasingly passive as an investment adviser. He restricted his telephone calls to several wealthy clients who were cordial but not actively investing. He also stopped following up on referrals.

Even simple inquiries by clients about their accounts seemed too stressful for Karl to handle. He spent hours reading investment newsletters and *The Wall Street Journal,* but took no action. Business had gradually picked up for other financial planners in his office, but Karl's commissions continued to decline. His income fell to $70,000 in 1988.

As his income continued to decline, Karl began bouncing checks, switching banks and setting up new accounts, and was late in paying many of his bills. Soon he began borrowing money from his wealthiest clients. Karl was on the verge of being fired when his company collapsed. He thus avoided the stigma of being fired. Karl found new employment in a salaried position in the trust department of a bank. Bit by bit he made good on past due bills. He now pursues a more modest life-style and often says to friends, "I wish the financial planning business hadn't gone so bad. I miss the chance to earn a really big income."[6]

How can the doctoral candidate who lost her dissertation and Karl, who lost his nerve, be helped? Much depends on how deep their problem lies. Fear of success sometimes stems from a neurotic behavior pattern, driven by an unconscious need to reject success. If so, the person who runs from success may need many sessions with a psychotherapist to overcome the problem. An important part of such therapy is to confront the patient with repeated instances of his or her fear of success. In Karl's case he would have to explore intensively what he didn't like about earning such a high income.

Not everybody requires psychotherapy to overcome fear of success. The majority of such instances are motivated by concerns about the heavy demands placed by others, or by a desire not to hurt other people's feelings or to ruffle their feathers. If a person is an outstanding success, some friends and family members may become envious or feel slighted. To avoid dealing with such awkward situations, a person may back off from being really successful.

Emotional support from family and friends can help a person overcome a fear of success that is not driven by unconscious desires and disturbing childhood experiences. Significant others can help a person overcome fear of success by offering reassurance that the person will still be loved despite his or her outstanding accomplishment. Losing close friends is a real possibility after outdistancing them in worldly achievement. Reassurance and cooperation are thus very helpful. Karl's wife might have told him repeatedly, "You had a great year in 1986, Karl, but don't worry about it. I'm not expecting miracles again. Savor your good times."

Many people fail to receive the emotional support they need from family and friends because they do not know how to ask for it. If you need emotional support, but are not adept at requesting it, do the following:

1. *Be specific about what you want.* Telling someone that you are in trouble and have no idea what to do next hands them a complex problem. A practical way of being specific in asking for help is to point to exactly the type of help you need. You might say to a friend, "I think I'm afraid of success, and I want to run my thoughts past you."

2. *Be as positive and self-confident as possible.* Instead of saying "I feel overwhelmed and out of control," say "I'm faced with an important problem to solve. I want to get your input on whether I'm thinking sensibly."

3. *Translate your request for help into an even exchange of ideas.* A

suitable expression is: "I would like to exchange some ideas with you on a problem I'm facing." Even if you really want some specific advice on solving your problem, presenting your request in a way that emphasizes an even exchange makes both parties feel more comfortable.

4. *Flatter the person from whom you wish to receive support.* Indicate that you respect the other person's advice because you respect his or her thinking, accomplishments, and judgment.

5. *Follow up any form of help with an expression of appreciation.* If the person is a friend rather than a spouse or domestic partner, write a note of appreciation.[7]

Poor Team Play

Team play is so valued that people who resist being good team players risk sabotaging their careers. To be accused of being a poor team player is to be seen as a misfit, particularly in a bureaucracy. If you own the company, conspicuous displays of team play are much less necessary. The team player emphasizes "we" instead of "I" and freely engages in group decision making. He or she also looks to exchange favors in such ways as taking care of problems when a co-worker is unavailable. The solo artist does little of any of this. To avoid self-sabotage, it is important to engage in team play even at an early stage in one's career. Conrad's experience illustrates why.

After graduating from college as an accounting major, Conrad fulfilled his ROTC obligation of two years of active duty as a military officer. He had a lot of respect for the army and the caliber of the officers with whom he worked. Yet Conrad felt he was not well suited for a career in the military. In his words, "I'm too independent. I like to make decisions on my own. I need more flexibility and space than the army can provide. I would be better off in business or industry."

Conrad's next career move was to obtain a position with a CPA firm in Boston as a staff accountant. While in the army Conrad prepared for his CPA exam. Within 18 months of working as a civilian, he passed all five parts of the exam. Conrad believed that his career opportunities were unlimited. His credentials were excellent, and his two years as an army lieutenant gave him more leadership experience than his competitors had.

Conrad went about his work diligently, rarely having lunch or after-hours drinks with the other accountants. He reasoned that he was more serious-minded than his co-workers. Conrad was intent on becoming the highest producer in his unit. He succeeded, attaining the highest number of billable hours among the junior accountants in his office.

When a supervising accountant position was created in Conrad's area, he was not chosen. Instead, the partners promoted a woman a little older than Conrad whose productivity was about average. Conrad was both perturbed and perplexed. Why would the partners not choose him for supervisor when he was the highest producer in the office and an experienced leader to boot? At Conrad's request, the managing partner of the office explained why: Conrad was indeed a competent and productive accountant, but he was too much of a loner. He acted as if he were in business for himself instead of working as a member of the firm.

Conrad learned early in his career that not being a good team player was blocking his ambition to advance toward management. If he wanted to stop sabotaging his career, he could adopt one of the two options available. He could stay with the firm, make more of an attempt to become a team player, and hope that he could reshape his image. Or he could seek employment in another CPA firm, begin afresh, and demonstrate the spirit of team work from the start. Because Conrad had solicited the feedback he needed, he could alter the personal style that was preventing him from achieving an important goal.

Because team play is so valued today, I recommend that you solicit feedback as to whether you are a good team player. If the feedback is negative, revamp your style and begin to cooperate more with others. Above all, start using the word "we" rather than "I."

Excuse Making

Deft excuse makers shift the blame for a negative event from themselves to an outside cause. They thus get off the hook temporarily. How often do you blame a computer malfunction for your failure to get results to your boss on time?

Repeated excuse making becomes self-sabotaging because the excuse maker is actually disclaiming responsibility for failure.

He is saying essentially, for example, "I'm no good with details. As you know, some people are better with concepts than details. It is therefore not my fault that some of the figures were wrong for our presentation to our biggest customer on Monday morning." Failing becomes easy when it is beyond one's control. Raymond Higgins and C. R. Snyder, two researchers on self-defeating excuses, describe a telling case:

Bob faced a dilemma. His oft-stated ambition was to be a social worker. In fact, he had been one briefly but had lost his job because he was unable to overcome his obsessive fears about things that might happen to him when he went to work. Over the course of several months he was absent twice as often as he was present. He ultimately agreed to "resign" his position. Now he needed only to complete a correspondence course to regain his certification.

As he thought about this situation, Bob realized that, if he were to become recertified, he might actually get a professional position. The prospect frightened him—he felt that he couldn't stand it if he were to try and fail again. As things turned out, Bob just couldn't find the time to work on his correspondence course. He had too many commitments and was making more all the time. Besides, every time he tried to read the course text, he fell asleep. Of all the available courses, why had he chosen this one? Something else would have been much better.[8]

Bob's case illustrates how self-defeating excuse making operates. His excuses did not get him through some hard times and enable him to achieve something worthwhile. Instead, they increased his chances of failure. Bob excused his high absenteeism from work by informing his supervisor and co-workers that he was suffering from chronic heart disease. (In fact, he did have a heart murmur.) His medical excuse concealed the real reason for his truancy (his obsessive fears) and helped him avoid being labeled as emotionally disturbed. Nevertheless, Bob's excuse making was self-defeating at another level. It reinforced his chronic pattern of avoiding dealing with the fears that were limiting his life and his freedom.

Bob's temporarily successful excuse making was also self-defeating because it eroded his self-esteem. The deceit inherent in the excuse was transparent to him. He eventually suffered from condemnatory self-statements and a growing sense of hopelessness about ever regaining control of his life.[9]

Excuse makers need to be pummeled psychologically by a few authority figures before they can learn to help themselves. One of the best illustrations of how to help an excuse maker happened to me at LaGuardia Airport. Stressed-out from the crowd, the noise, and the flight delay at LaGuardia, I could not locate my tickets. Feeling dependent and helpless, I said to the ticket agent at the check-in counter: "I've lost my tickets. What should I do now?" "Find them," he replied sternly. Rummaging through my attaché case, I did find them. The look on the man's face and the tone of his voice gave me no alternative.

Excuse makers have to be treated in the stern way adopted by the ticket agent by those who influence their lives. Suppose someone uses this excuse: "I won't be able to get the figures you need until next week because nobody is available to fix my computer." The manager in this case should reply, "I need the figures. It's your job to figure out how to get them to me. If you can't do it, take a one-week suspension without pay. In the mean time, we'll find somebody else to do the job." After one or two such constructive confrontations, the excuse maker will realize that excuses offer few long-range benefits.

Assume that no authority figure has confronted you about your excuse making. This could mean that you are not a self-sabotaging excuse maker. Nevertheless, it is to your advantage to conduct a self-audit to see if you have any tendencies toward an overreliance on excuse making. Answer the following:

☐ Do you attribute most of your mistakes to having had a bad day?

☐ Is it usually somebody else's fault when you fail to complete a project or fail to complete it on time?

☐ Do you attribute most of your problems to bad luck?

☐ Do you feel you would receive much better performance appraisals if your employer didn't have such unrealistic standards?

☐ Do you think you would be much more successful today if you had entered a different field?

Positive answers to the questions in the box could mean that you are placing too much blame on the outside world for your short-comings. Begin to think of yourself as the most important agent in whether or not you succeed. Only then can you overcome the self-sabotaging habit of excuse making.

Refusal to Negotiate

An intractable negotiating style is another form of self-sabotage. Tough-minded negotiation has some short-range benefits, such as a few big wins at the bargaining table. Yet in the long term the person who refuses to negotiate collects many enemies and few friends. Should a third party be required to settle a negotiating stalemate, that person will have little sympathy for the party who refuses to budge. Divorce lawyers sometimes demand preposter-ous settlements for their clients, and refuse to grant any conces-sions. Because of the lawyers' refusal to negotiate a mutually satisfactory settlement, such cases go to trial. In response to these attorneys' intractability, the judge is likely to order a minimum settlement for their clients.

Howard Raiffa, in *The Art and Science of Negotiation*, refers to the no-concessions negotiating style as macho-chicken.[10] *Macho* applies to the negotiator who acts very tough and masculine; *chicken* refers to the game in which two drivers head their cars directly toward each other. Unless one of the drivers gets out of the way (chickens out), a head-on crash is inevitable. The analogy is valid because both the driver and the negotiator are headed down a path of self-sabotage. The person who refuses to negoti-ate on the job often behaves similarly at home.

Marv, the vice-president of purchasing at a food processing company, prides himself on his toughness. He describes himself as "a guy who grants nobody any favors. Every dollar anyone gets from me is earned. I almost never grant concessions. Anyone who doesn't like it can do business elsewhere." As a parent he maintains the same firm attitudes. "I tell my children that if they want to drive the car, they earn the gas and insurance money. No exceptions. I never let the kids out for dates, athletics, or school events unless they have all their chores done. I'm the parent, I make the decisions. When they run their own households, they can make the rules."

Several times farmers have pleaded with Marv to compromise on the difference between the price they asked for their crops and the price he offered. One time, an orange grower explained to Marv that he would actually be losing $1.00 a bushel at the price Marv offered. Marv replied, "If you don't like my price, find another buyer or let your crop rot. Get back to us when you have reached your decision. You know our number."

The orange grower did sell at Marv's price that year. But the next season, the grower found other purchasers for his entire crop. Short of enough oranges to meet the demand for juice, Marv contacted the grower and asked when he would be ready to make shipment. The grower replied that he would not sell to Marv's company at any price, that the company could purchase oranges from California or South America. Marv knew that he would be held responsible for the extraordinary price his company would have to pay for oranges this season. Because competitors did not have to pay so much for oranges, Marv's company would have to absorb the cost. Orange juice profits were reduced to zero that year, and so was Marv's salary increase.

Marv also experienced some upheaval in his home life. His son left home to live with a group of friends while still in high school. He contended that since he was treated with no warmth or understanding at home, he preferred to live outside the family. Marv's daughter dropped out of college, stating that she would return to college at some point when she could afford to pay all her own expenses. She resented her father's implication that he was granting her an enormous favor by making small contributions to her college expenses. Following these defections by the children, Marv's relationship with his wife became strained. She blamed some of the children's confusion on Marv's authoritarian attitudes as a parent.

At first Marv found plausible rationalizations for the negative consequences of his unyielding negotiating style. The orange grower who refused to sell to them was just being spiteful, and his children were just being normally rebellious. Nevertheless, Marv was rational enough to see the underlying thread in these two setbacks. Unless he found a way to grant more concessions to people, yet still save face, he would further sabotage his work and personal life.

Marv knew the human resources director at his company well enough to ask her what he might be doing wrong in dealing with people. She advised Marv to attend a negotiating workshop and to read extensively on the topic. Marv has a way to go, but he has become more flexible. He is beginning to understand emotionally that both sides can win at negotiation.

If you, like Marv, have developed an inflexible negotiating style, it is time to practice the art of concession making. A refusal to negotiate is doubly self-sabotaging in a business climate like the current one, in which cooperative relationships between people are emphasized.

Failure to Empathize

Closely related to a refusal to negotiate is a failure to empathize with people. When a person cannot understand another's viewpoint, concessions are not likely to be granted to that person. Failure to empathize can be self-defeating because the individual or groups whose viewpoint is not understood may rebel. For example, an executive who cannot understand why a group of workers is dissatisfied about advancement opportunities may soon face discrimination charges. Failure to empathize can also be self-defeating when the issues are technical.

Fay was placed in charge of a brand-new software quality assurance (SQA) group. Six years of technical and managerial work in SQA together with many seminars and conferences on the topic resulted in Fay's becoming a zealot. Fay wrote a presentation on how to start an SQA program. She gave the presentation many times, both within and outside the company. Fay was promoted to manager of the quality assurance department, which included both hardware and software. Yet software quality assurance remained her true allegiance.

Fay was given the chance to become an adviser on software engineering to the general manager of a division. She jumped at the opportunity to have an influence on policy over the entire division. Despite her new position, Fay has continued to act as if she were still heading up SQA. She speaks regularly to software engineering groups within the division, trying to convince them to change their development methods. Her words appear to have no effect.

Fay turns her audiences off the minute she steps into the room. She wears buttons and carries a tote bag with SQA slogans. Fay refers to herself as an SQA engineer. She pushes hard for more test and SQA involvement in the software development process. Because Fay will not put aside her old role as an SQA engineer, development engineers do not take her seriously. They see Fay as another quality assurance person trying to tell them what to do, not as a spokesperson for their general manager.[11]

Unless Fay learns to empathize with her audience, and hears her message the way they hear it, she will continue to behave in a way that defeats her purpose. She wants to inspire people, but she frames her messages in a way that leaves them suspicious and skeptical. Until she learns that her failure to empathize is her biggest obstacle, Fay will never be successful as a division consultant for the total software engineering process.

Empathy is not easy to learn, but Fay has to take some constructive action if she is to adequately fill her professional role. A feasible approach would be the type of training now being used to help people become more sensitive to cultural diversity in the workplace. People from majority and minority groups are brought together in small groups to thrash out differences in attitudes and perceptions. In the awareness group proposed here, hardware and software professionals could talk about the type of person they want to serve as a general adviser. In the process, Fay would undoubtedly be taken to task for the insensitivity of her SQA buttons and tote bag.

If the feedback you have been receiving is that you are short on empathy, and long on seeing things your own way, take heed. Hold a group session with people who are dependent on your output. Initiate a discussion on how well your group is able to understand its requirements.

Drifting Into Obsolescence

Another gradual and subtle way of committing career self-sabotage is to become obsolete through lack of appropriate knowledge or skills. Obsolescence is often thought of in terms of technical knowledge and skill. However, a person can also become obsolete for lacking knowledge and skills about administrative matters or people. An example is the manager who never acquires the appropriate skills and sensitivities for dealing comfortably with a culturally diverse work force. Gradually that person becomes obsolete as he or she is perceived as practicing job discrimination. Persisting in a leadership style that is inappropriate to the circumstances is another path to obsolescence and self-sabotage.

When President Frank Marant gained control of Great Southern Foods from his uncle five years ago, one of his primary goals was to impose a system of financial controls over the $800-million processed foods conglomerate. The thirty-eight-year-old Marant was able to accomplish this initial objective. His controls were of some value in salvaging the company when it lost $36 million four years ago. Paradoxically, Marant's tight controls led to his recent downfall.

Insiders say controls were an obsession with Marant. He centralized management to the point of frustrating leading executives in the company. His insistence on checking and rechecking caused many delays in decision making. Operations were virtually strangled in paperwork and electronic messages. An example is that Great Southern's most recent annual report claimed that the company would spend $8 million this year to open twenty-five more processing operations. Yet six months into the fiscal year, little work has been done on the projects. Because of Marant's insistence on such a thorough analysis of each project, decisions have been postponed.

Such delayed decision making can be particularly harmful in the fast-moving field of processed foods. The constant parade of new products in this field makes quick reaction a necessity. A human resources director said: "Marant's situation is a perfect example of how a bungling president can mess up a company and bring about his own demise." The same director was among the fifteen people participating in a palace revolt when Marant was stripped of his authority.

A downward turning point for Marant came when two inside directors, Joe Palaggi and Dean Wilson, became upset about the company's lethargy in the fall. During the same time span, a number of key managers in Great Southern had complained to Palaggi and Wilson that Marant's leadership style had been demoralizing. When it seemed that Marant was about to fire two key general managers, Palaggi and Wilson blew the whistle. They went to an outside director to explain how the company was heading toward a rapid decline. Palaggi and Wilson spearheaded a drive to build a dossier on Marant's shortcomings as a company president.

The end for Marant came when Palaggi, Wilson, and three outside directors met in Atlanta. A special board meeting was called. Three dozen operating executives threatened to quit unless Marant was deposed from his chief executive position. The board moved swiftly, stripping Marant of his titles as president and chief operating executive. He was reassigned as vice-president of special projects at a 50 percent cut in pay.

Marant said that the whole affair was a conspiracy to remove him because he wanted to run a sophisticated, finely tuned business. A confidant of Marant said that what Marant's antagonists really objected to was his plan to bring in two new marketing executives from the outside. A counter-charge made by one of the inside directors active in Marant's dethroning was, "Frank just wasn't willing to accept the fact that you can't run a business by reading computer printouts and sending memos. If you don't get out and visit the troops, they'll eventually get rid of you."

Marant contributed to his own demise by blindly employing a leadership style that may appear modern and effective on the surface but that is becoming obsolete. Marant focused so much on computerized controls that he neglected the human touch of "management by wandering around" or "hands-on leadership." Because Marant's basic personality probably lends itself to managing from a distance, he chose a leadership style that was a natural fit. Yet had he studied current information about leadership style he might have realized that some adjustments were necessary. By ignoring the human relations aspect of leadership—and therefore becoming an obsolete executive—Marant created the conditions for being deposed. Marant appears also to have ignored early-warning signals, such as comments from key personnel, that his obsession with controls was dysfunctional.

Have you checked out your leadership style lately? Does it fit your current organizational climate? Ask co-workers, superiors, and team leaders for their opinion. Make adaptations if you are out of sync with the needs of your company.

Being Controlled by Primitive Thinking Patterns

As far back as the era of Greek mythology, it has been postulated that inside everyone's brain lie some primitive, angry, wild impulses seeking expression. Psychologist Albert J. Bernstein labels these impulses the Dinosaur Brain.[12] Inside each human brain lurks the brain of a dinosaur. It is irrational, emotional, and easily enraged. One moment people are normal, rational people; the next they are little better than reptiles. People get into trouble when they use their primitive thinking patterns instead of the rational parts of their brain. Allowing these primitive thinking patterns (lizard logic) to take over frequently can be self-sabotaging. Letting loose the Dinosaur Brain even once can sometimes severely damage one's career.

Bill, a successful pharmaceutical sales representative, was a prime candidate for promotion to division sales manager. He had already had his second interview for an opening in West Virginia. As division manager, Bill would never have to make another sales call except to observe a junior sales representative. After nine years of selling, Bill had had enough of spending so much time driving to physicians' offices. He was also frustrated because the physicians granted him so little of their time, and he rarely received a warm welcome. Bill often felt he was wasting his time.

Bill was confident that he would be promoted to the division manager position within the next thirty days. Now was his one chance to act out a long-standing fantasy. He wanted physicians to come to him, instead of the reverse. Bill leased temporary office space and a secretary. He covered most of these expenses with his own money, and hoped to hide some of the costs in an expense report. Bill then telephoned each physician in his territory, inviting them all to his office to hear his presentation on an individual basis. If only a handful of physicians accepted the invitation, Bill thought it would be well worth his time, effort, and money.

To Bill's chagrin, not one single physician considered his invitation. To Bill's shock, his division manager found out what he had done and, with the support of top management, had Bill fired immediately.[13]

What Bill did was to give free rein to his primitive thinking pattern. Welled up inside of Bill was an uncontrollable urge to have physicians come to him for product demonstrations. Many sales-people have the same fantasy. When a product or service is in high demand, it can happen that people knock on your door. If Bill's company had offered a clinicially proven cure for AIDS that retailed for $5.00 per dose, physicians might have rushed to his office. Poor Bill was allowing lizard logic to prevail. He should have disclosed his fantasy plan to a confidant before implementing it—especially the idea of funding it in part with company money.

Your primitive thinking pattern can be controlled (and one form of self-sabotage avoided) by following Bernstein and Rozen's suggestions:

- *Stop and think.* In dealing with another person, or acting alone, think before you act [Bill didn't].
- *Listen to your heart, literally.* If your heart rate is up, you are probably too emotional to think clearly. Calm down before acting or deciding.
- *Hold your immediate response.* Especially in an argument, your first response may be dominated by lizard logic.
- *Ask yourself, "What do I want to happen?"* Base your actions on your goal, particularly on what you want to achieve in the long term. Bill wanted physicians to come to his door, but he didn't want to sacrifice his promotion to division manager. He should have coordinated his efforts with his boss.
- *If the other person is yelling, do not act until he or she stops.* Say something like, "Can you run that by me slowly?"
- *Remember that explaining your point of view will not help.* Defending yourself and explaining reflect primitive thinking because they are part of fighting back. First identify the problem causing the altercation between you and another person, then offer your explanation.
- *Let the other person know that you have heard.* Restate what you have heard with a phrase such as "You're upset because we didn't deliver the equipment when you needed it."
- *Ask, "What would you like me to do?"* Volunteering to assist another person forces him or her to act rationally toward you, and will prompt you to do something constructive.
- *State what you want.* It is better to rationally explain what you want than to attack the other person. For example, "I need you to lower your price $3.00 per unit" is better than "You're overcharging me."
- *Negotiate.* Failure to negotiate can be self-sabotaging.
- *Get verbal encouragement for what you both have agreed to do.* Say something like, "You will rate me above average on my performance if I can increase my productivity by 25 percent during the next two quarters."
- *Let the other person have the last word.* The primitive thinking in us wants the parting shot, but this can undo all the good

that's been accomplished in problem solving with the other person.[14]

Imposing a Crippling Workload on Oneself

Carrying a heavy workload is impressive to higher-ups. It demonstrates ambition and a commitment to the organization. But carried too far, it becomes self-defeating. A bone-crunching workload may create so much stress that our judgment, concentration, and accuracy suffer. Furthermore, we may lose perspective and work in a mechanical, noncreative fashion. As a result, quality suffers.

As we attempt to do more and more analytical or paperwork, we typically neglect building relationships with people. Grinding away at one's desk or at the controls of a computer is true productivity to the workaholic, whereas dealing with others is time away from real work. Losing contact with people is self-defeating, of course, for managers and professionals.

The quality problem is critical. If you produce shoddy work, it will not be forgiven just because your workload is excessive. People will remember the shoddy work, not the fact that it should be attributed to overwork.

Kerri, a computer programmer, was already under severe stress from working seventy-five hours a week. Part of her heavy workload could be attributed to her willingness to help more people than her job description required. Kerri was also the president of the local computer science society. One day she was assigned the task of modifying software so that it would run the laser printers just purchased by the firm. One hundred copies of the modified software were distributed throughout the company. Within days, Kerri was flooded with phone calls from users who insisted the printer wouldn't work properly with the modified software. Letters and reports throughout the company were delayed while Kerri attempted to find the error. She rectified the problem within a day, and sent corrected disks to everyone. The problem was fixed, but Kerri's reputation was damaged. She was identified as the programmer who created chaos, and was passed over for promotion.

A self-imposed crippling workload occurs when we voluntarily grab on to more work than we can handle. When the heavy load is imposed by the organization, you have some responsibility for informing your boss about the situation. For example, you could say: "I'm working sixty hours per week at top speed. I still can't get everything done. You expect quality work from me, and I want to give it. How can I get help from somebody in our firm who has a little slack time?"

A secondary technique for preventing a punitive workload from becoming self-sabotaging is to deal with the stress that is causing the problems in concentration, judgment, and quality. If you cannot reduce the workload that is causing the stress, choose a sensible method of stress management. Find one that is time-efficient, such as jogging around your neighborhood or visualizing a peaceful scene, to avoid loading your schedule further. Every bookstore and library has available books, videocassettes, and audiocassettes dealing with stress management. In addition, most community centers conduct stress-management programs.

Revenge Through Poor Performance

In response to criticism and punishment, or even the threat of punishment, some people become passive-aggressive. They do not perform as expected (passive) in order to take revenge (aggressive). Occasional heel-dragging is understandable, but when prolonged or intense it is self-sabotaging. A woman in line for a company presidency allowed her desire for revenge to disqualify her completely:

Ever since Preferred Investments was established twenty-five years ago, Bill Axelrod and Jane Walton had been president and executive vice-president respectively. Bill's pending retirement in a year made it necessary to name a successor soon. To strengthen the organization, Bill hired Brittany Farmer, a young and intelligent financial analyst, as a staff assistant.

Jane immediately perceived Brittany as a threat to her chances of becoming president. The smooth working relationship between Bill and Jane that had existed in the past quickly changed. When Jane, Bill, and Brittany were in the same office together, tension was apparent. Jane became progressively more intimidated. Instead of confronting Bill with her concerns, she chose to rebel by diminishing her work output. She began coming to work an hour later than starting time, took extra-long lunch breaks, and left work early. At times she would leave work for a quick trip to a nearby bar, then return semi-intoxicated.

Bill spoke to Jane several times about her unacceptable job behavior, and told her that if she didn't return to normal she would be fired. During the time of Jane's deteriorating performance, Brittany was working extra-long hours and dedicating herself to the company. Jane's performance slipped further, and Bill finally asked her to resign. Brittany was awarded the presidency.[15]

Bill and Brittany were hardly innocent lambs in this episode. Rumors circulated that they wanted to force Jane into resigning. Nevertheless, Jane's losing time from work and drinking on the job were self-defeating. She self-sabotaged by not confronting Bill about her chances of becoming president and by not dealing properly with her disturbed emotions. If discussing the situation with Brittany did not help Jane regain her equilibrium, she should have sought professional counseling. Jane's family can also be faulted for not intervening in some way, as, for instance, by giving her the support she needed when she was floundering.

Staying in a Downward Spiral

As the process of career self-sabotage begins, the saboteur often digs himself or herself into a deeper and deeper hole. For example, a person accused of being a poor team player may become suspicious of others and thereby create conditions that are even less conducive to cooperating with the group. The story of Phil, a commanding officer of a naval reserve unit, illustrates how the potential downward spiral in career self-sabotage works.

Lieutenant Commander Phil's naval career started out with great promise. He graduated from college in the Naval Reserve Officer's Training Program, then entered active duty as an ensign. While on active duty, Phil earned an MBA degree with tuition paid by the navy. Phil performed well on his assignments and received promotions on or before schedule.

Three years ago, Phil was given the desirable assignment of head of base intelligence at Norfolk, Virginia. His fitness reports were outstanding for the first two years of the assignment. Then during one inspection, several criticisms were made of his operation. They included an allegation that security was not as tightly controlled as possible. Shocked by the charges, Phil was disrespectful to his superior. He sarcastically commented that this officer was not qualified to evaluate security measures. The disrespect led to a very poor officer fitness report.

Phil was passed over for promotion the next time he was eligible. Phil became embittered, and the navy assigned him to command a reserve center in Detroit. Realizing that he was now in a less prestigious assignment, Phil became more sullen. Several officers below him in the command purposely leaked the news to higher command that Phil had become negligent in some of his responsibilities. Phil was again passed over for promotion, and because of this lost his commission. Having left the military before serving his full twenty years has made it difficult for Phil to find civilian employment at a suitable level.[16]

Lieutenant Commander Phil is in a downward spiral that began with a negative evaluation of the security procedures under his command. It is unfortunate, but forgivable, that Phil behaved irrationally once (by showing disrespect for a superior officer). The poor fitness report he received started Phil on his downward spiral. Instead of sabotaging himself, Phil could have recovered the ground lost by saying to a superior: "My fitness reports haven't been as good as I would like. I would welcome any suggestions you have that might help me to regain my reputation."

Phil could then have responded positively to one of his superior's constructive suggestions. When a person is spiraling toward self-defeat, even one positive experience can initiate a countercycle. If you should be unfortunate enough to be caught in a downward spiral, reach out for help. Get one sales order, one compliment, one warm smile of congratulations to help you get back on a success track.

6

Self-Sabotage at the Top

*S*ome people wait until they become senior-level managers before they begin to sabotage their careers. It's not that these executives are consciously trying to self-destruct. The problem is that the nature of an executive's job exerts many subtle pressures leading to self-sabotage. By being an executive, some formerly rational and happy people are tempted into self-defeating behavior. One example is the temptation to carry off enormous personal profits. Many of the Wall Street deal makers who have been convicted of illegal transactions were not so gluttonous earlier in their careers. But placed in an executive position, and immune from the scrutiny of others, they became greedy on a grand scale.

In this chapter, I examine several aspects of executive self-sabotage, including the built-in hazards at the top and the most common forms of self-sabotage. I also explain how you can avoid executive self-sabotage and continue to enjoy the happy and productive career that enabled you to become a top executive in the first place.

Psychological Hazards of Being at the Top

It is always puzzling why some managers derail when they attain executive status. Why do people who are intelligent, interpersonally skillful, and well adjusted suddenly "lose it" when they become chief executive officers? A plausible reason is that certain psychological forces come into play. Some of these forces are within the executive, and others are within the subordinates. Whatever their source, they can create a multitude of problems.[1]

One problem is that occupying a top leadership position can be isolating. Instead of having peers, the top executive is separated from others. As a result, the executive's normal dependency needs for contact, support, and reassurance are frustrated. The executive becomes overwhelmed and uncertain. In response to these confused feelings, some executives become hostile toward their key people.

A second problem is that, consciously or unconsciously, employees expect their leaders to be infallible and gifted with magical powers. A new president was brought into an organization troubled by a declining customer base and eroding morale. Employees throughout the organization waited for him to make substantial improvements. But instead of taking any dramatic action, the president continued to spend time introducing himself to people and studying the organization's problems.

Hoping for an immediate solution to their problems, the employees became increasingly anxious and angry. They began to mock the executive behind his back and to show signs of frustration when dealing with him face to face. As a consequence, the executive became unsure of himself and more tentative in his actions.

A third psychological force is that the executive may have guilt feelings about his or her success and fear that it will not last. The combined force of the guilt and the fear leads these executives to unconsciously cause themselves to fail. The executive may do such seemingly irrational things as provoking disputes with major customers or firing well-liked old-timers.

The three forces just described can combine to adversely affect a leader, as illustrated in the following case history:

As a result of the unexpected death of his predecessor, Ted Howell was appointed president of the Latrix Corporation. The company manufactures and sells electronic equipment. Howell had been found with the help of a headhunter who had highly recommended him. He had previously held a senior staff position in a company in the same line of business. Howell's knowledge of the industry had been a key factor in convincing Latrix's board to take him on.

Soon after his arrival, Latrix's board members saw signs that Howell was having difficulties in dealing with the pressures of the job. A number of rash decisions made in his first week at the office were the first indication of trouble. But in spite of these mistakes, everything initially turned out better than expected. First, one of the company's main competitors went out of business, which freed up an important segment of the market. Second, one of Howell's employees came up with an excellent marketing idea that he quickly adopted and that proved very successful. Some executives were disturbed because their colleague never received credit for it. Nevertheless, these two factors helped get Latrix back into the black.

Unfortunately, this success apparently went to Howell's head. After the turnaround, he embarked on a dramatic expansion program, ignoring cautionary remarks made by his employees, consultants, and bankers. He took other steps, including the relocation of the company's headquarters to what Howell thought were more suitable surroundings. Howell also spearheaded the acquisition of an expensive company plane.

These two actions put a heavy strain on the company's finances. Those executives who expressed disagreement or concern about the new moves were fired. Consultants who suggested that Howell change course suffered the same fate. In the end, only sycophants who were willing to go along with his grandiose schemes and accept his aggressive outbursts were left.

As expected, the unrealistic plans and high expenditures put the company into the red. However, Howell was unwilling to admit his role in the debacle. When questioned at directors' meetings, he would become defensive and deny any responsibility for the losses. Instead, he would blame them on faculty moves made by his predecessor or on vindictive action taken by executives no longer in his employ. In his opinion, an upturn was just around the corner. To an increasing number of board members, however, Howell's behavior was becoming unacceptable. Eventually, having become impatient with the continuing losses and with Howell's imperious, paranoid behavior, they managed to remove him.[2]

The situation of Ted Howell and others like him is not hopeless. Executives should be aware of the psychological forces that are potential trouble spots. To prevent stress reactions and irrational behavior from surfacing, executive leaders should engage in a regular process of critical self-evaluation. Leaders might attempt to answer these questions:

☐ How accessible am I?
☐ How do I react to bad news or criticism from group members?

☐ Am I able to discuss any problems or ideas with colleagues?

☐ Do I think of my employees in terms of those who are "with" me versus those who are "against" me?

☐ How realistic is my vision of the company's future? Is there a large discrepancy between my perspective and that of others?

☐ Am I willing to accept responsibility if things go wrong, or do I blame others?

☐ Am I quick to take offense and to feel unfairly treated? Do I have a great need to blow my own horn?

☐ Do I feel anxious and guilty when I am successful?

☐ Do I have difficulty believing that my success results from my own accomplishments rather than from sheer luck?

Stopping to answer these questions serves as a reality check. It is an important process because the potential for losing touch with reality is especially acute in executives.

Executives can take preventive action in another way. Encouraging frank feedback from outsiders, such as board members and consultants, can help counteract the psychological forces that have a sabotaging impact. People from outside the organization often have an objective viewpoint, and may be willing to criticize an executive. Kets de Vries urges selecting a strong, independent board that is really willing to enforce its auditing role. An objective board might have told Howell that he was behaving irrationally. And Howell might have been able to prevent self-sabotage if had asked the board, early on, for feedback on his performance and behavior. The company, too, might have fared much better.

Abuse of Power

Power can be an intoxicant. Sooner or later, many executives are tempted to see how far they can stretch the power and prerogatives stemming from their positions. The most common form of power abuse is coercing employees into doing things that go way beyond their job descriptions. This would include demanding that employees spend company time running personal errands for them.

Demanding sexual favors from employees is another way of coercing people into going beyond their job descriptions. Current thinking on sexual harassment looks upon this practice as an abuse of power. Although the law is on the subordinate's side, he or she often feels pressured into submitting to the sexual advances of an organizationally more powerful superior. Executive power abuse can also take the form of misappropriating company resources, such as using company cars and planes for personal use.

Abusing power is self-sabotaging because the executive is rarely an absolute monarch. The board of directors, an outside agency, or the employees themselves will find a suitable way of getting even. Such was the fate of a high school principal, as described by a guidance counselor who worked at the school:

"Quentin, our principal, became the center of a stormy controversy. At first, he was well liked and respected by everybody. Quentin would talk to students in the hallway. He would listen to the concerns of faculty, staff, and students. His popularity was so high that he was the leading candidate for becoming the next superintendent of the school district. All the members of the school board were in favor of Quentin assuming that position.

"Quentin's popularity soon took a nose dive, however. Some serious allegations arose that led to an internal investigation by the school. He had been spotted late at night siphoning gasoline out of the school bus fuel tanks into his own car. The investigators concluded that Quentin had been doing this for about two years. He was also found to be using the school postage machine to mail many of his personal letters. Another charge was that Quentin had occasionally borrowed the school district's four-wheel drive truck to tow his boat to the lake on weekends. The caper was so easy to spot. The school's name was on both doors of the truck.

"The controversy over Quentin's behavior became even more heated when he and the school nurse developed a relationship. They frequently came to school and left together. The affair with the nurse led to a separation from his wife. Quentin and the nurse announced their engagement after Quentin and his wife's divorce came through.

"As a result of all these actions, Quentin's contract was not renewed. Rather than put up with the continuing gossip, Quentin's new wife resigned.

The two of them then left town. When last heard of, Quentin was planning to work in a family-owned whiskey store. His wife was looking for new employment as a school nurse."[3]

Quentin may have a difficult time recapturing the status and admiration he enjoyed as a high school principal. His present marriage may be satisfying, but he probably suffers from having left his children behind. Quentin stretched his formal powers beyond their limits. He didn't own the gasoline he stole, the truck he misappropriated, or the school postage meter he used. His position as principal didn't exempt him from the taboos about flaunting his romance with the school nurse while still married.

How might Quentin have averted the chaos that overtook his career? What he failed to do was to question his actions. As he siphoned gas under the moonlight, he might have said, "Is what I am doing at this present moment making any sense?"

As he towed his boat with the school truck or ran his personal mail through the school postage machine, he should have asked, "Why am I flaunting my power?" As he arrived at work in the morning with the nurse, he (and the nurse) should have asked, "What am I trying to prove? This is a conservative town, which has a very conservative school board. Do I want both of us to be fired for being inappropriate role models?"

Anytime your actions veer too far from the norms of your employer, occupation, or community, ask yourself some of the questions Quentin should have asked. The most universally applicable of them is, "Is what I am doing at this present moment making any sense?" Finding answers to questions such as these takes considerable self-understanding. Asking them repeatedly, in addition to checking out your perceptions with another person, will help hone your insights.

Insensitivity to the Human Relationship Factor

Many an executive has made a mistake in handling people while trying to be productivity-minded and highly analytical. Ignoring the human factor is often a by-product of becoming obsessed with controls and financial analysis. (Remember Frank Marant, the food conglomerate executive who spent so much time with computerized controls that he neglected his management team?) Ignoring the importance of human relationships can be self-sabotaging because most management systems fail without effective teamwork.

A related problem occurs when an executive takes literally all traditional notions about management. The result could be so mechanistic that you could lose the support of the people you are trying to manage. Phyllis, a newly appointed store executive at one branch of a chain of home-improvement centers, fell into this trap. Shortly after arriving on the scene, she decided to reorganize the branch. In the process, she broke up the old cliques of people who had worked together as teammates on various projects. Here is what happened, as described by one of the team leaders:

"Phyllis thought she was a productivity expert. She concluded that we were goof-offs. Her reasoning was that the members of each team had become buddies as well as work associates. Phyllis hoped that by forming new teams, productivity would increase. The opposite proved to be true. We missed the loose and easy work practices that we had had in the past. Being out on assignment with my team was more like fixing up my own house than being paid an hourly wage to fix up somebody else's place. Now the old feeling of camaraderie was gone.

"I tried to explain to Phyllis that the reorganization was a mistake. But she wouldn't listen. Instead she kept stressing the importance of increasing productivity and the fact that she wasn't in the happiness business. With four new teams created, many problems arose. Cooperation declined. People became huffy about which responsibility was theirs versus which responsibility was somebody else's. All of a sudden people became very rigid about taking a full lunch break and leaving a job early enough to wash up.

"Phyllis pleaded with us to improve productivity, and threatened us with firings if the situation didn't improve. Profits were sinking and she was looking bad in top management's eyes. The more she urged us to get our work done faster, the more we dragged our heels. Nobody was willing to rescue Phyllis because she had ignored our requests to maintain systems that had worked for several years.

"Phyllis finally recognized that breaking up the old teams and forming new ones was unworkable. So she reorganized us back into our original teams. Something had been lost in the process. The time we spent completing a job showed a spurt of improvement. Yet we never reached the level of productivity we had attained before Phyllis arrived. She finally resigned. I think top management helped her reach that decision."

Glossing over the importance of human relationships in teamwork proved to be self-sabotaging for Phyllis. She was not aware that giving team members a say in choosing teammates is likely to improve productivity. Even is Phyllis was not aware of that tidbit of human relations knowledge, she could have avoided a serious career setback. Phyllis should have solicited input from experienced workers before plowing ahead with her reorganization. If asked, the team leaders would undoubtedly have explained why their system of self-selected teams was working.

Part of Phyllis's problem was that she had become too smug and self-contained. She began to believe that she did not need help from others in making decisions. Are you falling into the same trap? When was the last time you asked somebody for advice before plunging ahead with a major decision? The best decision makers are confident, but not so smug as to avoid the input of others.

Delegation Problems

Virtually all executives have heard or studied about the importance of properly delegating authority and tasks. Nevertheless, many of them continue to have problems in under- or overdelegation. Because delegation is the lifeblood of collective effort, ineffective delegation can be self-sabotaging.

Underdelegation

Most of us have worked for a manager who attempted to do most of the significant work himself or herself. Such managers work longer hours than anybody else in the office, make all the important decisions, and constantly check on the work of group members. They make it difficult for their subordinates to grow and develop. As a result, their more talented people often leave. Another problem with underdelegation is that the executive doesn't capitalize on the suggestions for improvement coming from team members.

Kelly Gillen, an entrepreneurial executive, experienced many of these problems. Kelly's is a group of three deep-discount drugstores that she founded. Each store sells brand merchandise at an average of 45 percent below list price. Although called *drug*stores, these outlets sell hundreds of items in addition to pharmaceuticals, including stationery, watches, laundry materials, garden supplies, and beauty aids. By comparison with some discount stores, Kelly's sells only high-quality merchandise. Kelly explains why and how she started her own business:

"I had a wonderful career with a big chain. They hired me as a store manager trainee right after I completed my degree in business. At age 21, I saw no limits to my potential as a retailing executive. My career dreams were coming true. At age 35, I was promoted to a merchandising vice president. One year later I faced a career setback. My company was bought by a larger chain and they decided to cut most of our home-office staff. I was given six-months' severance pay.

"I couldn't find the job I wanted in my town. I didn't want to relocate either because of my husband and two children. Then it hit me that our city lacked a quality deep-discounter. So I founded Kelly's with some of my own cash, a home-equity loan, and money borrowed from a commercial bank. Getting started, I did everything that needed doing in the store, often working seventy hours per week. I merchandised. I unjammed cash registers. I hired employees. I even helped unload a truck when two of our warehouse employees were out sick. The business was an immediate success, and I was able to expand to two more locations.

"Despite the fact that demand for our retailing concept is still strong, I've run into some serious internal problems. My managers are rebelling. Griff, my most senior manager, told me I keep him on too short a leash. He told me it drives him up the wall when I straigthen out merchandise in his store. The last straw for him was when I told one of his supervisors to go home and change into a freshly ironed blouse. Griff quit in anger.

"Bridget, my most recent hire, has already told me she can't breathe. She says that although I'm a retailing wiz, I shouldn't be telling her how to do everything. The way I look at it, I founded the business, so I should be making the big decisions.

"Milt, my third manager, is an older man whose experience adds credibility to his opinion. He told me Kelly's could be expanding regionally by now if I weren't such a one-person band. Milt says that my striving for perfection is killing potential growth. He claims that because I have to approve everything, there are too many delays.

"I think I can still realize my dreams of taking Kelly's national. That's if I can change my ways. With my reputation, I may have some trouble hiring some new managers."

So far, Kelly Gillen has only given herself a minor wound in the foot. Fortunately, she had enough managerial skill to listen to the critical feedback from her team members. It won't be easy, but Kelly now has enough insight to begin to let go. If she can comfortably grant decision-making authority to her team members, her dreams of expanding her empire may come true.

Overdelegation

Overgenerous delegation can be self-sabotaging in two ways. One problem is that the overdelegator can appear underoccupied, overly detached, and downright lazy to others. Executives who have delegated most of their work to others are likely to be perceived as superfluous. This puts their jobs at risk. Not to engage in at least some important work is therefore politically self-defeating for an executive.

Overdelegation can also lead to self-sabotage because it results in a loss of control. The executive who delegates too much, and establishes no checkpoints, may lose touch with the organization's problems. People down the organizational line are hesitant to tell top management about serious operating problems. The chief executive who does not actively solicit such information may not know about major problems until disaster has already struck.

Nolan Bushnell, the creative spark behind Atari and other businesses, has had substantial problems with overdelegation. At Atari, he and other members of top management were unaware of a massive inventory buildup of computers on dealers' shelves. By the time they were informed of the problem, it had brought Atari to the brink of bankruptcy. He had similar problems at Pizza Time, another of his business ventures. When he finally paid attention to these problems it was too late. Bushnell analyzes what happened (as quoted in *When Smart People Fail*):

> We were emaciated managerially. In a food franchise business, managers can move [to other companies] quickly, due

to the competition. I simply had not realized how fragile my management was. Often, when I went to make collections, I would find a nineteen-year-old kid in charge of the store. It was really terminal, and I just hadn't paid attention."[4]

Bushnell thus contributed to the sabotage of his business, and to himself because he was a principal. Other entrepreneurs who derive their thrills from starting rather than operating a business face a similar potential for self-sabotage. They can prevent such self-defeating overdelegation by studying the subject of management more seriously. A constructive attitude executives can take toward a management development program is: "Okay, this material might be interesting, but how does it relate to me personally? How can it make me a better manager?"

To help find the balance between underdelegation and overdelegation, keep these suggestions for effective delegation in mind. By so doing you will avoid one more potential form of self-sabotage.

1. *Assign duties to the right people.* Without competent team members, delegation can backfire.
2. *Grant people sufficient authority to accomplish the delegated tasks.* You will be perceived as an underdelegator if your team members lack the clout to accomplish their mission.
3. *Retain some important tasks for yourself.* Managers need to retain some high-output and sensitive tasks to perform by themselves. In general, any task that involves the survival of your unit should be handled by you.
4. *Recognize that managers cannot delegate final accountability.* You are not off the hook just because you delegated something.
5. *Provide the necessary support to those receiving the delegated task.* If you do not help team members get the job done, the delegation may fail.
6. *Be willing to let others make mistakes.* If you don't give team members the freedom to fail, you will be perceived as an underdelegator. Besides, spending so much time helping people avoid mistakes defeats the purpose of delegation.
7. *Trust others.* Delegation will be severely hampered or will

not take place at all if you do not trust the people reporting to you. Frequent checking destroys delegation.

8. *Step back from details.* The biggest problem of the under-delegator is getting too involved in technical skills.
9. *Recognize that the manager is a coach, not a player.* Your role is not to do all the tasks but to help others accomplish theirs.

Failure to Groom a Successor

A major reason executives do not train successors is that they are insecure. They fear that they will be declared redundant if a replacement is readily available. In the current era of slimmed-down organizations, there is some merit to their logic. A higher authority might terminate an executive when a competent successor is waiting to fill the position. On balance, however, it is self-sabotaging not to train a replacement. It makes the executive appear weak and unprofessional. Not training a successor is also self-defeating because it may block the executive from being chosen for an even bigger assignment. A case in point is Geraldo, who was blocked from becoming a vice-president of a national trade association. Geraldo's explanation for the impasse was this:

"My boss cannot promote me unless I can find a good associate director who can replace me. It's too bad, but the associate director I have now will never be ready to take my place. She just doesn't know how to handle major responsibility."

The associate director has a different perception of why she is not considered ready for promotion to director: "On several occasions the director agreed that I should complete an important assignment. But within twenty-four hours Geraldo turns around and says he would rather do it himself. He won't give me the chance to get the experience I need to be prepared to become the director.

"Geraldo likes to set unrealistic goals for me. This makes it very hard for me to meet deadlines. Recently he gave me a fund-raising goal that was 20 percent higher than the previous year despite a downward trend in gift giving in our area. When I came in below target, Geraldo just couldn't understand what went wrong. He tells me I can't handle big jobs, but he hands me impossible tasks.

"I'm not alone in my viewpoint. During Geraldo's reign, there have been three other associate directors who have been either pushed out of the organization or demoted. Geraldo likes to get involved in day-to-day details instead of spending most of his time out in the community. A director should spend most of his or her time networking outside the organization. He also expects unrealistic turnaround times. When things can't be done in the time frame he wants, he puts you down as being unable to handle big responsibility.

"Geraldo has just reorganized the department. His new structure will make it even more difficult for him to be replaced by an associate director. I am going to be demoted to a team leader position, and Geraldo is promoting a secretary to become his assistant. Since the assistant is not a professional position, she would be out of the question as a potential director."[5]

Geraldo's surface problem is that he has failed to groom a successor. Underlying this problem are poor delegation practices. He takes back interesting work and he sets unrealistic goals. Geraldo's problems could be deep-rooted. He claims to want to be promoted to a vice-president, but his shoddy management practices and his recent departmental reorganization are revealing. They suggest that he may be trying to undermine his own promotion. Geraldo should sort out his feelings about career acceleration. If he is convinced that he really does want to become a vice-president, he can establish a sensible plan for grooming a successor.

Vacillation Over Major Decisions

Some people who have been reasonably decisive as middle managers become indecisive once they reach a senior position. A major problem is that the consequences of an executive's decisions are greater. If the executive makes a wrong decision, he or she will be perceived as ineffective. After all, decision making is the true measure of an executive. If an unpopular decision is made, the executive will incur resentment.

As a result of these fears, vacillating executives choose one of two courses of action. One is to delegate decision-making responsibilities to key subordinates, or, in some cases, to a superior. (This is difficult for a chief executive officer to do.) Another course is to take no action at all in the hope that the problem calling for a decision will resolve itself. For example, an executive might delay firing a subordinate in the hope that he or she will quit or take early retirement.

Howard, a chief hospital administrator, exemplifies the executive who avoids making decisions for both reasons. He fears being seen as wrong and therefore as ineffective. And he also wants to avoid resentment.

Nicknamed The Human Cipher by his subordinates, Howard is nevertheless admired by some for his cautiousness, restraint, and ability to look at problems from a balanced point of view. One day Howard received a letter from a patient complaining about inadequate hospital facilities. Three pages in length, the letter included charges that the water carafes were unclean and that the bed sheets were abrasive. Of greater significance, the irate patient implied that she was thinking of filing a malpractice suit in relation to her foot operation. Howard replied:

> Dear Ms. Fitzhugh:
>
> Your letter to this hospital has been referred to my department. It has been read by me personally. I will investigate and report back to you at a later date.

Another incident provides further understanding of Howard's reluctance to commit himself to a course of action. A new company in the community acted as a service bureau to hospitals and other organizations by taking complete charge of client billings. When the company representative was referred to Howard, his response was: "A decision of this nature can only be reached after a prolonged group study of the problem."

Howard sees himself as an effective manager. "I believe strongly in delegating responsibility," he says. "There are few decisions that the top executive must make. In a well-trained unit every person is capable of making decisions that affect his or her own welfare. I try to lead, not push. [*At this point Howard takes a piece of string out of his pocket and places it on top of the desk. He demonstrates that pushing the string won't move it. However, when it is pulled, or led, it moves quickly.*] An effective manager has a clean desk. He or she should be thinking, not doing."

Managers like Howard who avoid making important decisions are usually destined to failure. Ultimately, they will be deposed. They have been indecisive in order to protect their self esteem. But being indecisive eventually hurts their self-esteem as they fail. To avoid self-sabotaging indecisiveness, the executives in question must find other ways of satisfying their needs for self-esteem and for being liked. The methods they choose must be ones that do not interfere with their decision making. For example, an executive can inspire the admiration of others by doing good in the community. Eric Flamholtz and Yvonne Randle, two management consultants and authors of *The Inner Game of Management*, offer these three suggestions for overcoming executive indecisiveness on the job:

> 1. Vacillating executives who are information seekers need to learn to become risk takers. They must develop the courage to make decisions without complete information. One helpful approach is to set a time limit for gathering all information relevant to a decision. When the time limit is reached, the executive must make a decision with or without complete information. Waiting too long to make a decision can be disastrous. A tenet of crisis management, for example, is to act quickly when a crisis (such as a poisoned batch of product) is at hand. Further delay may cause irreversible negative consequences such as consumer sentiment building up against the company.
>
> 2. Vacillators who are buck passers need to learn to accept the decision-making responsibilities of managers. They must confront the reality that along with the privileges of being an executive comes the responsibility of making key decisions.
>
> 3. Vacillators who agonize over decisions facing them must learn to act on their beliefs about the best course of action. They must become aware that procrastinating about major decisions only results in a loss of respect from superiors, subordinates, and co-workers. A helpful approach is to practice making a decision within a reasonable time frame, and then making an effort not to worry about it. After a while vacillators will experience the feeling that making decisions is more comfortable than agonizing about them.[6]

The Godfather or Godmother

The Godfather or Godmother executive is styled after the underworld character who requires submission to his power in return for patronage and generosity.[7] To be liked by a "Godparent," you must continually defer to his or her superior judgment and wisdom. The sanctions for not submitting to the Godparent include being transferred or demoted, receiving bad assignments, or even being fired for trumped-up reasons.

Godparents have a compelling need to control group members. Sometimes the purpose of pulling people's strings is self-protection. As long as people are controlled, they cannot rebel. Another purpose of controlling group members is to humiliate them in order to decrease one's own feelings of inadequacy.

The Godparent approach to executive leadership is often self-sabotaging. The strong need for control characteristic of Godparents prompts them to insist that members of the organization acknowledge their superiority. To maintain this attitude, they implement two strategies. The first involves hiring weak people or keeping on the payroll people who are loyal but not necessarily competent. These people remain under the Godfather's or Godmother's control because they respect the executive's ability and look to him or her for direction.

The second strategy involves hiring competent people whom the Godparent wants to dominate and control. By virtue of having strong people under his or her tight control, the Godparent projects an aura of strength.

Godparenting executives are detrimental to the organization in the long run. One problem is the highly political environment they foster. Promotions and raises are based on loyalty and submissiveness, not competence. A great deal of political infighting takes place, as subordinates compete with each other to please the Godparent. The organization built by a Godparent may become a personal, private playground. Profits often become a secondary consideration.

The president of a company, who could afford whatever he wished, liked to be "entertained" by vendors seeking his favor. In return for lavish entertainments, he would purchase materials for his company. However, his purchases bore no relation to the company's needs. It was estimated that the company's inventory of raw materials would last for twelve and one-half years at the current rate of consumption. Nevertheless, the Godparent was still buying more.[8]

Another detriment to the organization is that the Godparent fails to identify and train a replacement. Godparents jealously guard their power and attempt to block others from gaining the experience needed to become a successor. Similarly, these executives block team members from developing an overall, strategic view of the organization. They accomplish this by not bringing the team together to discuss the overall strategy of the company.

Overcoming Godparent Executive Behavior

Behaving like a Godfather or Godmother is a slow and indirect form of career self-sabotage. The people the Godparent attempts to control may rebel and find ways of undermining his or her authority. For example, a whistle-blower might complain to the board of directors that the Godparent deliberately hires weak people. Unless the Godparent is the owner of the business complaints will be lodged concerning excesses indulged in.

To overcome being a Godparent, your first challenge is to recognize that as an executive, you can be powerful without totally dominating others. Your self-esteem does not have to depend on being the strongest and most controlling person. Instead, you should attempt to receive satisfaction from helping others develop.

Another challenge is to increase self-acceptance. A problem that Godparent executives have is that they feel positive about themselves only when they are in control of others. Similarly, they feel competitive toward their subordinates. Taking an inventory of your other accomplishments in life, such as having acquired business acumen or raised a nice family, can help you to begin building self-acceptance. A positive consequence of the inventory of accomplishments approach is that you can then feel positive about your accomplishments without comparing yourself to others.

Playing Jekyll and Hyde

Jekyll and Hyde managers have split personalities. When they deal with superiors, customers, or clients, they are pleasant, engaging people—much like Dr. Jekyll. Yet when dealing with subordinates, they become tyrannical—much like Mr. Hyde. Employees who deviate from Mr. or Ms. Hyde's expectations are publicly reprimanded (but not in front of Jekyll and Hyde's boss). The basic strategy of such managers is never to allow their superiors or peers to see their Hyde side. Consequently, their superiors (including board members) tend not to believe a subordinate who complains that his manager is being tyrannical.[9] As complaints persist, however, self-sabotage begins.

Jekyll and Hyde executives and bosses actually have a need to be liked by their subordinates. However, they believe this need is inconsistent with their need to control and their need for self-esteem as an executive. They firmly believe that an executive's main responsibility is to control the actions of team members so as to achieve organizational objectives. Jekyll and Hyde executives believe that they will enhance their self-esteem if they do control people and get them to perform well.

The difficulty in handling people arises because Jekyll and Hyde executives believe that being friendly with subordinates is inconsistent with exercising control over them. By contrast, they believe that being friendly with superiors *is* part of the executive role. This two-faced management style usually creates career self-sabotage. The Jekyll and Hyde manager's poor reputation with subordinates ultimately arouses the suspicion of top management, and a formal or informal investigation ensues. If the results of the investigation confirm the suspicions, the Jekyll and Hyde executive is replaced. Such was the case with Roger, the vice-president of claims in a medical insurance company.

Roger began his career as a management trainee in the San Francisco office of a nonprofit medical insurance company. He quickly impressed his superiors with his above-average productivity. Although abrupt with people, Roger was promoted to claims supervisor in three years. His superiors attributed his abruptness to his strong desire to achieve high levels of productivity and to satisfy clients. Roger bragged about the short turnaround time on claims achieved by his unit.

Roger continued to impress his superiors with his dedication and high performance. The turnover rate in his unit was above average, but not high enough to sound a warning to upper management. During an exit interview a claims processor who had worked for Roger complained about his abrasiveness toward employees. When Roger was confronted with this information by the director of human resources, he convinced her that these were the comments of a disgruntled, low performer. The human resources director was reasonably satisfied and decided not to share the incident with upper management.

After three more years of satisfactory performance, Roger was promoted to director of claims. The vice-president of claims, noting that Roger had a few rough edges in handling people, had some reservations about promoting him, but because of a freeze on hiring imposed at the time, promoted Roger nonetheless.

Roger now supervised a large staff and attended administrative meetings held by the CEO. With one more promotion, Roger would become a vice-president and a member of the Executive Committee. His popularity with the supervisors, however, continued to erode. Deborah, one of his supervisors, provides a firsthand description:

"Most of us knew Roger from before he was promoted to director. He was always a little heavy-handed with people. He used to rant and rave if a claim was disputed, or if somebody's productivity fell too much below quota. When Roger was promoted to director, he became much worse. Power must have gone to his head. Half the time in staff meetings was devoted to his reviewing any little mistake that had been made since the last meeting.

"Roger would get the angriest when he thought a supervisor was not pushing employees hard enough. He didn't seem to understand that a medical insurance company was not the place for a slave driver. He once chewed out a supervisor in front of everybody else. He accused her of reading *The National Enquirer* on company time. The woman was really just taking a late lunch.

"What irritates me and the other supervisors the most about Roger is that he is two-faced. When he deals with the vice-presidents or important visitors, he becomes Prince Charming. So tactful, so polite. It makes us gag. Roger reminds me of a head waiter I worked for when I was a teenager. He would rant and rave when he walked into the kitchen. As soon as he went through the swinging doors into the dining room, his snarl changed into a smile. He was a tyrant toward the help but a charmer toward the guests."

Roger's career advancement with the company was soon blocked. A job satisfaction survey revealed low morale among his staff and many negative comments about his handling of people. The human resources director was then asked to make a thorough review of Roger's people-handling skills. The investigation turned up so many negatives that Roger was reassigned to a position as a senior systems analyst. His pride was hurt, but his pay was not cut. Roger is now attempting to improve his interpersonal skills, and hopes someday to return to a management position.

If you're a Jekyll and Hyde executive, how do you learn to emphasize Dr. Jekyll and deemphasize Mr. Hyde when dealing with group members? First, you must understand that you don't have to exercise ultimate control over subordinates in order to be successful. Organizational goals can be achieved by giving group members the freedom to make decisions, and by not abusing them for making mistakes. The Jekyll and Hyde executive also has to learn that the need to be liked can be satisfied through subordinates. Many effective leaders are adored and respected by their group members.

The first action step is to practice showing the Dr. Jekyll side of your personality to subordinates. Try treating them as if they were your superiors, and then gauge their reactions. Some Jekyll and Hyde executives fear that being cordial to subordinates will be perceived as a sign of weakness.[10]

As with the prevention of any other type of self-sabotaging behavior, the Jekyll and Hyde executive must be on the alert to external signals of problems. For example, when the claims processor resigned, Roger might have inquired about the results of the exit interview. Periodic consultation with human resources professionals can bring to light problems in one's handling of people.

Greed, Gluttony, and Avarice

During the 1980s an alarming number of financiers sabotaged their careers by using illegal and quasi-illegal means to amass great fortunes. The money they amassed was often far more than they could ever plan on spending. Michael Milken, for example, earned over $550 million in one year. The financiers in question displayed boundless avarice, apparently driven by greed and gluttony for its own sake. It was said that Ivan Boesky wanted to be the biggest arbitrageur on Wall Street. The excesses of Boesky and Milken and their subsequent fines and imprisonment are well known. Less well known is that, on a smaller scale, many of us are capable of allowing the same sort of greed to sabotage our careers. Don Calhoun was one such individual.

The County District Attorney's Office conducted an investigation into Calhoun's alleged extortion of more than $1 million in his capacity as the former director of construction for a supermarket chain. The district attorney reported that company officials had asked his office to look into accusations against Don, who had left his job several months before the investigation opened. He had worked for the supermarket chain for more than twenty years.

Don said to friends and former co-workers, "I resigned because of lies and allegations based on misinformation given to the company. We are contesting the allegations. This is all my lawyer wants me to say."

The investigation focuses on allegations that Don received more than $1 million dollars in kickbacks from contractors. The grocery chain that had employed Don filed a civil lawsuit against him. It accused Don of accepting money over an extended period of time from Ferguson Enterprises. This construction company has been general contractor for many of the chain's projects, including a 100,000-square-foot superstore under construction and a child-care center.

A building inspector who knew Don said that he had not noticed anything unusual in his dealings with him, Ferguson Enterprises, or the superstore under construction. The director of assessments and building control who worked with Don said that the job was progressing marvelously. He also said that the quality of the work was excellent, and that Don was a real professional who kept a project moving when it bogged down.

Whatever the outcome of the district attorney's investigation, Don's career has been sabotaged. If convicted, there is very little chance that Don will ever regain a comparable position. If acquitted, there will still be a cloud of suspicion over him. Don will have considerable difficulty finding a high-level position in his field. He could conceivably become a business owner in a construction-related field, but it would be extremely difficult for him to obtain financing.

Assuming that he was guilty of receiving kickbacks, what could Don have done differently? The pat solution is to be moralistic, to say that Don should have internalized a stronger ethical code. More practically, he should have run a risk-versus-reward analysis of any potential unethical actions, especially when the temptation to accept kickbacks first arose. He might have reasoned:

> "If I accept an occasional dinner invitation or tickets to a sporting events from contractors, it would be relatively risk-free. Token gifts from vendors are within the acceptable range of company policy.
>
> "If I accept much more, I can lose my job, my reputation, and the emotional support of my friends. My self-respect would take quite a blow too. Suppose I get close to $1 million in cash from contractors. That would be a lot of money, but it could cost me my way of life. In terms of risk versus rewards, I'll stick with a few baubles from vendors. I can do honest work to get whatever else I want."

Failing to Size Up the Climate

All forms of executive self-sabotage contain some element of failing to size up the climate in one's work environment. To be out of touch with the political realities surrounding you is to risk sending your career into a tailspin. Look for straws in the wind suggesting that what you are doing, or not doing, is pushing you toward a setback.

One executive sabotaged his career because of his sexist thinking, as reflected in his speech. He didn't realize he was offending team members at his staff meetings by using such sexist phrases as: "Every manager and his wife is invited to our next management meeting," "I thought our personnel guy would be attending this meeting," and "The girls in my office work just as hard as the managers." This executive was not sensitive enough to hear the groans and observe the winces when he made such exclusionary statements. When asked about his suitability for the top job, several managers on his staff said, "His thinking is a little too provincial for the modern generation."

You may not always be able to discern your self-sabotaging behavior on your own. However, certain signals from the environment should suggest to you that it is time either to adjust something in your repertoire or to leave before your career is irretrievably lost. Here are a few such signals to look out for:

- You stop receiving intraoffice mail or electronic messages other than routine correspondence.
- You are rarely asked your opinion on important organizational issues.
- Your major customer has dropped its standing order, and now places orders less frequently.
- Your immediate superior becomes noncommunicative and evasive.
- You are not brought into discussions about a pending corporate takeover although your level of responsibility warrants your inclusion.
- Your performance evaluations have worsened and are characterized by much nitpicking by your boss.

If any of these or similar signals occur, investigate and attempt to uncover the real problem. If a real problem exists, and it relates to something under your control, take appropriate action. Stop the process of career self-sabotage.

7

Political Blunders

*E*veryone need not be a consummate office politician to get ahead or survive. But committing political blunders can put a serious dent in your career. It is self-sabotaging to do such things as step on the toes of powerful people or show indifference to the company's products or services. To avoid committing political blunders, you first have to develop sensitivity toward what constitutes such mistakes. Eleven recurring political blunders, and how they can be avoided, are presented in this chapter. Just in case you have recently committed a blunder, or may do so in the future, there is also a patch-up maneuver described.

Before reading ahead, take the "Blunder Quiz" to help sensitize you to whatever tendencies you may have toward blundering.

THE BLUNDER QUIZ

Indicate whether you agree or disagree with the following statements:

1. It's fine to criticize a company executive in a meeting so long as the criticism is valid.
2. Dressing for success is a sham. You should wear to work whatever clothing you find the most comfortable.
3. I am willing to insult any co-worker if the insult is deserved.
4. I see no problem in using competitors' products or services, and letting my superiors know about it.
5. If someone higher up than you in the company offends you, let that person know about it.

---

6. Never bother with company-sponsored social events, such as holiday parties, unless you are really interested.
7. If I disagreed with something major my employer did, I would voice my opinion in a letter to the editor of the local newspaper.
8. I'm very open about passing along confidential information.
9. I openly criticize most new ventures my company or department is contemplating.
10. I always avoid office politics of any kind.

Interpretation. The greater the number of statements you agree with, the more prone you are to making political blunders that can damage your career. You need to raise your awareness level about blunders on the job. Study this chapter carefully.

Bypassing Your Boss

Going over your boss's head to resolve a problem between the two of you can be a major political blunder. The more bureaucratic an organization is, the more hazardous the bypass. If done with extreme tact, you might be able to pull it off. But if you fail, your career can be damaged and your recourse limited. Your name can readily enter into your industry's network in an unfavorable way.

An important exception to the bypass taboo is when you are faced with an emergency situation. This would include working for a boss who is extremely incompetent or in violation of company policy or the law. Under these circumstances, a problem-solving session with your boss's boss might be appropriate.

Though the general principle is that bypassing your boss is a political blunder, it may become necessary when you get no satisfaction from speaking directly to your boss about an important problem. Asking your boss's permission to speak to a higher-up is another workable alternative. A sneak play is usually self-defeating.

Gerri, a customer service trainer in a bank, wanted to attend a three-day training seminar to enrich herself professionally. She took her request to her boss, Diana, who replied, "That would ordinarily be a reasonable request. But these aren't ordinary days. We are trying to conserve on costs. And besides, we need you here in the bank. If you want to learn more about your field, read some magazines or books. Bring up your request again next year."

Gerri was miffed that her boss rejected her demand. She waited for a spontaneous meeting with Grant, the human resources director, to plead her case. The next day she had a legitimate reason for meeting with Grant to speak about some upcoming training programs. Gerri then asked Grant if she might speak to him about a personal issue. She explained that Diana wouldn't approve her request to attend a professional seminar. Gerri also asked if Grant would be willing to reverse that decision.

Grant simply reported the conversation back to her boss. Diana in turn called Gerri into her office and delivered a straightforward message: "Grant tells me you disagree with my decision to turn down your travel request. In the future if you have a problem with a decision I make, thrash it out with me. Don't be a wimp and complain to Grant."

Gerri's sneak play thus backfired. She did not get to attend the conference, and her relationship with Diana deteriorated. Her next performance appraisal was worse than she expected. Gerri's political blunder has hurt her career, at least temporarily. A good relationship with your boss and an above-average performance appraisal are always important. Gerri should have stopped to think of the political consequences of bypassing her boss before complaining to Grant. Attendance at one company-sponsored seminar was not worth the cost of alienating Diana and sabotaging her future.

Should you be contemplating a bypass of your boss, assess the gravity of your reasons for doing so before taking action. Ask yourself:

- Is the gain I hope to achieve by the bypass worth incurring the wrath of my boss?
- Is my attempt at a bypass most likely to result in my boss's boss siding with my boss and leaving me without an ally?
- Is this issue so important that it is worth sacrificing my reputation as a loyal employee?

Criticizing Your Boss in Front of Others

The oldest saw in human relations is to "praise in public and criticize in private." Yet in the passion of the moment, we may still surrender to an irresistible impulse to criticize the boss within earshot of others. The boss who is criticized may not retaliate immediately and directly, but we can anticipate revenge later. Meetings are the most frequent settings for criticizing the boss in front of others. Slipups can also occur at parties and picnics, as Mary discovered.

Mary, an office manager, attended the annual family picnic given by her company. Jack, the president, strongly endorsed the picnic because he thought it contributed to company harmony. The company was still small enough for practically all employees to know each other. To show his enthusiasm for the event, Jack voted himself the role of hamburger and hotdog cook. After the hamburgers and hot dogs were consumed, Jack would play volley ball or just socialize with the employees.

Mary, who rarely drinks alcoholic beverages, drank about four glasses of beer from the keg. She sat down at a picnic table crowded with company personnel, including the president. Jack asked the rhetorical question, "How's everybody enjoying themselves today?" Mary responded, "I'm okay, but there is something I've been wanting to ask you, Jack." Others at the table looked quizzically at Mary.

Mary continued, "Why is an intelligent man like you so concerned about taking care of the homeless? You told us in our last companywide meeting that we were going to start doing something to help them."

Jack remarked, "That's right, Mary. This company is going to do something for the homeless. For example, we'll distribute to the homeless the food we don't eat today. I've also committed the company to hiring three homeless people this year."

"That's what I thought you said, Jack. But you really mean you are going to give jobs and food to bums. That's a disgrace. People choose to be bums. I hope you don't deny a decent citizen a job just to hire a bum."

Those at the picnic table became so silent that one could hear the whir of mosquitoes. Jack ended the silence by suggesting, "Why don't we all go back to enjoying ourselves?"

Two weeks later, the administrative services department was reorganized. Mary was demoted to the post of word-processing supervisor. When she asked Jack why, he explained: "To be a manager in our company, you have to have a social conscience. When your attitudes change, you'll be eligible for promotion."

Mary is stuck for now. She held her managerial position by virtue of her knowledge of company systems and procedures. Her limited formal education would make it difficult for her to find employment as an office manager elsewhere. It is easy to blame Mary's setback on having had one too many beers. But the "one drink too many" general-purpose excuse doesn't get to the core problem. Mary did not stop to assess the importance of the president's social conscience. Challenging these values was politically insensitive, and doing it publicly was self-sabotaging. Before attending the picnic, Mary should have vowed to herself, "As a manager, I must avoid doing anything in front of other employees that will embarrass anybody."

Should you feel impelled to criticize your boss in front of others, bite your tongue. As a sensible alternative, collect your critical commentary and then present it to your boss, diplomatically and constructively, in a private session.

Challenging the Boss's Judgment

Challenging the boss's judgment, whether privately or publicly, can be analyzed as a separate category of political blunder. Constructively criticizing a boss's opinions, or his or her facts, is much less politically risky. Well-adjusted bosses welcome tactful criticism, especially if you can help them avoid a damaging mistake. Challenging their judgment, however, implies that you question the quality of their thinking—a much more serious charge.

Ken, a systems administrator, took advantage of an open-door policy to challenge his boss's thinking.

Ken works for a small engineering company in its software research and development department. He was hired as a systems administrator, but expresses interest in becoming the manager of the software development group. From the standpoint of experience, talent, and education, Ken qualifies for promotion.

Historically, the company has been against rapid change. New ideas are slowly accepted, especially in regard to software development. Despite this facet of the corporate culture, Ken has been pushing for a new hardware configuration for the company. He has also told others that the department has low productivity, and that he can provide the right software to improve the situation. He regards the software written before his arrival as inferior. Ken is eager to take part in redesigning the company software.

Another key aspect of the company culture is that the president makes all the important decisions. For this reason, few employees confront the president, or even hint at disagreement. Ken believes that other people are needlessly fearful of the president, and that he would probably welcome some innovative thinking. Acting on this hunch, Ken began to challenge the standing procedures and policies formulated by the president. Several times he has entered the president's office to ask why the company continues to rely on such outdated software. He has also demanded to know why more change isn't initiated by the people most familiar with company operations.

Because of his open-door policy, the president has listened to Ken. But Ken observes: "The guy does listen. But I don't think I'm getting my message across. I'll have to step up the tempo of presenting my ideas for improvement."

During Ken's most recent performance evaluation, he asked about the company's timetable for promoting him. Ken's supervisor replied: "Hold on. The president has told me to keep careful watch on your performance. He questions whether you have the right stuff even to be with us very long." At that point, Ken began to question whether the company was deserving of his talents. He thought, nevertheless, that he might give the president one more chance to accept his ideas.[1]

As a systems administrator, Ken should be a force for constructive change in the company's computer systems. His approach to initiating change, however, is self-defeating. Ken has committed the political blunder of insulting the Big Boss's judgment. Ken did not stop to size up that aspect of the corporate culture that says all meaningful change is initiated from the top.

Ken might have been able to create change by volunteering to head up a task force to investigate the need for improved software. If the president had supported the task force, he might have supported its conclusions. Ken was also being politically naive when he took the open-door policy so literally. Ken's straightforward, hard-hitting approach to creating change was self-sabotaging.

Being able to create constructive change is a key requirement for effective leadership. If you want to be an agent for change, however, find a way to bring about change without insulting those people in the organization who want to preserve what already exists. Get them involved in your plans for change, but don't insult them.

Overt Displays of Disloyalty

Being disloyal to your organization or boss is a basic political blunder. Disloyalty takes many forms. Making it known that you are looking for a position elsewhere is the best-known form of disloyalty. Criticizing your company in public settings, praising the high quality of competitors' products, and writing angry letters to the editor about your company are others. You may not get fired, but overt signs of disloyalty may place you in permanent disfavor. When the budget cutters swing their ax, the disloyal often get the first whack. Seemingly trivial situations are often tip-offs as to the depth of a person's loyalty.

Marla had a promising career as an assistant to the vice-president of a company that manufactured and sold office equipment. The product line included electronic pencil sharpeners, desk fixtures, filing systems, and metal desks. The corporate culture emphasized paternalism. Employees were treated well, and management made many efforts to direct employees toward a healthy life-style. Among the programs contributing to this goal were a generous dental insurance plan, a wellness program that included a smoker's clinic, and discounts for "wholesome family entertainment" such as ice shows and circuses.

As a mark of appreciation for the company's hard-working employees, the president decided to begin a holiday turkey giveaway. On the Friday preceding Christmas, every company employee was eligible to receive a medium-size turkey to be taken home for cooking and consumption. The president thought such a gesture would foster the holiday spirit. He also hoped it would promote morale and improve communications. The senior executives would be responsible for handing out the turkeys, thereby interacting with all employees. Marla was assigned the task of organizing Turkey Day, to a large extent because of her reputation as an excellent organizer.

Tony, her boss, explained the assignment to Marla, and then told her that the president thought she would be the ideal candidate to organize the activity. Marla broke into laughter. As she continued to laugh, she said, "Great idea. My mission is to set up a company mission. The only employees who'll show up are those who can't afford their own turkeys. I'll go ahead and organize the affair, so long as you don't put 'Turkey Day Coordinator' on my résumé."

Despite her cynicism, Marla did a marvelous job organizing Turkey Day. While Marla was busily engaged in the paperwork of estimating how many turkeys were left for employees, the president said to Tony: "Thanks so much for lending us Marla for this event. She did a superb job." Tony offhandedly replied, "We're lucky Marla took the assignment. She thinks the whole idea is a joke." The president murmured, "How unfortunate. I had so much faith in Marla's dedication to the company."

Several months later when Marla's name was offered for promotion to director of purchasing, the president vetoed her nomination. He explained that despite Marla's high level of capability, she had not yet developed sufficient loyalty to the company to be promoted to such a key position.

Marla was not disloyal, but she made the mistake of poking fun at the PPP (president's pet project). Although a Turkey Day may appear trivial to a company outsider, such an event can be a sacred tradition to the executive who originated the idea. Marla was perceived as disloyal for poking fun at Turkey Day even though she performed superbly. She may have been judged unfairly, but such is the nature of politics within organizations.

Marla could have prevented her minor act of career self-sabotage by having the political sensitivity to realize that there are no secrets in organizations. Even if Tony was her advocate, there was always the chance that he would leak information about her extreme reaction to the planned holiday event. Marla didn't stop to think about the consequences of her actions, and it cost her a promotion.

Marla hurt herself, but her experience can help you. Before you make your next refreshingly candid comment, ask yourself: "Whose ox am I goring with this statement?" If the ox is a prized one, rework your comment until you can couch it in a constructive and complimentary way. Instead of saying, "The new cost-cutting plan is the pits. It will wreck customer service," try this: "I'm 100 percent behind the corporate effort to further reduce costs. However, thinning down customer service could have some dysfunctional consequences."

Being a Naysayer

Some people are paid to critically review the plans, budgets, and ideas of others. The reviewers render critical judgments, and then often request that others temper their plans and curtail their spending. Financial analysts, for example, are often placed in the position of having to vote against a proposed new product or acquisition. Even if it is within your role to say no to the dreams of others, it is best to avoid being regarded as an inveterate naysayer. If your role does not actually call for making critical judgments on the plans of others, being a naysayer can be even more damaging.

Perpetual naysayers generate negative vibes that make others uncomfortable. To be perceived in such a light is therefore a political blunder. It can block you from moving into a position that calls for a positive, charismatic person. Such was the case with Tracy, a merchandising manager at a department store with six locations.

Tracy began her career in retailing by happenstance, as a participant in a work-study program at Northeastern University. She was sorting through job opportunities in the placement office, hoping to find a work-study assignment for her junior year, when she noticed that a number of retailers offered work-study opportunities. She pursued matters further, and received a satisfactory job offer from a retailer with six locations. Tracy performed well enough in her temporary position to be offered permanent placement after completing college.

Tracy's job stability in an environment of high employee turnover helped her to advance rapidly with her employer. Tracy prided herself in her ability to control costs and not take unnecessary risks. As a merchandising manager, she urged buyers not to bring faddish merchandise into the store. She didn't want the store to get caught with merchandise that would have to be liquidated at a loss. As she explained:

"In retailing you have to be extra careful of costs. A wrong decision on one line of goods can wipe out profits from five profitable lines. The downside risk in retailing is very big. The chances of any one line of merchandise becoming a big hit is very small. That's why I like to take small risks.

"Another key principle of retailing I follow is to watch your head count. I would rather be understaffed than overstaffed. Some store managers hire more floor people than they need to make up for turnover and absenteeism. I can't accept that policy. It eats up profits too quickly."

Tracy's boss, Kim, has a different perception of her conservative business approach:

"Tracy has many good qualities as a merchandising manager. She sure is cost-conscious. But she carries it much too far. Since our stores are geographically dispersed, we allow local buying decisions. A few of our stores are more upscale than others. Tracy has been the merchandising manager in three different locations for us. During her tenure at each one, we never experienced a surge in profits. She never guesses right on hot merchandise. But on the other hand, our profits never dipped at those stores.

"The biggest problem we've had with Tracy is that she is so negative. She shoots down the buyers' most creative ideas. She spends more time with the returns department than she does with advertising and sales promotion. Tracy is Ms. Worst Case Scenario. She talks more about bankruptcies in the retailing business than about new successful stores.

"Tracy is also too negative with store personnel. She spends more time telling them what not to do than what to do. It's her style to be negative. Tracy can also be very negative with company executives. She was the lone dissenting voice when we talked about tentative plans to expand into a new suburban mall. Again, she focused more on what could go wrong than on what could go right.

"Despite her problems, Tracy is a good retailer. I hope she stays with us permanently. But we decided not to offer her a position as general manager of one of our stores because of her negativism. Her turning thumbs down on the mall expansion really ruined her reputation as a positive thinker. I can't see her as a good leader."

Kim's analysis is on target. Being negative, pessimistic, and dour are ill-suited to leadership. Tracy's negativism has helped her do a credible job of controlling costs and minimizing risks. Nevertheless, negativism as a general approach to business problems can be a major political blunder. Tracy's negativism is self-sabotaging to the extent that she wants to move further up the retailing ladder. Her negativism is also self-defeating if she wants to become a more effective leader as a merchandising manager.

Tracy can help herself by studying books and articles about effective leadership and then comparing her traits and characteristics with what is considered ideal. For instance, she might read that effective leaders are warm, expressive, and positive. Tracy can then ask herself, "How warm, expressive, and positive am I?" If Tracy is concerned about her negativism, she might undergo professional counseling to better understand the roots of her problem. The mere fact of questioning one's pessimism and negativism often starts the gradual process of change.

Reflect on your own behavior. Has the percentage of your negative comments climbed too high? If so, follow the suggestions offered to Tracy.

Being a Pest

Common wisdom suggests that diligently pressing for one's demands is the path to success. This may be true up to a point, but when assertiveness is used too often it becomes annoying to many people. The overpersistent person comes to be perceived as a pest, and this constitutes a serious political blunder.

Stuart Schmidt and David Kipnis, two industrial psychologists, conducted studies suggesting that refusing to take no for an answer (being a pest) can be costly both personally and professionally. People who were persistently assertive were labeled as "shotguns." It was found that such people received lower salaries and poorer performance evaluations than people who were more diplomatic and ingratiating. Shotguns also experienced high levels of job tension and personal stress.[2] A logical interpretation of these findings is that managers find ways to retaliate against pests.

Another form of being a pest is to complain constantly about work-related matters. Chronic complainers like to target such topics as the crowded parking lot, the poor quality of cafeteria food, the temperature in the office, the slowness of company mail, and the insufficiency of floating holidays. Large numbers of these complaints are self-sabotaging. The complainer is soon perceived as an ingrate or misfit—surefire labels for career retardation or plateauing.

Whether you are a pest about big issues, small issues, or a combination of the two, it can be self-defeating. It was for Brian, although he wasn't even aware what was holding back his career.

Brian was an administrator in the parking violations bureau of the city government. He enjoyed the relative security of his job and he took delight in knowing that his bureau paid for itself with the large number of citations it issued. Brian thought the city should get what it deserved from parking violators. Similarly, he thought he should get what he deserved from the city.

For Brian, getting what he deserved meant squeezing every possible dollar from his employer. When he was asked to attend a meeting in the next county, Brian filed an expense report claiming mileage allowance. He cited the appropriate city regulation to support his claim. Once when Brian was given a performance evaluation of 3.5, he demanded written documentation as to why he was not rated 4.0. The 4.0 rating would allow Brian to participate in a merit increase on top of his automatic cost-of-living adjustment. When his supervisor did not comply with the request for written documentation, Brian filed a grievance.

Brian's boss recalls the incident that finally compelled him to recommend in writing that Brian be excluded from consideration for promotion to supervisor:

"I was getting ticked off at Brian pushing for the maximum in so many situations. Then one day he pushed me over the edge. Once a year employees get a computerized printout of their benefits. Brian requested a meeting with me to discuss a discrepancy in his benefits report.

"Brian's statement said that he had accumulated 17 unused vacation days, and would be paid for them upon retirement, up to a maximum of 100 days. He was upset because he figured he was owed 20 unused vacation days. His argument was pointless, even if he was right about the three missing days. I knew he would easily accumulate the 100 maximum days long before retirement. The three extra days owed him were therefore superfluous.

"I told Brian to provide as much proof of his argument as he wished. It was his right. But as far as I was concerned, Brian would never become a supervisor in the Parking Violations Bureau."

Brian's problem is that he failed to examine the implications of his pushing for small gains. Angling to receive merit pay admittedly had some short-range benefits for Brian. But his abrasive method of demanding written documentation from his superior was politically unwise. The few extra dollars in mileage and the few extra days of accrued vacation pay were gains not worth pursuing. They branded Brian as being small-minded.

Brian committed a career self-sabotaging blunder that could have been avoided by carefully examining his own behavior. A general antidote for self-sabotage is to periodically review how you are handling people and situations. Ask yourself:

"Am I proud of how I handled that?"

"What kind of message did my actions communicate to others?"

"Is what I contemplate doing cost-effective in terms of my career advancement?"

Declining an Offer From Top Management

If you are already overworked, it is understandable that you turn down requests with a polite no when asked to take on another project. The well-accepted principle of time management—learn to say no—says you are right. A countervailing argument is that turning down top management, especially more than once, is a political blunder. You thus have to balance sensibly managing your time against the blunder of refusing a request from management. Here is an example of this scenario in action:

Rich, the vice-president of marketing in a media company, was also in charge of corporate acquisitions. The company was in a cash-rich position while many smaller media companies were struggling. One of the many projects Rich had going was doing a feasibility study on acquiring a cable TV station in a distant city. He needed somebody to visit the company and to prepare a thorough financial analysis of its worth. The project could easily occupy six weeks of one's time.

Rich approached Bev, the accounting manager, with a request to take on this feasibility study. He explained that he knew Bev was already saddled with a heavy work load. Rich also emphasized that this acquisition was a very important one, and the company needed a first-rate analysis. Bev replied that she would like to take a rain check. She explained that in order to do a top professional job she would need to spend more time on the project than she could possibly find.

Rich shrugged his shoulders, saying that he would find somebody else to do the study. He gave the assignment to Patricia, the supervisor of financial analysis, who reported to Bev. Patricia wedged the job in along with her regular responsibilities. She was able to accomplish it by delegating many of her regular responsibilities to two accountants in her department. The cable company was acquired, and three months later Patricia was offered a position as its controller. Bev was confused and upset about what had happened. She wished she had the opportunity to become the controller of a subsidiary.

Bev committed a political blunder that may have cost her a desirable promotion. Her first impulse was to turn down the marketing vice-president's offer to conduct the acquisition study. She submitted to this impulse instead of searching for an alternative solution, satisfactory both to Rich and herself. She might have explained that she had a crushing workload, but could take on the study if her burden were lightened. Following this logic, she could have requested authorization to hire one or two temporary accountants. They could have taken over some of the work of Bev's subordinates. In turn, the subordinates could have taken over some of Bev's work.

Instead of suggesting the delegation alternative (or any other feasible one), Bev impulsively made a blunder that kept her out of the running for a quick promotion. It can also be assumed that Rich is not enamored of Bev's inflexibility. It never helps your career to have a key executive downgrade his opinion of you.

The lesson here is that if you face a burdensome work load, and top management asks you to do even more, do not flatly refuse. Instead, negotiate a workable compromise that will enable you to take on the new assignment while divesting yourself of some of your present duties.

Being an Ethical Zealot

The many business scandals of recent years have brought renewed attention to the importance of business ethics. Many business schools have even hired members of the clergy to teach courses in the philosophy of ethics. Although ethics is in, it can still be a political blunder to beat the drum too loudly for scrupulously honest behavior. This is especially true in a corporate culture where ethical behavior is preached more than it is practiced. The misfortunes of Dave exemplify this problem.

Dave, a retailing manager, was an extremely hard worker. He believed in exerting himself in order to reach personal and organizational objectives. Starting out in the women's apparel department, Dave moved up the ladder quickly. His store associates enjoyed working for him even though Dave had extremely high standards.

Dave had strong religious beliefs that he carried along into his professional career. He was extremely fair, treated everyone with respect, and was known for his integrity. Dave made sure that customers got what they paid for, and his employees received what they were promised. Dave's hard work seemed to pay off. He was promoted to regional manager of women's apparel.

About a year later, a truck delivering a shipment of furs to the store was involved in an accident. The impact of the collison forced open the truck door, scattering the furs in the snow and slush. Dave had all the furs dry-cleaned. He planned to sell them at a substantial discount and to fully inform customers of what had happened. The shipper agreed to pay the difference between the sale price and the intended retail price because it accepted responsibility for the damage.

When Dave's boss heard what had happened, he called him into his office. The boss had seen the furs on their return from the cleaners, and he thought they looked brand-new. He wanted Dave to sell the coats at their original price because customers would not be able to tell the difference.

Dave thought through what the boss wanted him to do, and decided that it was against his moral principles. Dave went to the boss and told him that he would be selling the coats at the sale price. His boss told Dave that either he would sell the coats at the intended retail price, or he could turn in his resignation that afternoon. Dave returned to his boss that afternoon with a signed resignation. His boss accepted it without another word.

Dave began to look for a new job the next day. He thought his track record would enable him to find a comparable position quite easily. As the months passed by, Dave had few interviews and no job offers. After a year without an offer in the women's apparel field, he finally found a position as the manager of an office supply store. Dave took a substantial drop in pay and growth potential, but he was happy again to be leading a productive life.

Two years later, while at a business lunch, Dave uncovered the reason for his inability to find another job in women's apparel. His boss had enough connections to black-list Dave in the women's apparel field in his city.[3]

The easy solution for Dave would have meant not being so ethical. Submitting to the inner voice of his ethical code, instead of the demands of his boss, was assuredly a political blunder. It wound up sabotaging Dave's career in his natural field. He was forced to enter another phase of retailing, at much lower pay and with much less chance for growth. But sometimes a person has to make a career sacrifice in order to behave ethically. How would you have behaved in Dave's situation? Much depends on whether you place ethical obligations above the welfare of your career. Perhaps in such a situation being ethical is more important than avoiding self-defeating behavior. In the long run, you will feel better about yourself.

Whistle-blowers face the same dilemma as Dave. A whistle-blower discovers that management is doing something unethical or illegal. The person then informs the government or the media. Legislation prevents the whistle-blower from actually being fired for making the company's misdeeds public. However, the whistle-blower is likely to suffer career retardation or to spend the rest of his or her business life in limbo.

Balking at Revising One's Work

Hierarchical authority is less emphasized today than it was previously. Nevertheless, most managers still like to exercise the right of asking subordinates to revise written and numerical reports. Often the revisions requested are quite valid. Managers can act as outsider observers and thus serve as effective critics. They may also have a good perspective on the information requirements of higher management (the people who will ultimately read the report). At other times, the revisions requested may not be so valid. Some managers feel negligent if they don't request at least some revision of a subordinate's report.

Whether or not a request for rework is valid, it is usually a political blunder to balk at making revisions. The person who resists rework is likely to be regarded as stubborn, uncooperative, or, worse, poorly motivated.

Bob was the manager of financial planning and analysis at a large company in the chemicals industry. He had a thorough understanding of both the technical operations and the cost accounting of the business units for which he was responsible. After seven years in this area, Bob had developed heuristics (numerical rules of thumb) that enabled him to make quick assessments in a continually changing environment.

Bob's team was well respected for the accuracy and thoroughness of its analysis. Because of the technical skills of himself and his group, Bob had a keen understanding of the amount of work that was created by after-the-fact analysis of his groups' reports. Executives would often come up with thoughts for additional analysis after they had read the reports prepared by Bob's team.

Bob and a few of his team members would meet regularly with outsiders who used their output. During these meetings Bob would respond angrily when an outsider identified yet another way of presenting the data for analysis. Bob would complain that top management was already requiring too much data, and that they were suffering from "analysis paralysis." He would urge them to make a decision based on the data already presented. On many occasions Bob would ask the managers who used his information to justify their requests for revising the reports generated.

The members of upper management who attended the meetings with Bob and his group soon perceived him as uncooperative and arbitrary. The suggestion was also made that Bob was being disruptive to the mission. Despite his grumbling, Bob and his team were quick to respond with the additional information requested. Management thus was not concerned about the output of Bob's group but rather about the negative attitude Bob displayed when asked to do additional analysis.

Over the years, this negative perception haunted Bob as he tried to move into another position in financial management. Blocked by his negative image, Bob gave up his career in financial planning and moved into an accounting position in manufacturing.[4]

Bob's recalcitrance negated much of the fine work he and his group were providing the organization. He thus contributed directly to his own career setback. The other team members did not incur damaged reputations because it was Bob alone who was perceived as argumentative. Things could have worked out much differently for Bob, and he could be happier today. During the excitement of the meetings he allowed his self-centeredness to rule his rational side. Instead of rebelling at reanalysis (which he usually performed anyway), he might calmly have discussed his concerns about analyzing data beyond the point of diminishing returns.

Bob might also have taken a broader and more constructive viewpoint. He and his group were getting paid to do the rework. Furthermore, the additional analysis ensured that his group would be kept occupied performing tasks valued by the organization. Many staff groups suffer from the opposite problem. They don't have enough requests from top management. Consequently, they dream up ideas for useful projects that they then have to sell to management. Instead of taking this broad point of view, Bob kept his hackles raised and burrowed down the path of career self-sabotage.

If you face a situation in which you are asked to do tiresome rework, keep Bob's undoing in mind. So long as your meter is running, why be so resistant to rework? The issue might be worth a few constructive suggestions about not allowing work to reach the point of diminishing returns. However, career self-sabotage is a heavy price to pay for resisting rework.

Resisting the Dress Code

Rigid conformity is no longer a virtue in most successful organizations. Nevertheless, deviating too far from an important custom such as a dress code is a political blunder. The dress code is obviously not the same for every organization. Proper standards of dress can be gleaned from observing both fast trackers and members of top management. To flout these standards can be self-sabotaging.

Carla, a patent attorney, worked for a prestigious Toronto law firm. She chose to wear short-sleeved blouses to work during June, July, and August. Her supervising attorney advised her repeatedly that short-sleeved blouses and shirts were not suitable attire for lawyers in their firm. Carla brushed aside these comments as an infringement on her personal freedom.

The supervisor retaliated by placing a memo in Carla's file stating that she was not a good candidate for partnership in the firm because she did not fully respect its values. Four year later, Carla had still not been invited into partnership. Disgruntled, she resigned to join a very small law firm that wanted to have one patent attorney on its staff. Carla sorely missed working with other patent attorneys.

Carla's problems could be easily dismissed. If she hadn't been so stubborn about something as inconsequential as wearing long-sleeved blouses in June, July, and August, she would be a partner today. But beneath that problem could lie a deeper reason for her career self-sabotage. Carla might be using the form of self-sabotage called self-handicapping or excuse making. By not adhering to the dress code, she is giving herself a good excuse in case she fails to be invited into partnership. She can blame her failure on wearing short-sleeved blouses. In this case, the self-handicapping was too severe. It was guaranteed to do the job.

To prevent many forms of career self-sabotage in addition to violating dress codes, it is necessary to ask: "What handicaps am I imposing on myself that give me an out in case I fail?" Common self-imposed handicaps include not completing a degree, staying obese, refusing to learn how to use a computer, and using vulgarities in the office.

Burning Your Bridges

A potent political blunder is to create ill will among former employers or people who have helped you in the past. The best-known form of bridge burning occurs when a person departs from an organization. A person who leaves involuntarily is especially apt to express anger toward those responsible for the dismissal. Venting your anger may give a temporary boost to your mental health, but it can be detrimental in the long run.

Mark, the vice-president of marketing at a building materials company, had a basic disagreement with the company president about his job. Mark thought he should concentrate his efforts on the future of the company's marketing. He spent considerable time attempting to assess what kind of building materials would be needed to meet the changing demographics. He was also keenly interested in how the trend toward energy-efficient homes would affect the business. The president, in contrast, wanted Mark to spend more time dealing with current problems.

The dispute between the two men ended when the president asked Mark to resign. Upset by this incident, Mark wrote a letter to the board of directors accusing the president of being a "short-range thinker, preoccupied with matters that should be taken care of by first-level supervisors." The president retaliated by inserting a memo in Mark's personnel file. The memo described Mark as a dreamer who also showed poor judgment in handling differences of opinion.

The employment references the president gave Mark were so lukewarm that it prevented Mark from obtaining the specific kind of marketing position he really wanted. Ten months later, Mark finally found a position as a marketing director at a small company. He still regrets having written the angry letter to the board of directors.

Mark sabotaged his career because he allowed his right brain (the emotional side) to take over his left brain (the logical side). In the midst of his rage, he should have implemented the standard antidote to the urge to write a nasty note: Write the letter, but don't seal or mail it for forty-eight hours. When two days have passed, read your letter and decide if it's really a good idea to send it. Ninety-five percent of the time your decision will be no, and you will have warded off an acute self-inflicted wound.

How to Patch Up a Blunder

Patching up blunders is an important skill. To avoid self-sabotage, it is expedient to patch up the immediate damage as quickly as possible. The suggestions offered here apply to political blunders and blunders in general (such as misquoting a price to customers). The two are related: Not patching up an ordinary blunder can be considered a political blunder.

1. *Break the bad news to your boss before anyone else does.* If the blunder has taken place in front of your boss, this step is already taken care of. Suppose, however, you have insulted your boss's boss in a meeting. Word will quickly get back to your boss, so take the initiative by telling your boss directly. If you are willing to accept responsibility for your mistakes, your boss and others will be more forgiving.

2. *Avoid defensiveness.* Demonstrate that you are more interested in recovering from the blunder than in trying to share the blame for what happened. Focus on solutions to the problem rather than on faultfinding. Suppose you have been far too critical of your boss in a recent staff meeting. Explain that your attempts to be constructively critical backfired, and that you will choose your words more carefully in the future.

3. *Stay poised.* Admit that you made a mistake and apologize, but don't act or feel inferior. Mistakes are inevitable in a competitive work environment. Avoid looking sad and distraught. Instead, maintain eye contact with people when you describe your blunder.

4. *Have some answers ready.* If fixing your blunder will involve your boss, make suggestions as to how he or she can help. Suppose you disappointed a higher-up by not having some things ready for an important meeting. The executive in question wants to know what's wrong with your department. Give your boss some facts to work with that will help explain the delay. Encourage your boss to hold you responsible for the problem. Disarming the boss in this way will usually make him or her want to help you. Instead of focusing all the blame on you, your boss is more likely to present your blunder to higher management as a team effort.[5] Isn't that better than sabotaging your reputation?

8

Sex Roles and
Self-Sabotage

$\mathcal{A}$t times the things people do and the choices they make, as determined by what they think is appropriate for their sex, can damage their careers. Expressed in another way, the way you think you should behave on the job as a man or as a woman can sometimes interfere with your success. Let's begin with extremes. If a male executive thinks a man in power should be patronizing toward women, he may sabotage his career. He may fail to gain the cooperation of the women colleagues and the staff he needs to achieve his objectives. If a female executive thinks she should defer to men and be dependent on them, she may not be commanding enough to achieve her objectives.

Although most men and women are not locked into sex roles that doom them to career self-sabotage, it is true that stereotyped beliefs about how one should behave as a man or a woman can create severe career problems. Being either too traditional or too nontraditional with respect to sex roles and sexual preferences can be self-sabotaging.

Women Who Lower the Ceiling on Their Success

Robin Dee Post, a psychotherapist who specializes in helping career women, has made a revealing observation about her clients. Despite many remarkable accomplishments, successful career women often struggle with conflicts that undermine their effectiveness. These conflicts only add to their burden of coping with such demanding careers as being a small-business owner, accountant, attorney, lawyer, or physician.[1] Conflicts surrounding their sex role have not prevented these women from being successful, but they can lower the ceiling of further success. Six "ghastly traps" plague many successful career women, and all of them can be self-defeating:

1. *Being self-critical and perfectionistic.* Many high-achieving women are self-critical and perfectionistic. (So are many men, but the problem is even more common among successful women.) They set unreasonably high standards for themselves, and are overly conscientious. In extreme cases, they feel guilty if they violate their self-imposed high standards. Despite what they have achieved, many successful women feel inadequate and dissatisfied with themselves.

Perfectionism can lower productivity. Seated at her desk, for example, a packaging design engineer perfectionistically revamps the same package for an infant auto seat a dozen times. She could have completed five package designs in the time it takes her to produce one. Furthermore, the package design for an infant seat may not be a critical selling point. At this pace, she will most likely stay on a career plateau.

2. *Failure to prioritize and overcommitment.* High-achieving women frequently find it difficult to establish their own personal goals. Or they may give them low priority. They feel compelled to first meet responsibilities to superiors, subordinates, customers, and family members. All these responsibilities must be met before they feel entitled to attend to a self-development program.

Because these women are talented and conscientious, they are asked to participate in a variety of projects and community activities. They have difficulty saying no when a worthwhile project is involved. When asked to serve on a prestigious task force, one woman worried that she might never again be asked to do something so important. She therefore agreed to participate although she did not have the time.

Many high-achieving women are overextended, and feel overcommitted. As a consequence, they lead pressured lives, and have difficulty finding time for creative activity, reflection, and relaxation. A bank vice-president said, "Lots of people are on a treadmill, but my situation is different. I have three treadmills going at the same time. My career, my family, and my community obligations. I'm a candidate for cardiac arrest."

The bank vice-president may not see it, but her dilemma is self-imposed. She may need her career and her family, but why can't she drastically curtail her community activities? Her over-commitment is perhaps driven by a desire to prove herself to the world. If she invested some time in reflecting on her own behavior, she might no longer be a candidate for cardiac arrest.

3. *Procrastination and the avoidance of conflict-laden tasks.* Many of the successful women observed by Post put off activities that are anxiety-provoking for them. One woman kept putting off writing up a family evaluation in an acrimonious custody battle. The longer successful women avoid these unpleasant tasks, the more objectionable and insurmountable the tasks become. Procrastination usually produces self-blame and uncomfortable pressure as deadlines approach. It interferes with creative problem solving and productivity because the unfinished tasks detract from concentration.

Although the procrastination engaged in by such women may be driven by personal conflicts about success, it can still be overcome. Aside from using the procrastination antidotes described in Chapter 4, these career women can confront their own behavior by asking themselves:

"What is blocking me?"
"Is there a deep-rooted reason why I'm dragging my heels on this project?"
"Why can't I break loose and get things done?"
"I'm capable of getting this project done. Why can't I use my capabilities?"

4. *Excessive modesty.* Women often hesitate to acknowledge their own expertise and competence. A financial planner who is recognized as a local authority on investment strategy cringed at the prospect of giving a talk on investments. She doubts that she

has anything worthwhile to present. Some women with successful careers have trouble accepting recognition. They feel unworthy of receiving accolades for their legitimate accomplishments, and rarely toot their own horns.

Undue modesty can be self-sabotaging because self-promotion is an important ingredient of sustained success. Rachel, the vice-president of information systems at a savings and loan association, suffered from a modesty problem. She finally began to overcome the problem while attending a career development program. As the various high-level managers in the group presented their résumés, the thought struck Rachel that her credentials were well above average. As her self-regard increased, she became an even more forceful member of top management. The message here is that using objective data to compare your accomplishments with those of others can help you overcome undue modesty.

5. *Reluctance to resolve problems through confrontation.* A sales manager felt frustrated because one of her sales representatives was not putting enough energy into customer relations. The manager was hesitant to confront the employee for fear of hurting her feelings. Because the manager did not confront the sales representative, she continued to feel angry and guilty.

Perhaps the sales manager thought it was inconsistent with her nurturing role to be confrontational. A manager who fails to confront when necessary will not reach her full potential as a manager. Overcoming the dislike for confrontation is not easy, but a useful starting point is to confront a person about small things, such as an improperly completed expense report. If this confrontation over a small issue goes well, the manager can move on to confrontations that involve progressively more controversial issues.

The sales manager also has to ask herself what is so bad about confrontation. So what if the errant sales rep becomes upset? Being upset is part of life in a competitive business environment. The manager should also think through her role as a manager. Confronting group members about problems is an important aspect of the managerial role.

6. *Putting others' needs first.* Many successful women feel

selfish when they put their own needs ahead of the needs of other people, even in the pursuit of their careers. Some middle managers spend considerable time helping their subordinates with work problems and listening to their personal problems. From the standpoint of the organization, this is desirable. An important role of managers is to develop others.

The problem is that the middle manager who devotes too much time to subordinates will miss out on activities that more readily lead to promotion. Among them are preparing suggestions for productivity and quality improvement, and networking with people who can help your career. A ninety-minute lunch with a powerful executive will do more for your career than the same amount of time spent listening to employees' problems.

I am not suggesting that callousness and Machiavellianism replace human kindness in the workplace. However, the woman who does not want to subordinate her career needs to those of others must strike a balance. Investing even a couple of hours a month in forming alliances with the right people can pay enormous career dividends.

Do you recognize yourself here? If so, there are steps you can take to overcome the traps just described. Something can be done about the sex role stereotypes that compel successful women to sabotage their chances for achieving even greater success.[2] Four approaches are recommended, all centering around the idea that the culture breeds self-defeating thinking among some successful women.

General Approaches for Women Overcoming Self-Imposed Limits

1. *Challenge your negative self-beliefs.* Women who set limits on the levels of success they can achieve need to challenge their unrealistic and negative beliefs about themselves. Being critical of assertive or self-protective actions is particularly damaging. A manager might believe, for example, that her anger at a careless subordinate is proof of her nasty disposition. The manager has to challenge herself in words such as, "Getting angry at the right

person is a sign of goodness. How will a goof-off ever learn without my being confrontational?"

Another successful woman might feel guilty because her overcrowded schedule makes it difficult for her to accept any additional outside directorships. She must challenge her thinking in such terms as, "True, I am a company president who happens to be a woman. It doesn't mean that I have to submit to every demand that accompanies my success."

2. *Recognize the constraints placed on you by sex role socialization.* Early-life experiences condition some women to accept certain beliefs that can inhibit high levels of success. Typical of these self-sabotaging ideas are that—

- Successful women are often unattractive to men and therefore may not find a long-term relationship with a man. It is unwomanly to engage in such aggressive behavior as expressing anger, exercising power, and boasting.
- It is bad to be selfish.
- Other people's feelings and interests should be put ahead of one's own.
- It is important to assume responsibility for the well-being of other people.

Laying out these stereotyped beliefs and taboos helps identify their capacity for pushing a woman toward career self-sabotage. After exposing these ideas to sunlight, they can be challenged. The next step is for the successful woman to consciously modify her behavior, as needed.

3. *Assert yourself.* As an extension of the point just made, women must develop assertiveness in areas where they previously felt constrained. One area for change would be to clearly communicate feelings, including anger and disappointment. Limits must also be set on the unacceptable actions of others. Suppose, for example, that a customer assumes a woman is an assistant—and not the vice-president—because of her sex. The vice-president, who in the past would have let the incident slide, might now appropriately assert herself by saying matter-of factly: "I'm the vice-president with whom you have an appointment.

How can I help you?" (Notice that the woman makes her point, and probably feels better, without having belittled the sexist thinker.)

   4. *Achieve self-acceptance as a woman who is competent and successful.* Many successful women have a difficult time convincing themselves that they deserve their success. Remember the imposter complex described earlier? Achieving self-acceptance can be a long struggle, but it is worth the effort. The highest-placed woman in manufacturing in her company told a group at a management conference: "I want many of you to follow my lead. I deserve my success. I've worked hard, and I know my stuff. I enjoy the measure of success I've achieved. I also accept the fact that I have limitations. But they don't bother me. I have what it takes to run my unit of the organization."

Men Who Lower the Ceiling on Their Career Success

Women who lower the ceiling on their career success, in the context described here, are responding to cultural programming. They are sabotaging their chances for even greater success because they have not yet been able to shake the external limitations placed upon them. These women impose limits on their success because they accept certain stereotypes. In contrast, some men lower the ceiling on their career success because they reject a pervasive stereotype about the male role.

   The rejected stereotype is that managerial and professional men are more interested in worldly success than they are in family or personal relationships. From the standpoint of leading a balanced and rewarding life, these men may be better off than their traditionally minded counterparts. The latter are willing to sacrifice family and personal relationships for an extra rung or two on the organizational ladder.

   Two groups of managerial and professional men reject the male sex role with respect to career growth: those involved in a new passion, and daddy-trackers. Members of the first group may do so unwittingly. Members of the second group are making a conscious choice to reject certain stereotypes about the male role. Career men with new-found passions and daddy-trackers may have laudable motives and may be leading well-balanced lives. Nevertheless, they are usually setting limits on further career growth.

New-Found Passion

Some corporate ladder climbers suddenly become passionate about something other than their work. The sudden diversion is most likely to occur as part of a mid-life crisis. The passion is often a new romance, but could also be a participant sport or a social cause. Whatever the new commitment, the man invests so much energy in his new passion that his work begins to slide. Instead of arranging his personal life around work, the man begins to squeeze in work around his personal life. The result can be an intensely enjoyable personal life but sheer sabotage to his career.

Adrian, the distribution manager for a chemical manufacturer, supervised a staff of ten people involved in purchasing, warehousing, shipping, and customer service. His tour of duty in distribution was designed to add breadth to his experience as a marketing manager. If Adrian performed well in this assignment, he would be a leading contender for a vice-president of marketing position in the future.

Adrian had been divorced for three years. His two teenage children lived with their mother just three miles from his town house. Adrian began to rebuild his social life while separated from his wife, but had not been involved in a serious relationship. Returning to his Detroit home base from a business trip, Adrian had a two-hour layover at O'Hare airport in Chicago because of a flight delay.

After one-hour of shuffling through some business mail and reading *The Wall Street Journal*, Adrian decided to rest. As he closed his attaché case, he looked across the aisle. Seated across from him was a friendly-looking woman, about age 30, who appeared to be traveling alone. Adrian waved hello, and to his surprise, she reciprocated.

Such was the beginning of a torrid commuter romance between Adrian Markham and Heather Gladstone. Heather, a software training consultant, was on a business trip to Detroit, but lived in a suburb of Chicago. At least 400 miles and plenty of travel time separated them.

Adrian and Heather fell passionately in love, but with Heather remaining a little more committed to her work than Adrian was to his. During the week he would daydream about Heather. Adrian began to leave the office early on Fridays in order to get to Chicago. At first Adrian would fly, but as the costs mounted, he turned to driving. If the road conditions were favorable, Adrian would leave the office by 11 A.M. on Friday, and be at Heather's home by 8 P.M. Heather did make some trips to visit Adrian, but Adrian volunteered to do most of the traveling.

Adrian became preoccupied with scheming how to spend more time with Heather. He decided to begin taking vacation days on Fridays and Mondays and planned more and more business trips to the Chicago area. Although many of Adrian's times away from the office were legitimate vacation days, he gave the appearance of being negligent. On many Mondays when Adrian was physically present, he was visibly fatigued. Other times, he was so preoccupied with planning his trips and thinking about Heather that his concentration suffered. After leaving Adrian's office, staff members would often gesture toward his assistant with a quizzical look and a shoulder shrug.

Adrian's boss did try to intervene. He asked Adrian several times if he were experiencing a personal problem the company could help him with. Adrian assured his boss that he had never felt better and that he was going through some very positive changes in his life. Finally, his boss told Adrian that he had to show greater mental involvement in his work and be a more reliable physical presence. If he did not make these changes, he was told, he would have to accept the consequences.

Adrian discussed the problem with Heather. She suggested that he spend less time visiting her in Chicago. Heather also recommended that a little less time together would be helpful to their relationship. If they could retain their closeness despite less time together, it would be a sign that the two of them should live together or marry.

Instead of feeling reassured, Adrian panicked. He interpreted Heather's suggestion as a sign that she wanted to cool down their relationship. Adrian now telephoned Heather even more frequently, and insisted that he use up more of his vacation time so they could be together.

Thirty days later, Adrian was demoted to distribution analyst in the company. He was also told that if his performance was not satisfactory in this new position, and if he did not spend more time in the office, he would be terminated. Adrian now felt that his career and personal life were in a tailspin. Within several months, however, Adrian did solidify his relationship with Heather. The two became engaged, and planned to live together within one year. Adrian hopes that Heather can move to Detroit because he wants to remain near his children. Adrian is now performing satisfactorily as a distribution analyst, but hopes again to become a manager at either his current or another company.

Adrian's story has a reasonably happy outcome. He is only one promotion away from regaining a managerial position, although he has sabotaged his hopes of becoming a vice-president of marketing at his present company. If his relationship with Heather endures, one might argue that Adrian has made an excellent trade-off. A great romance is certainly worth a career sacrifice. The outcome might have been even happier for Adrian had he explored ways of salvaging his managerial position and his candidacy for a vice-presidency while carrying on his new romance.

Adrian ignored gentle hints from his assistant that his superiors and subordinates were questioning his behavior. He even failed to act on the verbal warnings of his boss. Adrian might have done much less damage to his career if he had confronted himself in this way:

> "Heather is my passion, my preoccupation, and my great romance. For now, she is the driving force in my life. After the surge of excitement is over, I will still love Heather. But I will probably also need my career.
>
> "My career was a passion of mine for many years. It has subsided now, but I will need it again. No use throwing it overboard. Heather will still love me if we can just work things out so that we spend ample time together without my being derelict in my job responsibilities."

Adrian might also have followed Heather's approach to juggling romance and career. She was more hesitant than Adrian to set aside her work for the sake of the romance. Finally, other people have pursued commuter relationships without sabotaging their careers. Adrian might have sought out such people and investigated how they balanced work and personal life. If you are involved in a commuter relationship, follow the advice offered to Adrian.

The Daddy Track

Some men place themselves on a Daddy Track without much encouragement from their employers, or even much urging from the mother of their child or children. They have voluntarily reduced their work load in order to devote more time to parenting. Some men restrict themselves to forty-hour weeks, others to four-day weeks, and some take extended parental leaves. More accurately, these men are committing career sacrifice, rather than career sabotage. In order to be more active fathers, they are willingly sacrificing some career momentum.

For some Daddy Trackers, the career slippage is slight. Many men regularly take their children off to the child-care center and visit them at lunch. Although early morning and lunchtime can be classified as personal time, not being available at such hours can still hamper one's career. Many employers call meetings at 7:30 A.M., and many important business contacts are developed at breakfast or luncheon meetings. Chris is a man who is willing to accept moderate career slippage in order to be a more active father.

It's a typical weekday morning in Half Moon Bay, California. At 8:15 Chris is getting ready to leave for work. Two-year old Willie clutches a new toy football as he climbs into his child seat in the family car. Buffer, Chris's wife, also gets into the car. Chris gets behind the wheel. The family starts on a half-hour drive to the biotechnology company where the couple work as researchers.

The ride proves to be eventful. Chris and Buffer cruise behind a truck loaded with redwood logs and answer Willie's questions about trees and lumber and houses. They see a van on fire and quiet Willie's fears. Coming over a hill, they watch jets take off from San Francisco International Airport. Driving into the industrial park that houses the company's million-dollar day-care center, they pass a train depot. An obliging engineer toots a whistle and Willie beams.

The joy turns into trauma when Willie is reminded that he must leave his football in the car. No outside toys are allowed in the day-care center. The tantrum is still ringing in Chris's ears as he settles into his labor work around 9 A.M.

And so begins one more of the eight-hour days that for working father Chris constitute a career. At 34, after nine years at the laboratory, Chris has new priorities. As with his lab partners in the cardiovascular department, he used to work long weekends searching for miracle drugs. Now, on Saturdays and Sundays, he's home with Willie, hard at play. While his colleagues stay late on weekdays, attempting to unlock chemical secrets, Chris is picking up his son from the day-care center and dealing with the mysteries of childhood.

"I can't have my child in day care for a 12-hour day," says Chris. "He won't be my child. When you're all done, someone else will have raised him." As part of his commitment to being an active parent, Chris took off three months during Willie's first year to get to know him better. The leave also gave Buffer the opportunity to return to work.

So Chris works from 9 A.M. to 5:45 P.M. and resigns himself to treading water in his job, even as Buffer climbs past him on the corporate ladder at the company. "I'll sacrifice the career," he says. Then he corrects himself. "Not exactly sacrifice, but I'll kind of put it on hold."[3]

Chris has knowingly accepted a career plateau in order to be an active parent. If he is truly happy with his decision, he has not committed even mild career self-sabotage. However, his passion for spending time with his son could conceivably be clouding his judgment. It would probably be possible for Chris to sacrifice just six hours per week of parenting and still advance in his career. Maybe it will be to Willie's advantage in the long run for his dad not to make too big a career sacrifice. Suppose Willie's mother doesn't rise as high as she wants to in her career. Which parent then will be able to send Willie to the college and graduate school of his choice? Who will be able to purchase Willie the car he may want as a high school junior or senior?

Maybe Buffer could take over if Chris worked one or two twelve-hour days per week and one Saturday per month. This would still enable Chris to accomplish his parenting goals. At the same time, he would be preparing for the contingency that ten years from now he may wish that he had not shortchanged his career.

Machismo and Self-Sabotage

An exaggerated sense of one's masculinity can be self-defeating because it leads to sexist thinking. Sexual discrimination and sexual harassment are also sometimes a by-product. The macho-male may damage his career by thinking of women employees as being suited only for support positions. He may make frequent use of such terms as "dear," "honey," and "be a nice girl" when conversing with women employees and customers. Even more troubling, he may create a harassing work environment by telling sexually oriented jokes or taking liberties degrading to women.

A man's belief, arising from machismo, that women are best relegated to support positions, can damage his career because it often means that he cannot accept working for a woman. Nick experienced this problem to the point where it sabotaged both his career and his marriage.

Nick was a well-respected manager at IBM with twenty-six years of experience. Co-workers saw him as a dedicated and responsible worker who had continued to develop his managerial skills. Nick was known as a traditional thinker, someone who was satisfied both with his family life and with his career.

Nick had three grown children, two of whom were out on their own. His youngest daughter was in college. He frequently talked about their achievements with his co-workers.

Nick enjoyed working for his boss, Joe, with whom he had an excellent working relationship. He was disappointed that Joe was to being transferred to another department, but accepted the fact that IBM encourages managers to acquire broad experience. Nick's disappointment turned to outrage when he was informed that his new boss was going to be a woman younger than himself. Nick didn't know how he could take orders from a woman. He wondered how he could tell his wife and friends that he was now working for a "girl." Driven by a sense of humiliation, Nick resigned without having first conducted a job search.

Nick's sudden resignation stunned people at the office, and created turmoil at home. He and his wife, Nancy, had been living in the same town for the better part of their married life. Nancy had developed close ties with friends and neighbors, and was emotionally attached to their house. Despite Nancy's attachment to the community, Nick wanted to make a fresh start and leave town. He also had little choice because managerial job opportunities in their area were very limited.

Although Nancy valued her relationship with Nick, she decided not to move because of his irrational act of resigning from IBM. She tried to convince Nick to plead for his old job back, but he refused. They continued to fight over the issue of leaving town, but Nick was intractable. As the couple continued to fight, their relationship deteriorated. They agreed to separate, and Nick finally relocated to the south, hoping to find new employment and a better life.[4]

It won't be easy for Nick to regain the stature and relatively high income he enjoyed at IBM. He may also soon regret having precipitated the breakup of a good marriage. Nick's resignation in response to having a female boss was but a symptom of his underlying problem. Nick's macho conception of the world created his sense of humiliation when he heard about his new boss. He didn't even stop to give the relationship with her a try. Nick could very likely have avoided his problems if he had at any point stopped to compare his old-world thinking with the real world as it is today.

Nick's employer, IBM, is one of the most advanced companies in the training and development programs it offers its employees. Nick could have taken advantage of an awareness development program tailored to his needs. Such programs help people to confront their attitudes and develop empathy and toleration for people of different demographic characteristics. Should you have difficulty overcoming traditional thinking about power relationships at work, diversity awareness training could prove helpful to you.

Ultrafemininity and Self-Sabotage

Just as a man's attempt to be overmasculine can hurt his career, a woman's attempt to be overfeminine can hurt her career. Many people have observed, for example, that women who are very glamorous, sexily dressed, and overly feminine (as defined by cultural stereotypes) limit their promotability. Women who rate very high on physical attractiveness are readily welcomed into secretarial, clerical, support, and sales positions. However, a woman who is perceived as too glamorous and physically attractive is less likely to be nominated for a high-level managerial position. In recognition of this problem, wardrobe consultants typically advise managerial and professional women to avoid wearing large earrings, dangling jewelry, and spiked heels. In addition, they are advised to wear their hair at shoulder length or above.

In what way does being very feminine, charming, and glamorous sabotage a woman's chances of climbing the managerial ladder? My investigation into this matter has revealed several themes. The male executive who promoted the glamorous woman may be accused of being unduly influenced by her appearance. To avoid having this judgment questioned, the male executive will thus shy away from promoting an ultrafeminine woman, other factors being equal. If no other well-qualified candidate is under consideration, a glamour image will not handicap the woman.

Male executives who promote unusually glamorous women to high-level positions may be concerned that they will be accused of being romantically involved with them. One executive expressed his concern that he would find it distracting to work closely with a beautiful woman executive. He said he would have a difficult time controlling his feelings of physical attraction toward her. Asked whether the same problem would extend to working with women below him in rank, he replied: "To some extent, I do have that problem with any beautiful woman in the office. Yet it's a bigger problem if you work closely with a woman day in, day out, and go on business trips with her. To keep any possible romantic feelings from distracting me, I hire women who dress and groom professionally. It has not been a problem in our company. This is an office, not a posh retail store. Almost all our women employees dress in a professional manner." He went on: "I'm just saying that I wouldn't hire an assistant who was so glamorous that I thought of her as a sexy woman. On the job I prefer to think of a woman as just another member of the team, not as a prospective sexual partner."

Finally, ultrafemininity handicaps a woman's access to higher-level positions in a way that involves circular reasoning. Wardrobe consultants, human resource professionals, and business schools tell women to deemphasize glamour in order to appear more professional (and promotable). Such information is widely disseminated and accepted as true. People in power therefore buy into the idea that an overglamorous image is not very professional for women. (The same is less true for men.) Dressing and grooming in an overglamorous manner, including wearing enticing perfume, is therefore a negative factor when a woman is considered for a middle- or top-management position.

Margot, an office supervisor in an insurance company, regularly received satisfactory (or better) performance evaluations. Her unit of the company was in charge of the paperwork involved in reinsurance (sharing part of the company's insurance risk with other insurance companies). A vacancy was soon to be created at the next level of management because of a retirement.

Margot did not know if she would automatically be considered as a candidate for the manager of reinsurance. She therefore took the initiative telling her boss that she would like to be considered for the vacancy. Her manager said that she would pass this information on to the next level of management.

Two months later, Margot read on her electronic mail that another supervisor had been promoted to the post of manager of reinsurance. Margot was disappointed, but not shocked. The woman who did receive the promotion also appeared to be qualified. As the weeks passed, Margot's curiosity grew as to why she had not been chosen. She also wondered why she was not given an explanation.

When Margot asked her boss why she had not received the promotion, her boss told her that she would arrange an interview for Margot with the vice-president in charge of the selection committee. The vice-president told Margot candidly, "I guess this is something somebody should have told you a long time ago. You have a reputation for having an unprofessional image. You act one way toward men, and another way toward women.

"I recall a meeting we had to discuss staffing in your department," he explained. "You acted in a flirtatious, almost seductive, manner when pleading your case to a man at that meeting. You act in a much more professional manner toward women. The point also came up in the selection meeting that your appearance needs toning down. After all, this is an insurance company. No other woman supervisor dresses the way you do."

Margot was initially enraged with the feedback she received. Her first thought was that she was being denied a promotion just because she attempted to be charming and took pride in her appearance. She also wondered if she might be a victim of sex discrimination. Margot dismissed that idea quickly because the person chosen for the position was a woman.

Margot's third thought was more constructive, and one that could in time reverse the sabotage she had already imposed on her career. She would make a conscious effort, while in the office, to relate to men and women in the same way. She would also conform more closely to the informal company dress code. Margot could still find ways to express her uniqueness in dress and appearance without creating a distraction.

Assume you are a woman who frequently sexualizes male and female relationships on the job. To prevent career self-sabotage, follow Margot's lead in relating to men in the same manner as you relate to women.

Ultrafeminism and Self-Sabotage

As the women's liberation movement became better understood, it was referred to by many as the sex role liberation movement. One of the purposes of the movement was to allow people, both men and women, the freedom to act outside of rigid sex roles. The sex role liberation movement soon came to be seen as part of a larger human rights movement. Its purpose is to free everybody from discrimination and from being locked into roles that are determined by sex, race, ethnicity, physical status, and so forth.

Despite the general acceptance of the sex role liberation movement, and the importance of human rights, being perceived as an unyielding and rigid feminist can be self-sabotaging. A woman who quickly attacks anyone who does or says anything that could even hint at sexism becomes an uncomfortable work companion. She puts men and women on the defensive when they are simply engaging in the normal social amenities or using only mildly sexist language. Here is a checklist of ultrafeminist responses or behavior patterns that could be self-sabotaging because they alienate others. (An ultrafeminist male could be equally guilty of some of these.) Below each ultrafeminist response is a recommended alternative that makes the same point but in a less hostile manner.

Ultrafeminist Response: When a man opens a door for her, she says: "Thank you, I am perfectly capable of opening doors for myself."

Better: "Thank you, but I actually enjoy opening doors. It tones my arm muscles."

Ultrafeminist Response: When a man says to her, "You look lovely today," she responds: "Loveliness has nothing to do with business. I don't want our relationship to be sexualized."

Better: "Thanks for the compliment. Now, about that budget we are going to discuss today. . . ."

Ultrafeminist Response: When a woman says to her, "I like your idea, I'll discuss it further with the girls in the office," she responds: "Since when has our company violated the child labor laws? To my knowledge, we only employ women."

Better: "Girls? Oh, I get it. You're referring to the women in your department. You had me confused for a moment."

Ultrafeminist Response: When a man says, "What would be the woman's point of view about this safety feature?" she responds: "There is no such thing as a 'woman's point of view.' I can only speculate upon a person's point of view based upon his or her life situation."

Better: "In my opinion, safety is a unisex issue."

Ultrafeminist Response: When a co-worker politely asks a woman out for dinner a third time despite two refusals, she responds: "Are you aware that badgering me to go out with you is a form of sexual harassment?"

Better: "Thanks anyway, but again I cannot accept your invitation. I keep my social and work lives entirely separate."

Ultrafeminist Response: When a male co-worker asks a woman if she would be willing to bake cookies for an office party, she responds: "Are you asking me just because I'm a woman? Why not ask one of the men in the office? They are equally capable of baking cookies."

Better: "Sorry, you've asked the wrong person. I don't enjoy baking cookies. What else needs doing? I wouldn't mind rearranging the desks for the party."

The initial statements just presented are certainly within the rights of a feminist thinker to make. Because of their strident tone, however, they are likely to make others defensive. Of greater significance for a person's career, they can erode a woman's base of support and head her toward self-defeat.

The ultrafeminist does not have to sacrifice her ideals in order to prevent career self-sabotage. Instead, she can capitalize on the sexist statements of others by using them to educate rather than to alienate. The reply to the "girls in the office" statement presented above is a good example of a response that informs rather than antagonizes.

Flaunting a Homosexual Life-style in a Traditional Setting

The climate for gay men and lesbians in the workplace is changing for the better. Gays and lesbians have traditionally received better treatment in some fields than others, but people known to be gay are now more easily accepted in a greater variety of fields. Part of this acceptance can be attributed to the human rights movement. Another part is due to the growing recognition that approximately 10 percent of the population is gay.

Of even greater potential significance, a growing body of legislation provides equal rights to gays and lesbians. For example, New York State has an executive order that prohibits discrimination against state employees based on sexual orientation. Yet despite this increasing climate of acceptance, it can be career-sabotaging for an individual to flaunt a homosexual life-style in most work settings. The more traditional the setting, the bigger the problem. A nurse describes what happened to a physician she knew:

"I met Dr. Chelsea when he was a first-year resident at a local hospital. He had arrived from the South with his new bride. She found employment as a medical secretary in the department of his residency. The couple settled in for four grueling years.

"After completing his residency, Dr. Chelsea, his wife, and infant daughter returned to the South to establish a practice close to home. Chelsea was not happy, however, because the type of medicine he practiced there was not as specialized or challenging as what he had worked on during his residency. As his discontent mounted, Chelsea was offered the opportunity to enter a successful group practice in the city of his residency. Although Dr. Chelsea and his wife were reluctant to leave the South, they both saw the move back north as a good professional opportunity.

"The Chelseas enjoyed all the trappings of a successful suburban family—a fine home and furnishings, expensive clothing, luxurious vacations, and the like. Soon after their return, the couple had an infant son. Life was truly pleasant for the Chelseas. However, their idyllic existence came to an end when Dr. Chelsea, after many years of doubt and self-recrimination, acknowledged that he had now chosen homosexuality over bisexuality. Mrs. Chelsea filed for divorce and returned with the children to her family's home in the South.

"Dr. Chelsea changed from a conservative manner of dress and behavior to one of flamboyance. He began wearing an earring on one ear and adopted some of the stereotypical mannerisms of an effeminate male. Chelsea became indiscreet with his relationships, often inviting his numerous lovers to meet him at the office during working hours. On occasion he would greet them with a buss on the cheek and a hug. He was sometimes seen around town walking down the street holding hands with a male companion.

"After much discussion, the partners decided that Chelsea's behavior was tarnishing their staid, professional image. Consequently, they asked Chelsea to resign from his position. Dr. Chelsea is now in a solo practice that he finds to be very time-consuming. The practice is also not very lucrative because his heavy expenses are not shared with others, and his patient load is moderate."[5]

The medical partners who asked Dr. Chelsea to resign might be condemned as narrow-minded bigots. They used the oldest excuse in the world for job discrimination: "It's not our attitudes. But what will our patients [customers/clients/stockholders/fans] think?" Another point of view is that Chelsea's flamboyant display of a nontraditional life-style created too much controversy, and the partners just did not want to deal with it. They may also have had some legitimate concerns about the impact of Chelsea's flamboyance on their practice.

At last report, Chelsea is not happy, nor is he as financially well off as he was. He has thus committed career self-sabotage. Turning from bisexuality to homosexuality is not the cause of Chelsea's self-sabotage. He has every right to pursue the sexual orientation that best suits him. Flaunting his life-style, despite working in a conservative medical practice, was his undoing.

Wearing an earring to work is no longer very unusual. Many heterosexual males have adopted this practice, originally initiated by gays. Meeting his lovers in the office and hugging them in front of patients, however, was self-sabotaging. If Dr. Chelsea really wanted to remain part of the group practice, he might have challenged his own behavior. The same should be done by every rational person engaged in self-sabotage. Chelsea might have asked himself: "Why am I doing this to my career? Why am I doing this to myself?"

9

Career-Choking Addictions

*A*ddiction to a counterproductive habit is a leading cause of career self-sabotage. Careers are wrecked every day by compulsions to do things that either harm one's physical and mental health or drain productive energy away from the job. Even if the addictive behavior itself does not severely damage one's career, its side effects can. For example, compulsive spenders can confine their shopping binges to nonworking hours. Yet the debts they accumulate, the creditors hounding them, and the inevitable family strife combine to interfere with work concentration. Engaging in addictive behavior, and dealing with its by-products, becomes a job in itself.

An unhappy fact about career-choking addictions is that nearly everyone can fall prey to one. The capacity to be addicted lurks inside us all. Every field of endeavor contains case histories of successful people whose addictive behavior did severe damage to or even ruined their careers. Here I describe the addictions that are most likely to create problems for career-minded people: addiction to failure itself, to alcohol, drugs, food, gambling, spending, and sex.

The traditional view of addictions is that they are strangulating diseases that create lifelong problems. Looked at in this way, the prospects of overcoming an addiction are quite slim. A more optimistic viewpoint is to regard an addiction as maladaptive behavior that is under a person's conscious control. Looking upon addictions this way suggests that you can overcome an addiction.

With most addictions, people have enough choice in the matter at least to prevent their habit from destroying their careers and personal lives.

Addiction to Failure

Some otherwise successful people become addicted to choking under heavy pressure. Just when peak performance is required, they perform at a level way below their usual level of achievement. Unlike most addictions, the failure addiction has no benefit that is visible on the surface. A person addicted to chocolates at least derives temporary satisfaction from eating them. The negative consequences (such as weight gain, temporary depression, or complexion problems) set in later. A failure addiction, however, does have a hidden gain. The person with such an addiction may have an unstated need for self-punishment, a need to wallow in misery.

Ted Stolberg, a specialist in turning around troubled companies, claims he can usually detect a company owner who is a failure addict: "He's the guy who orders two martinis, chain smokes, is 30 pounds overweight, talks real fast, and is twitchy. At his office, he yells at his secretary and surrounds himself with weak people who he can easily manipulate."[1] An important implication of this description is that people often suffer from multiple addictions. The man just described is addicted to failure, alcohol, and tobacco.

A distinguishing feature of the failure addiction is that it usually does not manifest itself until the stakes are high. Under these circumstances the person is being truly tested. Similarly, many athletes turn in superb, calm performances when they do not face a threatening opponent. Alan, a labor relations negotiator who suffered a mild addiction to failure but then recovered, describes how the problem affected him.

"Ever since I can remember my career goal was to become a top-flight labor negotiator. In pursuit of my goals I obtained both a master's degree in labor relations and a law degree. I became a labor relations attorney for a steel producer. But this didn't mean in any way that I was anti-union. If the opportunity had been right, I would have readily worked for a labor union.

"My career began by my helping to prepare labor-management agreements. It was interesting but tedious work. It also helped prepare me to get directly involved in negotiations. My negotiating experience began with my working on relatively small provisions of the agreement. I negotiated such things as disability insurance, wash-up time for employees, and how much the company would contribute to the cost of safety shoes.

"The issues I negotiated were resolved fairly well. We came to agreement on big points and small points without too much haggling. My company was satisfied, and so was the union. When it came time for me to lead the negotiation team over a big issue, it was a different story. I began to get the shakes. The night before negotiations over pay, I suffered from gastrointestinal discomfort. So much so that I thought I would have to call in sick the next day.

"My jitters were well justified. I bungled matters the next day by irritating the union with an insensitive remark about them being hogs. The union negotiators became so irritated that they prolonged negotiations a few extra weeks. I estimate that we settled for a dollar more per hour than we would have if I hadn't goofed.

"I was angry with myself because I had a history of choking in the past. I was known to have excellent presentation skills in college. Yet on two occasions I stumbled miserably when I had to give a presentation that was a big chunk of my final grade. I've had the same problem in golf. I shoot my best when I play by myself. But when it's a competitive foursome, I miss far too many easy putts.

"My company was not upset enough with my negotiating skill to bench me. The little successes I had achieved helped preserve my reputation. My work proceeded well for the next couple of years. Much of my success was linked to the fact that I was not faced with major issues to negotiate. Then came my big chance. Management and labor were negotiating some major differences over medical insurance for union workers. The union threatened to strike if they couldn't get what they wanted. It was my job, assisted by others on our team, to get them to settle without a strike.

"I had formulated some great tactics before the session. I would be conciliatory, and compliment the union for wanting to settle this important issue to the benefit of both sides. Unfortunately my strategy didn't work. The union reps accused me of trying to manipulate them with "mind games." Negotiations went downhill from that point forward. Finally, the company had its first strike in ten years. The strike only lasted five days, and we made a reasonable settlement. So my reputation was tarnished, but not ruined.

"At that point I decided I had to do something about my choking. If I wanted to be a good negotiator under fire, I had to stop screwing up at the big moment."

Alan did do something about his problem. He sought the advice of a psychologist who specialized in behavior modification. The psychologist explained Alan's problem in terms of his having extreme anxiety about performing well. Alan's performance anxiety was creating his choking today as it had in the past. He was anxious primarily when the stakes were high because this was when poor performance would be the most visible, and when he had the most to lose.

Alan's remedial program was to study a videotape on positive imagery intended to reduce stress and anxiety under pressure. He learned to visualize himself in a tough negotiating session, acting in a confident and self-assured manner. He thought of himself executing his strategy superbly, instead of fumbling his lines. The visualization technique worked for Alan. He now reports much more confidence and success in handling tough negotiating sessions. Another way of explaining Alan's use of visualization is that he mentally rehearses a good performance before entering a situation he anticipates will be anxiety-provoking.

You too can benefit from visualization if you frequently choke under pressure. Before entering into the situation in which you are concerned about choking, first force yourself to relax. Perhaps an hour before the command performance, exhale and inhale a few times. Then create a mental image of yourself giving a peak performance. Imagine yourself stating your point in crisp, impressive language. At the end of the meeting (or other important situation), the key people there are congratulating you for a job well done. Smile and savor your victorious moment.

Alcohol Abuse

Alcoholism is a major form of self-sabotage, self-defeat, and self-destruction among workers at all levels. In support of this fact, the treatment of alcoholics constitutes more than a billion dollar-a-year industry in North America.[2] Every reader knows at least one person who has suffered a serious career setback because of his or her alcohol abuse. A curious aspect of alcoholism among executives is that they often hold on to their positions for a long time before suffering a serious career setback. Ramsey is one such person.

Ramsey was the dean of social sciences at a state university, a position he held for seven years. Before that he was an associate dean at another institution. Above all, Ramsey is likable and noncontroversial. Youthful in appearance and affable, Ramsey was described by his supporters as "strong in human relations skills" and "sensitive to people." When Ramsey was not directly or indirectly under the effects of alcohol, he was an effective administrator.

A glimpse of Ramsey's operating style helps explain how he functioned as an academic dean, although an alcohol abuser. Ramsey surrounded himself with capable assistants and delegated substantial responsibility to them. Faculty, staff, and students, for instance, recognized that Ramsey's administrative assistant provided the answers to most minor problems.

When a faculty member wanted quick approval of a minor travel expenditure, the unofficial word was "Ask Marge. She'll get it approved." When a student required a class section change because of a personality conflict with a professor, Marge did most of the detailed administrative work such as course scheduling and budgeting. Committees were assigned to study all special problems that arose, such as whether to inaugurate an international studies major.

Ramsey would review reports and make action recommendations during the morning hours. As he told an assistant professor, "I'll discuss your committee report on academic standards with you in the morning. I think better on an empty stomach."

Ramsey drank heavily at lunch about three days a week. Marge protected him from visitors on those days by scheduling meetings only between 10:00 and 12:00 in the morning. Emergency meetings were scheduled between 3:00 and 5:00 P.M. on the days he drank heavily at lunch. Ramsey rationalized that "People can discuss their work concerns best over a drink." As a result, he would invite faculty and staff members to join him at a nearby cocktail lounge around 5:00 in the afternoon. For Ramsey a drink meant an alcoholic beverage, whereas many of those who joined him ordered sparkling water, tonic, or fruit juice.

Conventions and professional meetings allowed Ramsey to feed his alcohol addiciton for days at a time. One of Ramsey's former faculty members describes his social behavior at a convention:

"Ramsey is a great person to attend a meeting with. He has no intention of listening to presentations and bringing ideas back to the school. All he wants to do is glad-hand and drink. Few people I have met could keep up with Ramsey's drinking. During the three days of meetings, Ramsey kept on encouraging me to have a few drinks to loosen up a little.

"His recurring expression at the meeting was that since we work so hard, we should relax when we have the chance. Despite his heavy drinking, Ramsey was back in his office Monday morning. He would chat with people and tell them what a great professional experience the meetings were."

Word of Ramsey's excessive delegation and lengthy lunch breaks eventually got back to the central administrative staff of the university. Ramsey was confronted about the consequences of his drinking problem, and asked to step down as dean of social studies. He admitted sadly that he had a disease that needed to be cured. Given a four-month leave of absence to seek help for his drinking problem, Ramsey enrolled in an alcohol abuse clinic.

During his leave Ramsey decided that it would be too embarrassing for him to return to the college, especially in a capacity other than dean. With his drinking under better control, Ramsey conducted a job search. He found a position as an admissions counselor at a small liberal arts college. Although his pay and status were both substantially reduced, Ramsey looked forward to the new challenge. He hoped that his alcoholism was permanently under control.

What Ramsey should have done to prevent his drinking from sabotaging his career depends on your viewpoint of the nature of alcoholism. Ramsey followed the traditional, "disease model" of alcoholism. He waited until he encountered a severe problem, and only then did he go to a clinic to cure his disease. According to a Harvard Medical School psychiatrist:

"The central premise of the disease concept of alcohol is that the alcoholic cannot control his or her drinking—one drink usually leads in time to twenty. Alcoholism is a chronic, long-term disease over which one has no control and which has an inevitable downhill course. There is no cure except to stop drinking—completely and for good. . . . An alcoholic can no more control his or her drinking than a diabetic can control the malfunctioning of the pancreas."[3]

The more optimistic viewpoint contends that alcoholism is a counterproductive habit that can be broken. The disease interpretation of alcoholism leads many alcohol abusers to believe that because they are diseased some external force is required to cure them. By contrast, if alcoholism is regarded as a bad habit, the majority of alcohol abusers can learn moderation.

Many experts, in fact, believe that alcoholics can and do moderate their drinking. They consider the likelihood of relapse greater if the recovering alcohol abuser thinks that craving and loss of control are inevitable. Equally harmful is the belief that a single drink of an alcoholic beverage leads to uncontrollable drinking. At scientific conferences on alcoholism treatment, a return to social drinking is considered to be a realistic goal.[4]

If Ramsey had believed that his heavy drinking could be reduced to a comfortable level of social drinking, he might have curtailed his drinking much sooner. Ramsey's drinking pattern was significant. If he could confine his drinking to three afternoons per week, he could also have learned to reduce it even more drastically. An alcoholic rarely drinks in a church, on a subway, or while an airplane is on the runway. The reason is that they choose not to drink in those situations rather than face the outrage and ostracism of others. According to the counterproductive habit viewpoint, most alcohol abusers can learn to confine their drinking to limited situations and limited amounts.

Measuring Your Tendency Toward Developing a Dangerous Dependency

The first step in overcoming alcohol abuse, or any other substance abuse, is to determine if you have a problem. Why don't you take the self-audit "Do I Have a Substance Abuse Problem?"[5] The results could tell you whether you are developing a dangerous dependency. Respond to each question with "always," "sometimes," or "never."

We are all occasionally vulnerable to pressures that can create some of these symptoms. Breakups of relationships, problems with relationships, family illness, or career changes can often lead to depression, lethargy, frequent illness, or substandard job performance. However, if you responded "sometimes" or "always" to four or more of the above questions, it is time for changes in your behavior. Get your self-defeating behavior under control bit

---

DO I HAVE A SUBSTANCE ABUSE PROBLEM?

1. Do I show excessive absenteeism on Monday, Friday, and days before and after holidays?

2. Do I have unexcused and frequent absences?

3. Have I been tardy lately?

4. Have I been leaving work early?

5. Do I have altercations with co-workers?

6. Have I blacked out or fainted recently?

7. Have I had strong cravings for alcohol or other drugs?

8. Do I make demands on my doctor for refills of prescriptions before they are due?

9. Have I been disoriented and forgetful lately?

10. Have I suffered from memory lapses lately?

11. Do I have unexplainable status of apathy or elation?

12. Am I lethargic?

13. Have I been getting into accidents?

14. Have others told me that my appearance is deteriorating?

15. Has my job performance been slipping?

---

by bit, such as first eliminating all alcoholic beverages during normal working hours. Then move on to cutting your after-hours drinking to two or three drinks daily, a relatively safe level. If you cannot overcome your problem by yourself, get professional help.

Alcohol and drug abuse lead to predictable behaviors and feelings. Among them are absenteeism, especially on Mondays and Fridays; frequent accidents, ranging from minor to major; lateness; unreliability. Physical signs such as blackouts and chronic fatigue or emotional signals such as mood swings or irritability are common. Relationships with co-workers deteriorate because abusers are edgy or have to cover up.

Drug Abuse

Drug abuse among high-achieving managerial and professional workers is not uncommon. Approximately 5 percent of these people abuse drugs to the point of impaired job performance. Drug abuse appears to be particularly prevalent among people in high-pressure jobs. The average work week for managers and professionals is now fifty-three hours, up from forty-four hours twenty years ago. Heavy work loads of this nature cause job stress for many people, creating the conditions in which drug abuse flourishes. The person most likely to abuse drugs when faced with heavy pressures is someone with a low frustration tolerance and a need for immediate gratification.

Drug abuse leads to career self-sabotage for the same reasons that alcohol abuse does: It leads to mental and physical health problems, including impaired concentration and judgment. What is not widely recognized is that the abuse of legal (prescription) drugs can be as harmful as the abuse of illegal ones. According to Michael Cavanagh, legal drug abuse is more apt to go undetected because these abusers are typically middle-aged or older workers with conventional values and behavior. They don't fit the stereotype of the adventuresome young drug abuser.[6]

Nancy has been employed by the same company for the past five years. She is generally a friendly, high-performing worker. She recently went through a difficult divorce and is now a single parent with two children. During the last six months she has displayed stress symptoms at work. Nancy talks louder and faster than usual. Her poor concentration leads her to make careless mistakes. She interrupts people frequently without seeming to be aware of her rudeness.

The primary factor that brought Nancy to the attention of her supervisor was her attitude change. She went from being a person who was easy to get along with to one who regularly criticized the performance and behavior of her co-workers. On top of this, she recently got into a shouting match with her supervisor and threatened to quit.

The supervisor liked Nancy but found her changed behavior so intolerable that she referred Nancy to a counselor in the employee assistance program. Nancy resented the referral but followed through to satisfy her supervisor. She told the counselor, "Look, I will talk to you a couple of times, but you should really be seeing my co-workers and supervisor. They have more problems than I do."

The more the counselor tried to help Nancy see that her behavior was self-defeating, the more upset she became. Because Nancy's behavior changed around the time of her divorce, the counselor concluded that the pressures of the divorce had caused her problems.[7]

What the counselor did not know was that Nancy had been depressed during her divorce and that a physician had prescribed a stimulant (antidepressant drug) for her. Nancy had taken the prescribed dosage and found very little relief from symptoms of depression. At Nancy's request, her physician increased the dosage. Nancy also went to another doctor to obtain more anti-depressant medication. She therefore became an unwitting legal drug abuser, and its side effects led to behavior problems on the job.

Nancy's employee assistance counselor might have done a more thorough analysis of the factors surrounding her problems. He should have coordinated his efforts with those of the physician caring for Nancy. At a minimum, he should have taken a more thorough history. Nancy, and others like her, cannot be faulted for taking prescription drugs. She can be faulted, however, for deceptively getting another physician to prescribe similar medication for her. Being deceptive is part of Nancy's problem.

The key factor in preventing this type of career self-sabotage is to keep in the forefront of your mind that heavy drug usage is self-defeating. You should also remember that heavy job pressures or personal problems often create the stress that prompts people into going beyond recreational drug use. If you experience heavy job pressures, the sensible and productive antidote is to enroll in a program of stress management.

Eating Disorders

Compulsive overeating can readily become another type of career-choking addiction. One problem is that an overweight person cannot project the healthy, trim image many organizations prefer for their key people. This can result in losing an important promotion or assignment. A second problem associated with extreme overeating is the physical repercussions: lethargy and the reduced energy and mental quickness required to achieve peak performance.

Compulsive undereating can also sabotage your career. A person who looks anorexic (extraordinarily thin) projects a sick, unhealthy look. Such an appearance is perhaps even worse for your career than being obese. Someone who is more than 20 percent below the normal weight range for people in their age-height-build-sex category may go through some profound changes in personality and behavior. Unfortunately, these changes are all of a negative kind.

Anorexics or near-anorexics typically become irritable and unsocial. They become increasingly unable to concentrate on anything but food. Compulsive undereaters are forever pestering co-workers about the amount of calories, cholesterol, and fat in food. They brag about such things as not having eaten a candy bar, used salt, or eaten a Polish sausage in a year.

Other severe symptoms of excessive undereaters include apathy, loss of pride in personal appearance, and feelings of inadequacy. The predominant mood of the food-deprived person is gloom and depression.

Putting it all together, the overuse or underuse of food can potentially do as much damage to your career as alcohol or drug abuse. Many obese people believe that they are victims of job discrimination. Kurt, a 250-pound computer service technician (who is 5' 10" tall), explains why he thinks he was the victim of job discrimination:

"I'm so angry, I plan to take my case to the state human rights commission. I've done a top job making repairs at customer sites. And I've been doing it for six years. By now I should be a supervisor, or at least promoted to a senior service technician. I even think my raises have been lousy.

"When I joined the company I weighed about 200 pounds. That was 100 pounds lower than my top weight. The company never told me there were any weight restrictions for the job. After two years with the company, I experienced some personal problems. I got into debt and my wife left me. So I started to eat more than I should. My job also creates a lot of pressure to eat more than I should. As I travel from customer site to site, it's easy to stop off for a donut or a hamburger and french fries.

"My supervisor began mentioning that I was getting a little heavy. He told me that I wasn't projecting the right image to customers. I told him that our customers didn't care about images. All they wanted was to have their equipment up and running. My boss would start giving me little digs, like calling me "the donut king." My co-workers started doing the same thing. What bothered me was that these barbs were taking away from my professionalism. I was singled out for being some type of character. It prevented me from being seen as the dedicated worker I truly am.

"When I asked about being promoted to supervisor when a vacancy occurred, my boss started hemming and hawing. He told me that my image wasn't too great, that the company was worried about my health. When I tried to pin him down about my image, my boss said that a couple of customers had told him they were surprised to see such a heavy technician."

Kurt has a right to be angry. He probably is the victim of job discrimination. He could sue the company for job discrimination. But all the time, energy, and money spent in that direction would be much better invested in dealing with the real problem sabotaging his career. Until Kurt overcomes his food abuse, he will continue to have image problems on the job.

A crash diet-and-exercise program will give Kurt only a temporary change in body weight. Approximately 80 percent of the people who lose a substantial amount of weight gain it back within one year. What Kurt and others with eating disorders must do is to make lifelong changes in their eating and exercise habits.

The results of numerous studies and the advice of countless experts point to the same inescapable conclusion: Overweight people can maintain a lower body weight only by eating healthier foods and by burning more calories. Avoiding overeating is also important, but not as important as eating the right food. People who are biologically predisposed toward heaviness have to work extra hard at losing weight. Just eating normally leads them to be heavy.

Every literate person knows that a healthier diet and less food intake, accompanied by more exercise, is necessary for sustained weight reduction. The reason some overweight people do not use this information is that they have severe emotional conflicts about body weight. Others cannot control their weight for the same reason that they fail to control other forms of self-defeating behavior: They are not sufficiently committed to achieving their goals to develop the productive habits that would replace the counterproductive ones.

Developing constructive eating and exercise habits is often facilitated by getting the right type of professional help. The right type of help for some is a health practitioner specializing in food disorders. For others it might be a weight-loss clinic.

Compulsive Gambling

Gambling has become easier and more widespread with the computerization of betting parlors, the increase in government-run lotteries, and the building of ever more gambling resorts. The temptation to play feeds the potential career self-sabotage of the estimated 2–3 percent of the population who are compulsive gamblers. According to an article in *Psychology Today,* nearly all these people seek the sense of power and control that "the action" affords. The action and the "high" it affords become even more important than the potential winnings. The addiction to gambling is strengthened by the fact that many gamblers are striving to fill the void created by childhood feelings of rejection and isolation.[8] To the person who felt rejected and isolated as a child, something is always missing in life. Many of these people turn to gambling as the "missing something" to fill that void.

Compulsive gamblers pass through a predictable three-stage development of the problem. First is the winning phase, which pulls the person in by the thrill of the action. Second is the losing stage in which the gambler tries to compensate for losses by betting more and more. Gamblers are chasing the Big Score, which will wipe out previous losses. Third is the desperation stage, when the gambler becomes irrational and commits imprudent acts to obtain betting money.[9]

On the job, the compulsive gambler is usually irritable, nervous, and easily distracted. He or she gambles on company time, perhaps even organizing a sports betting pool. Severe financial problems also surface that require work time to manage. All these forces combine to produce shoddy job performance.

Gordon, now a member of Gamblers Anonymous, explains how gambling affected his career:

"I'm not currently gambling, even though I don't think I'm fully cured. My current job title is systems analyst. It suits me fine. It gives me a chance to be creative, to concentrate on something that makes a definite contribution to the company.

"An important feature of this job is that it doesn't give me too much freedom to place bets during the day. I share a small work area with another systems analyst. It would be very embarrassing for me to pick up our phone and place a bet.

"Being an analyst, I work under tight deadlines to accomplish a project, and it really helps. Before, I was a manager of a management information systems group. It gave me too much freedom to make phone calls or visit gambling parlors during the day. I had a good team of people working for me who really didn't need much regular help from me.

"Being a gambling addict was worse than having two mistresses in addition to a wife and two children. Of course, there were the money problems. When I was winning, finances were no problem. But when I was losing, I became frantic. It was pretty hard to concentrate on a management problem like a budget review when I was on the brink of bankruptcy.

"I remember attending a management meeting when I had a thousand dollars on a race that was being run at the very same moment. Somebody nudged me and asked me if I was still with the group. I told them I had a toothache and had trouble concentrating.

"The home problems that stemmed from my gambling created more of an interference with my work than the actual betting did. My wife would be on the phone with me at ten in the morning, pleading with me to stop gambling or to seek help. Once I hit our four-year old when he interrupted me. At the moment I was figuring out where I could raise some quick cash to get into a poker game coming up that weekend. Realizing what I was doing to my family made it difficult for me to concentrate on my work for a week.

"When I heard about some of the nicknames co-workers had given me, I knew my days were numbered. I was in the restoom one day when I overhead two programmers talking about me. They referred to me as 'Gambling Gordie' and 'Gordie the Greek.' By the time I joined Gamblers Anonymous, my employer had asked me to resign."

Losing his job jolted Gordon into understanding the gravity of his compulsive gambling. He then joined Gamblers Anonymous, which functions as a support group to help compulsive gamblers cope with their addiction. Like other people engaged in career self-sabotage, Gordon did not stop early enough to reflect on the consequences of his counterproductive actions.

Gamblers are often searching for thrills and excitement to help them overcome depression and boredom. Gordon might have found a more constructive arena for thrill seeking. Perhaps developing new computer games or security codes for computers could have satisfied his craving for excitement and thrills. In the process he would have been less bored and depressed. A big problem, however, is that a constant supply of thrills is needed to do the job.

Another approach to overcoming gambling is to seek professional help. One technique of psychotherapy adapted for gamblers is referred to as *imaginal desensitization*. Gamblers are given a brief, individual five-minute relaxation training period. They are then shown how to imagine themselves being stimulated to gamble, approaching a gambling situation, but not actually gambling, and then leaving the scene. Because the patients learn to relax, some of the tension associated with not gambling is diminished.[10] Gamblers can sometimes use this visualization technique on their own, without outside help. If gambling is getting out of control for you, give imaginal desensitization a try.

Compulsive Spending

Compulsive spending is recognized as another addiction that is as serious as compulsive gambling. Compulsive spenders can do as much damage to their careers as other addicts. The financial stress they face diminishes their judgment and concentration. As the compulsive spender goes more heavily into debt, family problems mount and he or she becomes distracted from work.

People put themselves into heavy debt for many reasons. A major factor driving indebtedness also causes addictions. The person is depressed and hopes that buying things will bring happiness. Some people are insecure and hope that purchasing gifts for others will gain them acceptance and friendship. Sometimes when a couple separates, one spouse will binge on credit spending as a form of revenge against the other spouse. Credit is sometimes overused because people believe that presents to themselves will make up for hurts experienced, such as the end of a relationship. Some people are low in self-esteem and think that the accumulation of possessions will make them feel better about themselves. Finally, poor impulse control leads some people to make unplanned purchases.

A complicating factor in compulsive spending is that the spender's partner often encourages the addiction. As a result, the careers of both partners may be damaged by the counterproductive spending habit.

Todd, a successful car salesman, was married to Lisa, a records supervisor with the state police. Todd and Lisa purchased their first home when they were both in their twenties. After making the purchase, cash flow became a problem. So Todd and Lisa began using a credit card for minor purchases. As credit-card application forms arrived in their mailbox, the couple took advantage of the borrowing opportunity.

Todd and Lisa decided that the house needed major repairs, and they began making them with borrowed money. Soon they were borrowing the maximum on all their credit cards. Trouble started when they were making minimum monthly payments on their charges. Around that time Todd shifted jobs because his income had plunged as a result of a lull in automobile sales. He was forced to take a temporary cut in pay while he trained as a security systems sales representative.

Todd and Lisa continued to struggle with credit card and mortgage payments on the house and a new car. Todd no longer had access to a dealer car, so he purchased a used truck with a $3,500 advance from a credit card. The couple continued to make minimum payments on their loans. Sometimes they would make a payment with money borrowed from another card.

The couple soon recognized that they were in serious trouble. As creditors hounded them, Todd became more frantic to earn sales commissions. Sales prospects called the office complaining about Todd's high-pressure tactics. Several customers who had signed contracts quickly canceled them, claiming that Todd had not been truthful about the terms of the deal. The company put Todd on probation. Lisa became so worried about their deteriorating finances that she mismanaged some important record systems.

As their financial turmoil increased, Lisa discovered that she was pregnant. Rather than do what they could to get out of debt to prepare for the new baby's expenses, Todd and Lisa bought elaborate baby furnishings and remodeled a room on credit.

Troubles continued to mount. A loan collection agency threatened to repossess their car, and the telephone company disconnected their service. Todd was too preoccupied to used a planned, well-reasoned approach to sales. After failing to make his quota for three consecutive months, he was dismissed. He found new employment as a management trainee in a fast-food restaurant. Lisa was threatened with demotion, and took a maternity leave of absence.

With Lisa not working, and the considerable expenses of raising an infant daughter, the couple struggled financially. They recognized the financial hole they had dug for themselves, and now refuse to borrow except for financial emergencies. They are fighting bankruptcy and continue to be pursued by creditors. With debts totaling $26,500, Todd and Lisa have entered budget counseling. Even with Lisa returning to work shortly, the couple has calculated that it will take them eleven years to become debt-free. Meanwhile, they are trying to regain their peace of mind, one minimum payment at a time.[11]

Todd and Lisa have taken a constructive step toward ovecoming their spending addiction by going through budget counseling. Full-fledged counseling of this type helps people deal with the underlying problem, such as depression or a hunger for affection, that breeds compulsive spending. To prevent a recurrence of unwieldy debt, the spending addict is also given suggestions for managing credit wisely. Most others can also benefit from such suggestions:

1. Prepare a monthly budget to determine how much debt (if any) you can afford to assume.
2. As a general rule, limit your total borrowing to 15–20 percent of your monthly take-home pay, not including a house mortgage payment.
3. Instead of carrying many credit cards, stick to one major credit card, and your favorite department store's charge card.
4. Before accepting any new extension of credit, review your budget to see if you can handle it easily.
5. If you have substantial equity accumulated in your home, consider a home equity loan for financing a major pur-

chase such as an automobile or educational expenses. The interest on a home equity loan is fully tax deductible.

6. Make monthly payments on your debts that are large enough to reduce the principal on your credit cards and other loans. Otherwise you may be paying almost all interest and making little progress toward paying off the loan.

7. Even as you are paying off debts, set aside some savings each month. Attempt to increase your savings by at least $25 per month.

8. If you are unable to pay your bills, talk to your creditors immediately. Explain your situation and let them know that you intend to meet your debt obligations. Agree to a payment schedule you can meet. Never ignore bills.

9. Choose bankruptcy only as a last desperate option. A bankruptcy filing will remain on your credit record for seven to ten years after filing. Future employers may be leery of hiring a person who was such a poor money manager. Of greater significance, bankruptcy may deal a substantial blow to your self-esteem.

The last point is very significant. Low self-esteem perpetuates addictions and just about any other behavior or attitudes that contribute to career self-sabotage.

Compulsive Sex

Some people are obsessed with sex to the point that it sabotages their career. Preoccupation with sex is more of an obsession or compulsion than a true addiction. Unlike an addiction, a layoff from sexual activity does not create physical symptoms of withdrawal. Nevertheless, a sexual obsession can lead a person to risk any kind of consequence in pursuit of sexual satisfaction.

An obsession with sex has several potential damaging consequences to one's career. As with addictions and other compulsions, it can divert time and energy away from work. An insurance underwriter was referred to the company medical department because of her excessive drowsiness. She explained to the company nurse that she was addicted to X-rated films. Because she had three young children, she had to wait until they were asleep before watching her adult videos. She often did not get to sleep until 3:00 A.M., despite having to get up at 7 o'clock.

A compulsive need for sex is a potentially greater problem. It can lead to an embarrassing exposure, sure to be unwelcome to a conservative employer. After public exposure for unusual or illegal sexual practices, the person's job may be in jeopardy. When such escapades are frequent, the probability of exposure increases proportionately.

Paul, the sales promotion manager at a pharmaceutical company, was a happily divorced man in his mid-forties. His two children were in college, he lived alone, and he had a long-term relationship with Norma, a woman he cared for deeply. They would spend much of their weekends together, and frequently got together during the week. The two of them shared an exciting and mutually satisfying sex life.

Paul's expression of his sexuality extended beyond his relationship with Norma. He frequented bars featuring nude dancers, and subscribed to five different magazines that specialized in photographs of nude women. On occasion Paul hired nude dancers to entertain him at home. When out of town on business trips, Paul would often hire prostitutes through escort services.

On several occasions at trade shows, Paul's commitment to the company was questioned because he excused himself from dinner meetings. He explained that he was physically not up to a late dinner. Paul missed one of these dinner meetings not knowing that his boss was an unexpected visitor. What Paul had in mind was to search for a bar with nude dancers.

That night he did find a bar that featured a beautiful woman taking a shower in a transparent shower stall set up on stage. The dancer's eroticism and sensuality aroused in Paul a disturbing sexual tension. As he walked away from the bar toward his hotel, he was approached by a young woman who said "How about a date?" "Sorry," responded Paul half-heartedly, "but a man can only get into trouble exchanging money for sex. It's illegal."

"Just this once, honey," said the attractive stranger. "Okay," responded Paul, "how much?" The woman said she would charge $100 for an hour, and Paul said, "It's a deal." In response, the woman flashed a police badge, and said, "You're under arrest for solicitation. Come with me to the police station. You have the right to remain. . . ."

Paul was detained overnight in the city jail. He pleaded guilty in the morning and paid a $200 fine. But his punishment didn't end there. He missed the morning meeting, and one of the other managers at the meeting found Paul's name in the newspaper. It was included in a listing of men caught in a sweep.

Paul was asked to resign because the president wanted only "people of high moral fiber" on the management team. In addition to losing his job, Paul almost lost his relationship with Norma. She finally forgave him after he promised that he would never repeat such a crazy stunt. After six months of trying to find a suitable job, Paul assumed that background checks conducted by employers had revealed his arrest. It would therefore be exceedingly difficult for him to be hired as a company employee. Paul finally resolved matters by purchasing the rights to open a submarine-sandwich franchise.

Paul might seek treatment for his compulsive interest in sex. He needs to contain his obsessive sexual interest at least to the degree that it no longer interferes with his career. As a self-employed business operator he will have to be on guard not to divert too much of his attention away from the store.

Paul was zapped badly for attempting to hire the services of a prostitute. It might therefore be naively assumed that he will not be a repeat offender. Perhaps not. A word to the wise may be sufficient, but a word to the obsessed is less effective. Many men arrested for soliciting prostitutes are repeat offenders—even those whose family, friends, and employers know of their previous arrests. Paul will need to exert considerable self-control to prevent any further career self-sabotage.

Few readers of this book face career self-sabotage because of daring sexual activity. But keep in mind that we all have inner urges that could get us into trouble if not channeled into a safe outlet.

10

Bizarre and Scandalous Actions

*M*any self-sabotaging actions erode a person's career; step by step, little by little, people dig themselves into a deeper and deeper career hole. Other people bludgeon their careers into a shambles with one sudden bizarre or scandalous act. An example would be the executive who appears drunk at an important command performance. Still others engage in a series of bizarre and scandalous actions over a period of time—until caught. Embezzlers, for example, typically continue to siphon off company funds until discovered and indicted.

Bizarre and scandalous behavior on the job is well worth examining. Almost anyone is capable of wrecking in a single blow, or a short series of blows, a career that has taken years to build. The experience has happened to bank presidents who have raided depositor funds as well as to politicians who have paid to have sex with teenagers. Awareness of the mistakes of others is an important preventive strategy.

Violent Temper Tantrums

An occasional mild temper tantrum may even boost your career. It shows that you are human and that you conduct your work with intensity and involvement. At the extremes, however, one violent temper tantrum in a business setting can send your career into a tailspin. Temper tantrums in business are taboo. Such outbursts are an extreme deviation from the cultural norm of gentility and politeness among managers and professionals. Professional tennis players can rant, rave, scream, and throw their rackets during a tournament. As a punishment they may be fined and banned from a future tournament or two. But a few tantrums will not ruin their careers because the contemporary norms governing the sport do not strongly oppose such behavior. In business, the situation is different.

January is performance appraisal time in the research laboratory of an East Coast energy company. Even when ample money is available in the budget for raises, it is a tense and difficult time for laboratory managers. When money for raises is limited, and promotional opportunities are scarce, managers experience additional stress. In recent years, budgets for most departments and divisions have been cut.

Double-digit raises have been replaced by single-digit ones, averaging 4–5 percent. Promotional opportunities, even for superior performers, have also decreased. The salary and promotional constraints have heightened competition and resentment among many of the scientific personnel. General dissatisfaction and low motivation have been widespread among support workers.

Bruce has been a solid-fuel research technician at the company for eighteen years. He has received generous raises, and a few promotions, in years past. For example, he received a 10 percent increase during six of those years, and was promoted to senior research technician five years ago. But because Bruce had performed the same job in his group for most of his career he had drifted into a pattern of not working very hard or showing much innovation.

Bruce had not received an above-average raise since his promotion to senior research technician. He believed that he was deserving of a substantial increase this time around. Weeks before his performance appraisal, Bruce began complaining to his co-workers that he was overdue for a sizable increase.

Laboratory employees believed that supervisors knew before meeting with them what general level evaluation they would give. However, they also believed that some room for negotiation existed. Bruce went to the scheduled meeting with his supervisor with the hope of convincing her of his outstanding performance. If convinced, she would then be obliged to give him a high evaluation.

When he walked into his boss's office, Bruce was ready to spring into debate if he did not hear words of praise. When she uttered the words, "Your performance has been somewhat disappointing this last period,"

Bruce lost emotional control. He shouted a few angry words about being underappreciated. Feeling overwhelmed by anger, he overturned chairs, then grabbed a personal computer and threw it against the wall. Bruce shouted "Go to Hell" as he stormed out the door. His blast of fury lasted about fifteen seconds.

Bruce's violence had immediate consequences. He was given a one-year suspension from work. He was instructed to attend company-paid counseling during his absence as a precondition for his returning to work. Bruce sought legal advice as to the prospects of having his suspension removed. Bruce's lawyer advised him that he had been suspended for just cause.[1]

In fifteen seconds of fury, Bruce sabotaged his modest career. If he chooses to return to the company, he must find interim employment. Should he return, he may never be forgiven for his burst of fury. Bruce's outburst was an unfortunate consequence of pent-up anger that had been accumulating for a long time. He made a few indirect attempts at discussing his feelings with co-workers, but he would have been better off discussing his feelings with a company counselor or his boss. Letting out angry feelings a little bit at a time often helps prevent a sudden, uncontrollable outburst.

If Bruce had attempted to calm down just before meeting with his boss, he might not have felt so wiresprung when he entered the performance appraisal meeting. But, as it was, he had talked himself into a frenzy.

What Bruce should do now is engage in a little old-fashioned fence mending, and write a note on personal stationery, offering his deepest apologies for his tantrum. He might ask to help pay for the smashed computer monitor. Most important, Bruce should promise to continue with counseling to learn how he can develop better emotional control.

How do you know if you have a problem with emotional control, and should therefore learn how to calm down in key situations? If three or more of the following statements apply to you, you may be subject to outrages on the job:

- ☐ I often swear and curse at team members or support workers.
- ☐ I start grinding my teeth when somebody disagrees with me.

☐ I often get into shouting matches with strangers in such situations as waiting in line for refreshments.

☐ I often blast my horn at people ahead of me who do not proceed immediately when the traffic light changes to green.

☐ I have struck my children or other family members on more than one occasion.

Expropriation of Company Resources

Greed, gluttony, and avarice have been described in Chapter 6 as a potential form of executive self-sabotage. The same unethical behavior is also a bizarre and scandalous way of defeating one's own purposes. Expropriation takes many forms, from the trivial to the consequential. Trivial expropriation occurs every day as employees reproduce menus and league schedules on company photocopying machines. When expropriation proceeds on a grand scale, it becomes a form of bizarre and scandalous behavior. Troy, a vice-president of marketing, expropriated company resources on a grand scale to enhance his life-style.

Troy began employment with his company twenty years ago as a sales trainee. He worked his way up the ranks to brand manager in ten years. Five years later, he was promoted to vice-president of marketing. One of his special assignments was to design and implement sales promotions to entice wholesalers and end-consumers into purchasing more of the company's products.

Troy's creativity and energy helped him design winning sales promotions. His salary and bonuses increased handsomely. As Troy began to achieve high earnings, he tasted personal luxuries. The more he tasted, the more he wanted. To boost his share of luxuries, Troy developed what he thought was an airtight scam involving wholesaler incentives.

In order to reach his sales targets, Troy had to offer incentives to wholesalers to buy his products. Troy started modestly, offering season tickets to the local university's football games. Then came offerings of fax machines and cellular telephones. Each succeeding year he offered larger and larger incentives. In the end he offered large-screen televisions, trips to the Caribbean, and 200 hours of limousine service. The company went along with these expensive incentives because they were achieving results.

Troy dutifully awarded the incentives to the wholesalers who met their quotas. In addition, he set aside a number of incentive packages for himself. Troy got away with his scam because he stayed within budget for incentives. Also, the company lacked internal control procedures designed to prevent this type of action. Troy's superiors were so delighted with his sales successes that they did not even suspect that some of the wholesaler incentives were being expropriated.

A year and a half passed by, and Troy and his family were still enjoying the unauthorized incentives. He saw no reason why his scam would not last indefinitely. One day another company vice-president and Troy played golf. Over a drink at the clubhouse, Troy casually mentioned that he and his wife would be going on an "incentive cruise" next month to Saint Martin. The other vice-president said, "What do you mean? I thought the incentive cruises were for customers, not for company personnel."

Troy attempted to cover by saying, "My mistake. I just got a little confused. I mean that my wife and I are taking the same exotic trip that our winning wholesalers take."

"Oh, I see," said the other vice-president. But he didn't see. Instead, he requested that an internal auditor investigate the incentive program with special attention paid to how the incentives were distributed. Within two weeks Troy was accused of fraud and asked to resign. While demanding Troy's resignation, the president told him that he had just blown a great career opportunity: "Three days before I learned of these allegations, I had recommended to the board that you be promoted to senior vice-president."[2]

Troy was ordinarily a rational, intelligent person. His personal assets included drive, ambition, creativity, and good interpersonal skills. He was doing fine without committing fraud. He sabotaged his career for a few luxury vacations, a large-screen TV, and limousine rides. On the basis of his superior job performance, he could soon have afforded to puchase all these things with his own money. If he had wanted extra money so badly, he might have used his creativity and business experience to find an honest way of earning it.

Troy got high on his own hormones. The excitement of big earnings stirred up his emotions. His judgment became distorted, and any dishonest tendencies lurking in the back of his mind surfaced. As with virtually all self-saboteurs, Troy needed to shake himself into reality. He might have said to himself: "Things are going great now. But hold on, many other mature people have blown things when they were going well. Is my little scam really worth the risk? What's the downside risk of expropriating incentives that are intended for our wholesalers? Biting the hand that feeds me is not really sensible."

Troy will know better next time, but next time may be a long time coming. His relationships with his wife and children are now severely strained, although his wife certainly encouraged his errant behavior. His job search will be painful, since there is little hope that he can regain his former stature in the short run. If Troy does rebound, he will at least have learned to confront his own thinking should he entertain any further self-sabotaging thoughts.

Many of us face the temptation from time to time to put our hands in the cookie jar. At the point of highest temptation, it becomes necessary to ask oneself, "Is the potential gain worth sabotaging my career?

Drunkenness During a Command Performance

"How can anybody be crazy enough to do something like that?" is the reaction often heard when somebody shows up for work intoxicated. Such behavior is even more perplexing when the drunk person occupies a key position and shows incredibly poor timing. One wonders if the person who is drunk at a command performance is secretly hoping for a way out of holding a responsible position.

At age 49, Arthur was the CEO of a public relations firm in Leeds, England. Along with an attractive salary and bonus, Arthur had a generous expense account. He drove a Jaguar sedan and had a sumptuous home in York. Arthur's family was happy, and felt financially secure until his career downfall. Much of Arthur's success in attracting clients to his firm could be traced to contacts he had made as a major in the Royal Scots Dragoons.

The holding company that owned Arthur's firm emphasized earnings competition among its member companies. After a year as CEO, Arthur began to experience considerable stress as a result of the rivalries among the several companies in his business group. In an attempt to cope with his problems, he began to drink earlier and earlier in the day. It appeared to other managers in the company that on several occasions Arthur was intoxicated at client meetings, but because drinking with clients was so prevalent not much was said about Arthur's behavior.

As time passed, Arthur was noticeably intoxicated at several other client meetings. One day the chairman of the board spoke with Arthur and told him he would not tolerate his being inebriated at business meetings with clients. Several months later, Arthur's parent company arranged an elaborate American tour for the company's four major international clients. Representatives from the British and American affiliates of the group of advertising companies would meet in New York City to conduct business and to be entertained. Based on Arthur's many personal contacts, and his keen ability to drum up new business, Arthur and three of his staff members were sent to New York.

One of the scheduled events was an evening chartered boat tour of Manhattan Island. Formal dress was required, the cuisine was international, and the champagne flowed. Arthur consumed glass after glass of champagne. As he veered from right to left and back again, Arthur made insulting comments about the brashness of American executives and the stuffiness of the British. Arthur ultimately lapsed into unconsciousness and had to be carried off the boat at the end of the tour by two of his staff members.

Arthur's vulgar display was reported back to headquarters long before his return flight landed in Leeds. He was fired immediately, and his reputation severely tarnished throughout the public relations community in England. After a year Arthur was still unemployed, and his savings and other assets were depleted. At that point he found a small public relations firm willing to hire him for a six-month probation period as an account director. The owners of the firm reasoned that Arthur could still get some mileage out of his old contacts.[3]

Arthur and others like him could prevent such self-inflicted career damage. He was giving signals that he found the competitive nature of his business to be overly stressful. For example, he began drinking earlier and earlier in the day. Arthur needed to decrease the job pressures, not to trash his good reputation. He might have thought through his actions and come up with a sensible plan for reducing the source of his distress without being self-sabotaging. Career counseling might have been helpful in this regard. A sensible alternative would have been for Arthur to become an account representative in his own firm. In a professional organization, such as a public relations firm, it is no disgrace to switch from administrative to technical work.

If you feel overwhelmed by job responsibilities, consider lessening your responsibilities before you resort to such counterproductive behaviors as drinking too much at company functions.

Hyperactivity in the Office

A fast-faced, energetic, and assertive approach to job responsibil-ities is an asset to your career. It is certainly far more impressive than lethargy. But when quickness and energy turn to hyperactiv-ity and mania, your mental stability may be called into question. Career self-sabotage is often the result. A co-worker describes the hyperactivity of a woman in her office:

"Dorothy has been with the company for twenty years, and has achieved a high level of professional respectability. However, lately, I've begun to worry about her. Dorothy used to come in each morning with a wide grin and a cheery hello. Nowadays she comes in tired and haggard. Any comments she has to make border on being cynical.

"The way Dorothy has been handling her work lately has aroused my concern. Others in the office are concerned too. Dorothy used to accept assignments with enthusiasm. Now every time the boss hands her something to do, she lets out a sigh. Dorothy seems to have this great sense of urgency about her. She attacks every job as if she is hurrying to meet some important deadline. It doesn't matter how trivial the job may be. Sometimes it appears as if Dorothy has lost control in the quest to complete her work. Her job isn't enjoyable to her anymore. All she cares about is getting it done. She never seems to stick to one job at a time. Dorothy is like a hummingbird going from flower to flower. Only she goes from job to job at the same hectic pace.

"Dorothy's hurry-up attitude extends beyond the work day. I get a ride home from her sometimes. You should see her on the road. She is always speeding to beat yellow lights. She honks her horn constantly and changes from lane to lane to get ahead of the rest of the traffic. It's scary.

"My husband and I are outdoor lovers, just like Dorothy and her husband, Ralph. So we often get together on weekends for biking trips or picnics. Yet we haven't done it in a long time. Most of the time Dorothy is at work on weekends. If she is at home, she is too wound up to relax. Ralph says that Dorothy is so obsessed with her work lately that she feels time spent at home is a waste. He is worried about Dorothy, and so am I.

"I have heard that there will soon be an opening for a top-level position in our department. Jack, one of the most senior people, is going to retire. Dorothy has the experience needed for the job. She is well-qualified to take the job since she knows our client requirements so well. However, I'm sure that Dave, our boss, is worried.

"Even though Dorothy is the heir apparent to Jack's job, her image in the department has been damaged by her hurry-up-itis. Dave must be concerned that Dorothy is out of control in her present job. She doesn't appear as if she would be able to handle the added responsibilities and pressures of the new job. It's such a shame. Dorothy doesn't know it, but she is building a large roadblock in her career path by her rushing through everything."[4]

Dorothy can be prevented from committing further career self-sabotage. One approach would be for her worried co-workers to express their concern to Dorothy, individually or at a small-group luncheon. The feedback would be useful to Dorothy in helping her to decide whether to seek professional help. A physician would probably prescribe sedatives for her. Dorothy might then be able to calm down enough to figure out what panicky feelings were propelling her into hyperactivity.

But Dorothy shouldn't have to wait for others to confront her about her bizarre behavior before taking corrective action. Despite her clouded thinking, she should still be perceptive enough to gauge people's reactions to her. Just looking at the expressions on the faces of co-workers should give Dorothy a clue that she is worrying them. She could then ask herself questions about what she is doing that is puzzling others, or she could solicit feedback from them. Because Dorothy has not yet done anything scandalous nor made major mistakes in handling assignments, her reputation is salvageable if she acts soon.

If you are working at a dizzying, manic-style clip, pause a moment from your frenzy. Ask yourself if you are being truly productive, or simply defeating your own best interests.

Maintaining a Swashbuckling, Reckless Life-Style

Employers today are much more tolerant of the after-hours behavior of managers and professionals than they were in the past. In earlier decades, a manager who rode a motorcycle to work or lived in a loft would have been seen as fitting poorly with the company culture. Today, these aspects of one's personal life-style are less likely to attract unfavorable attention. Such personal

choices may even go unnoticed. Yet there are outer limits to the
life-style that will be tolerated by upper management. A swash-
buckling, reckless personal life can lead the higher-ups to question one's judgment.

Eduardo was an excellent student at Pennsylvania State University. He
majored in business administration and was the president of a student
governance organization. With a wealthy family backing him, Eduardo
drove a Corvette and took lavish vacations during school breaks. After
graduating from Penn State, Eduardo went on to receive a master's degree
in international management at the Thunderbird School at the University of
Arizona. He was heavily recruited by several major business corporations.

Eduardo accepted an attractive offer from a multinational company
based in the United States that produced manufacturing control systems.
His goal was some day to become the vice-prersident of international
marketing. As part of his management training program, Eduardo was given
assignments in general accounting, auditing, credit, and sales. He was
immediately placed on the company's fast track, reserved for new managerial recruits of exceptional promise.

After a three-year stint in company headquarters, Eduardo was promoted to be the marketing manager of the company's branch in Mexico
City. During this assignment, Eduardo remained single and pursued the life-
style of an affluent bachelor. After six months in Mexico City, reports began
to trickle back to headquarters that Eduardo was having problems.

Eduardo's job performance was erratic, particularly with respect to
getting field reports completed on time. He was also getting into disputes
with local management about sales strategies. Eduardo's position was that
the Mexico City branch relied too much on existing customers to increase
business. He believed that new customers must be pursued more aggres-
sively.

Eduardo entertained prospective customers lavishly, including taking
them to bullfights. He especially enjoyed the bullfights because he was in
training to become an amateur matador. Local management was also
concerned that Eduardo was using his expense account to entertain too
many women who could not influence sales.

Around 1:00 A.M. on a Tuesday, Eduardo drove a company car into a
tree on the way back from a nightclub. He escaped with facial cuts and a
severely sprained wrist, but his companion was killed. Police reports
suggested that Eduardo was driving beyond a safe speed and, though not
drunk, that he had been drinking heavily. Headquarters responded by
recalling Eduardo to the United States and reassigning him to a market

research analyst position. Eduardo feels remorse about the accident, his family is angry at him, and he wonders how he will regain his career thrust.[5]

Eduardo did not deliberately get involved in a fatal automobile accident, thus sabotaging his career. But neither did he attempt to curb the thrill seeking that propelled him into recklessness, such as learning to fight bulls and lavishly entertaining people who were only quasi-legitimate business prospects. His confrontations with his superiors about their business judgment were also part of his recklessness. Eduardo's approach led his superiors to condemn his brashness rather than praise his innovative thinking.

Eduardo could have prevented his career setback by sizing up his situation in Mexico City and asking himself: "Which personal characteristics of mine can possibly cause me to blow this great opportunity?" A question of this nature would most likely have helped him to recognize the potential pitfalls of his bravado and recklessness. However low your predisposition toward career self-sabotage may be, it always helps to ask yourself what could possibly go wrong. Laying a potential problem out in clear view is the first step in preventing self-sabotage.

The Indiscreetly Conducted Office Romance

The office has now surpassed introductions by friends and singles bars as the most popular way of finding a date or mate. A contributing factor is that men and women now often work with each other on an equal level. Although finding romantic partners on the job is common, indiscretion and brazenness can still be self-sabotaging.

Robbie was in his late forties, and married with two children. He had enjoyed a successful career in the trucking industry, and had been steadily promoted by his long-term employer. Robbie was then recruited as an executive vice-president of a medium-size trucking concern. The president of the company was a former truck driver who had built the business over twenty years into a company with gross sales of $10 million annually. He knew the trucking business quite well but was a poor administrator. Robbie's mission was to establish better administrative controls, revitalize the sales and marketing organization, and improve rapport with the drivers.

After a year with his new employer, Robbie had reorganized business operations and recruited three talented new managers. He had accessed new markets by acquiring additional Interstate Commerce Commission (ICC) operating authority. The drivers respected Robbie as a doer and a person on whom they could rely. Robbie's accomplishments exceeded expectations, and he became recognized as someone who provided more leadership to the company than did the president.

Robbie had for many years been "bi-curious." From time to time he would watch adult movies of men engaged in sex with other men or attend gay bars. His preference was for masculine-appearing men, which made the trucking environment particularly pleasing. He began to extend dinner and hot-tub invitations to young male employees.

Rumors quickly spread of Robbie's dating offers. A manager who was leaving the company to take another position then told the president that he and Robbie had had sexual relations at his apartment. He also claimed that the two had engaged in sex several times in a company truck at lunchtime. Shocked, the president repeated the tale to his assistant. Word of the affair then became public knowledge. Robbie quickly lost the respect of company employees, and his leadership suffered. To prevent a crisis in leadership, the president requested that Robbie resign immediately.[6]

Admittedly, Robbie's office romance is more bizarre than most. Few people would be so indiscreet as to conduct a romance with a same-sex person on company premises. Furthermore, Robbie took great risks in requesting dates of men whose sexual orientation he did not know. Those who would conduct more traditional office romances can also profit from the following guidelines:

1. Act very professional with each other. Avoid walking around holding hands or kissing, touching each other, sending billets-doux through the office mail, or making frequent telephone calls to each other.
2. Maintain a high level of productivity so that others cannot fault your romance for lowering your productivity.
3. Don't arrive or leave with your lover, and don't discuss your glorious weekend trysts with co-workers.
4. Don't sit next to each other at staff meetings or play footsie under the table.

5. Be especially discreet if you are on a business trip to-gether. If there are other company members present, take separate rooms, perhaps even on different floors or in different hotels.
6. Have lunch together only occasionally. Lunch with other co-workers more frequently than you do with each other.
7. Consider keeping your relationship secret unless it's a committed relationship. It's usually not worth being the subject of office gossip for a short-term relationship.
8. Remember that a great relationship is worth more than one mediocre job. If the two of you are from the same department, one of you should consider requesting a transfer to another department or location.
9. Remember that a mediocre relationship is worth less than one great job. Don't proceed beyond the first date if you are convinced that the relationship will not last more than three weeks. Why do something that could be self-sabotaging for a brief surge of excitement, followed by a sense of embarrassment and defeat?[7]

Blatant Sexual Harassment

Sexual harassment takes many forms in the workplace. According to an article in *Personnel Administrator*, the three most blatant are sexual assault, sexual propositions involving threats of adverse job-related consequences, and sexual propositions involving a promise of positive consequences.[8] All three of these can inflict emotional wounds on the harassed and destroy the career of the harasser. Despite these overwhelming reasons for not committing blatant sexual harassment, almost every company has some employees who harass others. Even more reprehensible than those who harass their co-workers are those professionals who sexually harass the people they are supposed to be helping, such as patients, clients, or students.

Steve is a dentist with a general practice in a downtown office. At age 45 he divorced his wife of eighteen years. A contributing factor to his divorce was Steve's desire to lead a sexually diverse life. He imagined that by being single, healthy, and relatively prosperous, he would attract large numbers of young women. Steve was surprised that he met relatively few young women interested in spending time with him socially. Most of the women who were willing to date Steve were approximately the age of his former wife.

Frustrated and disappointed, Steve fantasized more and more about having sexual contact with young women. One day he decided to give free rein to his sexual fantasy of having physical contact with some of his younger patients. At first he hugged briefly two different patients. Because he met with no resistance other than a lack of responsiveness to his hug, Steve decided to progress further. In a period of ten days he kissed and fondled three of his women patients. One left his office indignantly, while the other two told him to stop immediately.

Steve realized that he had behaved offensively, so he decided to stop making advances toward his patients. He also hoped that the women would let the incidents drop. Steve was mistaken. Within one week he heard from a lawyer hired by one of the patients he had molested. Two days later he was informed by the county dental association that one of the other women he had harassed had filed a complaint.

The story of the sexual harassment charges leaked to the press. Steve received a formal censure from the county dental association, and reached a reasonable financial settlement with the patient who attempted to sue him. The third woman Steve harassed has not filed a complaint. But Steve's dental practice has declined so precipitously that he is now thinking of abandoning his practice.

Steve's acts of sexual harassment have been self-sabotaging even if they have not completely destroyed his career. If Steve never again makes a sexual advance toward any of his patients, he may be able to regain his reputation and rebuild his practice. However, he will have to drastically reduce his living costs until his practice is rebuilt. Steve let his sexual fantasies cloud his professional judgment to the point where he disregarded the rights of his patients.

Sexual fantasies are fine—so long as they remain fantasies. But Steve and the rest of us have to keep in mind that allowing a sexual fantasy to take over our rational thinking, or to act it out regardless of how inappropriate the circumstances, can ruin our reputations and careers.

Physical Violence

Remember the research technician who became so enraged over his performance appraisal that he wrecked company property? His temper tantrum badly damaged his career. An even surer route to career self-sabotage is for an employee to do physical violence to another employee. Company policies and labor agreements between the company and the union usually list physical violence as grounds for immediate discharge or suspension. Nevertheless, a physical outburst by a production worker against a co-worker is much more likely to be glossed over than one by a manager or professional.

Trudy, a company cafeteria manager, faced heavy job and family pressures. As a single parent of two preschoolers, she had to get her youngsters to the child-care center before going to work. Trudy could not afford the medical-care option that allows parents to take sick children to the child-care center. When one or both of Trudy's children were sick, she therefore had to scramble to find a backup person to take care of them.

Trudy's major on-the-job pressure came from having to get meals prepared in a short period of time. The challenge was heightened because she had to rely on part-time workers who had a high rate of absenteeism and tardiness. Despite Trudy's many pleas for more full-time help, the company chose to economize on cafeteria staffing.

In January a group of 100 stockholders were slated to visit the company, all of whom would eat in the cafeteria. Trudy's boss agreed to authorize the hiring of six temporary workers for two days to help handle the overload. Trudy knew that providing good service for everybody would be difficult, but she would do her best. Two days before the visitors were due, Trudy could feel her adrenalin pumping. A snowstorm hit the area the day before stockholders' day. Trudy worked her way through traffic to the day-care center, and arrived at work barely on time. Three of the six temporary workers called in to say that they couldn't get through to work.

Trudy made special arrangements to stay late that night to get as much work done for the next day as possible. The storm subsided that evening, and the roads were in good shape by the morning. All food had to be ready by 10:45 A.M. to accommodate the visitors and company employees who would first arrive for lunch at 11:00. As Trudy walked through the kitchen, one of the cafeteria employees put a ladle into the clam chowder. He sipped from the ladle, then suddenly spit it back into the pot, exclaiming, "How could you serve this ——— to anybody?"

Trudy doesn't have a clear remembrance of what happened next. One of the cafeteria workers said that she grabbed the employee by his shirt collar and began punching his face. After about five punches Trudy stepped back in horror. The clam chowder had been contaminated, the taster had a bloody nose, and Trudy was fired the next day. The taster was given a two-day suspension for violating the health code.

Many readers will empathize with Trudy. Some would want to hold the sampler's head in the clam chowder for five minutes. Nevertheless, Trudy committed a bizarre act that cannot be condoned. Being under such heavy pressure that day, she should have used an on-the-spot relaxation technique. Exhaling and inhaling a few times before inspecting the kitchen might have worked.

The consequences of Trudy's self-sabotage lasted only a few days. The company president heard about the incident, and found it amusing. He explained to Trudy's manager that he would not reverse her decision, and he could not condone violence. But he added that Trudy's outburst might be classified as "justifiable homicide." "Besides that," he commented, "the company clam chowder is excellent." Trudy's manager reconsidered, and Trudy was called back to work without a loss in pay.

The lesson from Trudy's experience is that at unpredictable times you may suddenly be called on to exert control over your emotions in order to prevent hurting your career. Try practicing emotional control by purposely placing yourself in situations where you have the urge to choke somebody. Try out a few verbal responses that may safely give vent to your anger, such as saying: "What you are doing bugs me. Please stop." A suggested practice setting is a crowded movie theater where people seated near you might be talking or noisily crumpling candy wrappers. Or how about standing in line at a supermarket while a coupon collector in front of you takes ten minutes to get her coupons credited?

Snooping

Unauthorized rummaging through company records is a surefire path to self-defeat. Rarely is the information obtained from snooping worth the risk of being caught. If you are looking for trade secrets, then you are committing a criminal act. If you just want to discover what the company has put in writing about you, there is an alternative. Freedom of information laws allow you to demand to see your personnel file. Demands of this nature may be a political blunder, but they are less damaging than being caught snooping.

Trevor, an ambitious junior in a management consulting firm, wanted to know what the company thought of his chances for someday being invited into partnership. He asked his boss's opinion on this topic over lunch one day. The boss said that it was much too soon for the partners to make such a determination.

Trevor wasn't convinced. His conversations with other consultants in the firm suggested that the partners kept a management inventory chart. The chart described the partners' collective opinion about the promotability of each member of the professional staff. Trevor decided to make an investigation of his own. Although the office wasn't officially open on Saturdays, many of the juniors used that time to prepare client reports and take care of paperwork. One Saturday morning, Trevor was the only person in the office. He wandered into the office of Foster Reinholz, the senior partner.

Trevor attempted to wiggle open Reinholz's top desk drawer, where he had heard the management inventory chart was kept. As Trevor knelt down in front of the massive oak desk, in walked Foster Reinholz. Trevor felt the blood rush to his face, and his lips began to twitch. The senior partner said in accusatory tones, "What can I help you with?"

"Nothing, nothing," fumbled Trevor, "I'm just looking for a yellow legal pad. The supply cabinet seems to be locked."

"I doubt you will find a legal pad in my desk. I'm not in charge of office supplies around here," said Foster.

The senior partner apprised others in the firm of Trevor's strange behavior. The incident was not discussed with Trevor, but his name was deleted from the list of people with potential for partnership. Foster said he did not wish to investigate the incident, but he would never approve for partnership any person he did not trust.

Intelligent and ambitious, Trevor did not stop to think of the implications of his actions. Snooping is no more welcomed by business associates than it is by spouses or roommates. Before sneaking into the senior partner's office, he neglected to ask himself a key question in preventing career self-sabotage: "If what I am contemplating becomes public knowledge, what will be its downside risk to my career?" Ask yourself the same question whenever you are contemplating a risky act.

11

How Organizations Commit Career Homicide

$\mathcal{I}$t is too simplistic to place all the blame for self-sabotage on the victims. Sometimes it is the fault of the organization. As psychologist Don Cole has concluded from his research: "Professional suicide is often not 'suicide' at all, but rather a kind of organizational 'murder' in which the brightest and most committed employees get killed off in a professional sense by the very organizations that are badly in need of the talents they offer."[1]

The incidence of career homicide was first formally observed in a major aerospace company. After a period of from three to five years with the company, some of the brightest, most talented, and hardest-working managers and professionals would either begin to deteriorate or withdraw from the organization. Some would—

- Quit their positions for other jobs that were far beneath their capabilities.
- Become disruptive and do things for which they must have known they would be fired.
- Quit working hard and little by little retire on the job.
- Fail to keep up with the technology and gradually allow themselves to become outmoded.
- Develop psychosomatic problems such as backaches, headaches, ulcers, and dizziness.
- Let themselves deteriorate to a point where they appeared

ripe for serious self-injury through excessive weight gain or the pressure of an exorbitant work schedule.[2]

In this chapter I describe seven of the most important homicidal tendencies of organizations, and how this needless destruction of careers can be prevented. But let's not forget that although the company can be a major contributor to career sabotage, we all have some responsibility for staving off our own victimization.

Leaving People Too Much on Their Own

Critics generally contend that most organizations exercise too much control over their members. People are not given enough freedom to pursue objectives they believe are worthwhile. This criticism may be valid, but there is a major problem lurking at the other extreme. Some organizations grant managers and professionals so much freedom that these people run the risk of working to achieve objectives that are of little concern to top management. If goals and objectives are not clearly articulated, people waste resources on inconsequential projects.

Shana, the director of safety and health at an office-equipment manufacturer, became quite interested professionally in "sick buildings." The term relates to the observation that workers in some office buildings have an alarming number of colds, skin problems, and viral infections. Allegedly, these health problems are created by toxins in the air produced by heated office machines and various chemicals such as photocopying machine toner.

Shana assumed that top management was genuinely interested in seeing to it that none of the company's buildings was "sick." After all, the company policy manual included a statement about the company's providing a safe and healthy work environment for all employees. Besides that, the company had hired her and given her a staff of two professionals and one assistant. Shana mentioned to her boss, Megan, the vice-president of human resources, that she would be investigating the problem of sick buildings. Megan said that the project sounded interesting and that Shana should do what she thought best.

Shana and one of her staff members, Tony, geared up to study the problem of sick buildings within their company. They attended conferences;

they networked with others across the country interested in the same problem; and they hired an outside consultant to help them. After one year they had completed their task, and prepared a sixty-page technical report.

Megan was somewhat supportive of Shana's study, which did indicate a high level of toxicity in the air of one building. This could mean that there was some potential for an above-average rate of employee illness. Curing the problem might cost several hundred thousand dollars. Shana and Tony were excited about their findings because they believed that they were on an important mission. Megan then attempted to arrange a three-way meeting among herself, Shana, and the president of the company.

When the vice-president of human resources explained the nature of the meeting she was requesting, the president said, "You take care of this, Megan. I'm not interested. It sounds like a bunch of quackery. Anything else we need to talk about today?" When Shana heard of the president's reaction she became first enraged and then despondent. She remained in a motivational funk long enough to receive two consecutive below-average performance appraisals over the next year. Shana's career had lost its momentum.

The organization was certainly at fault for letting Shana work so long on a project that the president did not value. However, a staff person can avoid Shana's predicament by investigating management's interest in a project before plunging ahead.

Emphasizing Negative Rather Than Positive Feedback

The most frequent complaint of employees is that management always lets them know when they do something wrong but not when they do something right. This complaint shows up in company attitude surveys, when outside consultants talk to insiders, and at social gatherings. One could argue that this state of affairs is desirable, because it reflects the philosophy of management by exception: The manager gets involved only when a problem occurs.

The flaw in management by exception is that it overlooks the fact that people need to be rewarded for the things they do right in order to sustain their efforts. In extremes, receiving virtually all negative feedback makes people feel unappreciated and alienated. The person whose good deeds go unnoticed, and whose mistakes are dramatized, can sometimes be triggered into career self-sabotage. Kip, a credit manager for an equipment-leasing company, explains the circumstances leading to his downfall:

"The results of my work are very visible. If we guess wrong about a customer's credit-worthiness, the company knows about it in spades. Management hears very quickly when customers don't pay on time, or don't pay us at all. We then have to go through the hassle of taking back the equipment. In the meantime, we've tied up the equipment and it has generated very little, or no, revenue.

"The default rate on the credit I have approved has been very favorable. We make the occasional mistake, but we are running less than 2 percent defaults. I'm proud of what I and my assistant have accomplished. Yet management hardly makes mention of our contribution to the company. At performance appraisal time, I usually get a handshake and a smile. I also get an occasional, 'Keep up the good work.' But other than that, nobody ever mentions when I've done a good job.

"Last year the company decided it wanted me to cut the default rate by 25 percent. I said it was a tough goal, but I would try. As it worked out, I cut the rate by 29 percent. I was very proud. Despite cutting back the rate, we had one very visible default. We leased a new robot for making quality-control inspections. Unfortunately, our first lessee proved to be a deadbeat.

"The vice-president of finance called me into his office. He started chewing me out for running a sloppy credit check. For me, it was the last straw. I couldn't control myself. I started ranting about not being appreciated, and yelling that nobody recognized the contribution of the credit department. I told the vice-president he could take a flying leap. Like a jerk, I ran out of the building.

"Later on, I came back and resigned in a sensible way. But it was too late. I had made a fool of myself in the equipment-leasing industry. I was branded a hothead. I'm now working for 30 percent less pay as the manager of an employee credit union in a hospital."

You can avoid Kip's unhappy experience by recognizing that it is not unusual for a manager to offer very little positive feedback, yet always to emphasize the negative kind. Anticipating the problem will help you avoid being crushingly disappointed when it occurs. You are therefore less likely to become enraged with negative feedback.

Confusion Over the Rules of the Game

By "rules of the game" I mean an understanding of what needs to be done to get ahead or to be otherwise rewarded by management. There is often a big discrepancy between what top management says is important for advancement and what actually counts. The folklore of the company may state that "dedicated, committed employees are those chosen for promotion." In practice, so long as a person performs adequately, currying favor with the people in power is a much swifter route to a good job than hard work and talent.

Another example is that in a sales organization, top management may state that good customer service is the number-one priority and that promotions and salary increases will be based on that accordingly. In reality, sales volume—with a special emphasis on new customers—is the true path to promotion and high earnings. The person who emphasizes customer service, and downplays sales volume and cultivating new business, is thus defeating his or her own purposes.

Below is a list of confusions over the rules of the game that were present in an aerospace company. The same confusion and conflict occurs in many organizations. Employees who take the company's implied promises too literally may be misguided and wind up in a self-defeating adversarial relationship with management.

Promise: If you do good work, you will be rewarded.

Reality: The only way to get rewarded is by threatening to quit.

Promise: If you develop a product, you will be placed in charge of your own division or works.

Reality: When a product is successful enough, it is given to manufacturing. You are then sent back to develop another product.

Promise: We want people who will seize responsibility.

Reality: The result of seizing responsibility is (a) you get more work to do, (b) people see you as a threat and get mad at you, and (c) you get less cooperation from the organization.

Promise: We want employees to push us (management) for the things they feel need to be done.

Reality: Management talks to you less and less when you are assertive.

Promise: Results count.

Reality: Results are not as important as how your boss or your boss's boss feels about you.

Promise: I want to know what you think regardless of how unflattering it may be.

Reality: If you express what you think, and it is not flattering, you end up being punished.

Promise: We are a rapidly expanding company, where there is considerable opportunity for you to get ahead.

Reality: We are in an industry that is static or declining, and there are in fact few opportunities here.[3]

By acting as if these promises were reality, you may stumble into self-defeating blunders. For example, it would certainly be self-defeating to make unflattering comments to your boss if he or she bristles at being criticized.

To avoid the problem of not knowing the rules, take the initiative to understand the true organizational norms. Speak to people from different parts of the organization about what aspects of performance really count. Observe carefully which people in the organization are favored, and what rules they tend to follow. Be on the alert continually for what activities really do get rewarded.

The Pursuit of Conflicting Goals

A major source of job stress is the pursuit of conflicting goals, such as happens when two of your supervisors give you conflicting orders. With too many goals, you'll feel trapped—because you are bound to get somebody angry whatever goal you attain. When you get the wrong person angry, the result can be self-defeating. Sherri, a major account manager in an insurance company, explains the problems she encountered:

"The purpose of my job is to take care of several major accounts. I am supposed to solve their problems, and look for openings to save them money on premiums. I'm also supposed to expand their coverage wherever possible. Another key part of my mission is to make sure the account does not slip away to another carrier. In the insurance business, you have to stay alert to the competition. They forever snipe at you, promising to offer better service at lower cost.

"I know my accounts very well. Some of them just want to deal with the facts of insurance. It's strictly business. Others like the relationship part of dealing with an insurance company. They expect me to make small talk with them, and take them out to lunch and dinner. I sell these clients insurance, and I help cure their loneliness.

"For whatever reason, some of my customers would rather spend an occasional dinner with me instead of being with family and friends. It's okay with me. I'll do what needs to be done to hold on to an account.

"I started to get into trouble with the company after a new austerity program was announced. Some guy with an MBA convinced management that the company's sales-retention costs were too high. This boils down to meaning that people like myself were spending too much money entertaining our accounts. I wish it weren't true. I would like to spend much less of my time and the company's money entertaining my clients. The fact is, however, that several of my accounts will jump to the competition if they are not entertained royally.

"Shortly after the austerity program was announced, the company imposed some very fancy premium targets. This meant that I had to generate some more business, big time. If I cut back on entertainment expenses, I knew I would lose business. It had already proved to be true in one company. I told the insurance manager at one of my accounts that I would be doing less business entertaining. Thirty days later, he turned over a big chunk of our business to a competitor.

"Generating more business also meant that I would incur heavy entertainment expenses. It usually requires a lot of entertaining to start a new account. So there I was running up heavy entertainment expenses to hold on to old accounts and get new ones. I was moving toward reaching the new sales targets. At the same time I was going over budget on entertainment.

"My boss told me that top management wanted me to keep up the sales but lower my sales expenses. That's like telling a firefighter to put out more fires but save on water. As a result of all this, I was getting into squabbles with two layers of management. They were pleased with my premium volume, but they were getting on my back for my cost of sales.

"My boss would tell me to be more innovative in saving money on entertainment. My response was to make comments about entertaining accounts at Burger King. They didn't see the humor. I explained that my entertainment was cost-effective, so what I was doing made sense. We kept up this ridiculous dialogue.

"Finally, two of my biggest accounts were assigned to another major account manager. I was given a couple of lesser accounts in their place. My boss and his boss were much cooler to me than in the past. I had hurt my reputation with the company. Because of an ailing insurance industry at the time, I decided it was no time to look for another employer.

"Maybe I was a little too stubborn, but the company put me in an unfair squeeze. I have a less lucrative position, and I really didn't do anything wrong. I don't know how I'm going to work my way out of my dilemma."

To minimize the chances of being sabotaged by conflicting goals, Sherri should have confronted management tactfully about the squeeze she faced. She could have asked management to assign priorities as between generating new business and controlling entertainment expenses.

Putting the Lid on Innovative Thinking

Many victims of career homicide have an entrepreneurial spirit, characterized by an urge to innovate. They want to launch new ventures for the organization and improve on what already exists. Entrepreneurial thinkers have a strong need to accomplish things for the sake of accomplishment. They are primarily concerned with end results and have less concern for the means by which these results are achieved.[4]

In contrast to the typical bureaucratic-style manager, the entrepreneurial personality is willing to make waves and does not fear taking politically unwise actions. Entrepreneurial personalities may not be political blunderers, yet they are not overly concerned as to how their opinions will be received by people in power. Instead, they become single-mindedly committed to an objective, and in their drive to reach their objective they often alienate their superiors.

Innovative people do not want to be told how to do their job, particularly when they are convinced that they have developed a better way. They believe that it is their responsibility to get the job done, and they do not welcome direction on when, where, or how to do it. Part of their bravado comes from a feeling of professional security. Entrepreneurial thinkers typically believe that they can readily find new employment or start their own business.

Standard operating procedures are often cast aside as innovators seek better and quicker ways to reach objectives. This creates problems for a rigidly bureaucratic organization that prefers to accomplish things in a standardized way. (Most organizations think of themselves as innovative, and none would accept being called rigidly bureaucratic.)

Traditional managers, who respect routine and standard operating procedures, often find ways of putting the lid on highly innovative thinkers. The entrepreneurial type is labeled a "blue sky thinker" or accused of being "insensitive to price considerations" or "unwilling to accept what can't be changed." He or she is denied promotion and choice assignments.

When this clash does occur between the entrepreneurial thinker and the bureaucrat, the former may suffer a career setback. From one perspective, the entrepreneurial thinker is self-sabotaging. Putting less emphasis on innovation would probably be better for his or her organizational survival. Or the episode can be regarded as career homicide. It takes place because the organization has not developed the management skills and attitudes necessary to accommodate this kind of worker.

In some instances, innovative thinkers who are driven out of large bureaucracies go on to found successful new businesses. Most entrepreneurs in the computer field, for example, were at one time fired from a larger corporation that rejected their innovations. At other times, the organization can wreck the career of an entrepreneurially-minded worker. Gary explains what happened to him.

"I worked for ten years in the product development end of the plastics industry. Among the many household and industrial products we manufactured were plastic trash bags. Our company had a reasonable share of the market, and was looking to expand. An area of uncertainty was that plastic-bag manufacturing became a political hornet's nest. Many environmentalists were opposed to plastic bags; yet our industry had collected solid data showing that plastic bags were better for the environment than paper.

"The uncertainty in the industry made our management more cautious than ever. It was an unfortunate situation for me because I had some big plans. Our group had developed a way to make stronger bags at a lower price. But it meant considerable investment in new technology. The start-up costs would therefore be enormous. Yet my analysis suggested that within a few years the new bags would be a booming success.

"I was told to cool it because top management was not going to invest in new technology when the whole plastic bag industry could explode at any minute. I wouldn't cool it. I kept on making presentations, sending memos, and grabbing people in the halls to get them to listen to me.

"The company got its retribution by demoting me to a lab supervisor. My revenge was to quit and build a new company based on my idea. I poured all my savings into an attempt to start a plastic bag business based on new technology. Months went by as I tried to borrow money and find investors. I encountered as many deaf ears on the outside as on the inside.

"After five months I gave up the idea of revolutionizing the plastic trash bag business. A few months later I found employment as a product development engineer in a small company. What's really eating my heart out is that I had a breakthrough idea. In recent months, a new company has been formed by somebody else to produce virtually the same bag I had in mind."

Gary's problem is difficult to resolve. One approach taken by corporate employees whose ideas for new products are rejected is to form their own companies. Another approach is to put the first great idea aside and develop another idea the company would be willing to sponsor. Attempt to discover the type of innovations the company is able to support and promote.

Crisis-Oriented Management

Everyone has heard of the manager who proudly proclaims, "I do not get heart attacks, I give them." Although a cliché, such a pronouncement can be true. Researchers Larry Pace and Stanley Smits have shown that crisis-oriented managers create overwhelming stress for some team members. They are often substance abusers themselves, addicted to drugs and alcohol or to their own Type A behavior.[5] People with Type A behavior are impatient, demanding, aggressive, and hostile.

Crisis-oriented managers use crises to motivate themselves and others. They relish sudden business downturns or budget cutbacks because such conditions legitimize pushing people into a frenzy. One executive who specializes in turning around troubled companies recommends that during a crisis members of the management team be supplied with cots in their offices. In this way, they can minimize the need to take time from work to sleep at home.

Managers who thrive on the crisis mode commit career homicide by creating so much stress that their subordinates engage in self-defeating behavior. Stressed-out team members with a predisposition toward counterproductive behavior may be triggered into substance abuse and other forms of escapism, such as absenteeism, lateness, daydreaming, and denying that problems exist. In the turmoil, someone like Doris may suffer a severe career setback.

Doris worked in the state education department as a program supervisor. Her particular assignment was to coordinate activities to ensure that licensed health-care professionals enrolled in a three-hour seminar on detecting child abuse. New legislation had made this seminar a precondition for professionals renewing their licenses and registrations with the state. Doris believed strongly in the mission of the program, and enthusiastically pursued her objective.

Mitchell, the agency head to whom Doris reported, worked at a frantic pace, and expected his key people to do likewise. At his regular staff meetings Mitch would forever focus on the pending budget cuts. His favorite saying was, "The taxpayers are demanding more and more, but the legislators are giving us less and less." Although Mitch often cried "wolf", heavy budget cuts did in fact take place in the midst of Doris's child-abuse awareness program.

Doris lost one professional staff member and one assistant from her program. Already overworked, she pleaded with Mitch to get an extension on her deadline for completing the first phase of the project. Mitch berated Doris for her callous disregard of the taxpayers' needs. He told her to be a true professional and work as many hours as required to complete the program on time. Doris explained that she was already working sixty hours a week. Mitch replied that he did not want to hear excuses. He also told Doris to prepare for the next round of budget cuts.

Doris soon lapsed into physical and emotional exhaustion. She began overeating and overdrinking, and developed severe dermatitis. A physician working for the state recommended that Doris be given a thirty-day medical leave of absence. Mitch approved the leave, at the same time writing a memo for Doris's personnel file stating that she could not tolerate much work pressure.

Assume that you feel trapped working under a crisis-oriented manager, and believe that the situation is adversely affecting your health. Request a transfer and explain to others the real reasons why you would prefer to work for a different manager. Specify that working continually in a crisis mode is bad for your productivity and health.

Recruiting Mostly Outsiders for Key Positions

In many instances, recruiting outsiders for key positions makes good organizational sense. Needed experience and talent can be brought into the company when it is not available internally. The outsider may introduce an objective viewpoint and a broader perspective that insiders lack. Also, the outsider may be able to take courageous leadership actions because he or she has no internal political ties.

Despite the potential advantages of bringing in outsiders for key positions, if overdone it can contribute to career homicide. Competent, hardworking company employees become discouraged and demoralized if they perceive themselves as ineligible for choice promotions. As an extreme response, a disaffected employee may even leave the organization precipitously to take a lesser job in a lesser organization. If the organization promoted more company employees into key positions, fewer people would damage their careers by making impulsive job changes.

Barry was a regional marketing manager for a national chain of nursing homes. He concentrated his efforts on creating a market for the nursing homes through such means as speaking to sources of referral, advertising, and obtaining publicity. Barry believed strongly that the nursing homes he represented were making an important contribution to society. They were well designed and well staffed, offered excellent elder-care programs, and were competitively priced.

In Barry's assessment, he was not being paid well enough for a marketing manager with so much responsibility. He explained to the corporate staff that he wanted to advance. Barry was reassured that he would be in line for future promotions. As the future unfolded, however, Barry's promotion was not forthcoming. He was passed over for three promotions that went to outsiders.

Each time a new person was brought in from the outside, Barry wanted to know why he had not been given the nod. He was told each time that his performance was fine, but that the outsider chosen had special expertise or experience needed by the company. Barry countered with the argument that the nationally based nursing care industry was so new that his experience was almost as lengthy as any outsider's. Barry was told by the president that he should be more patient and that organizational needs were more important than individual ambitions.

Barry could no longer tolerate being passed over in favor of outsiders. He hastily looked for a new position and within a month found a marketing manager's position with a fledgling chain of child-care centers. But because the company was severely undercapitalized and could not meet its payroll while waiting for an adequate revenue stream, Barry was laid off after six months. He now felt that his career was in a tailspin. Unable to find another position directly in his field of experience, Barry accepted a position as a marketing manager for a public utility.

Barry now earns substantially less than he was earning at the nursing home chain, and his prospects for promotion look slim. The utility is a stable organization with very few changes in management.

To avoid the trap of working for a company that fills key positions primarily from the outside, investigate a company carefully before joining it. Speak to both current and former employees. If you are currently working for a company that offers few promotions from within, discuss your concerns with top management. Maybe your discussion will prompt management to look at internal people more carefully before recruiting externally.

Preventing Career Homicide

Organizations can prevent career homicide by avoiding the practices that contribute to the problem. The seven negative practices described here are major contributors to career homicide. Career homicide can therefore be substantially reduced if management—

- Does not leave people too much on their own, without goals or guidance.
- Emphasizes positive rather than negative feedback.
- Clarifies the rules of the game.
- Minimizes conflicting goals.
- Encourages innovative thinking.
- Avoids crisis-oriented management.
- Allows ample opportunities for promotion from within.

In addition to addressing the specific contributors to career homicide, organizations can also take the following steps to increase the effective utilization of their people:

Step 1. *Establish specific organizational goals.* Being specific reduces the ambiguous character of organizational goals and helps prevent people from pursuing inappropriate goals. If people know what organizational goals they should be pursuing, they can better mesh their personal goals with those of the company. Working toward specific goals is also a potential stress reducer. Accomplishing something tangible always makes people feel refreshed and less tense.

Step 2. *Initiate performance evaluations at regular intervals.* A well-constructed evaluation system increases the chances that people will be rewarded for achieving good results rather than for merely impressing others.

Step 3. *Initiate training and development programs that teach managers how to be constructively candid with people.* If these skills are developed by managers, fewer people will be deceived and disappointed. As a result, they are less likely to impulsively damage their careers or to burn their bridges completely. Constructive candor also helps people to overcome self-defeating behavior. If they know what they are doing wrong, they may be able to take remedial action.

Step 4. *Provide opportunities for decompression and the periodic release of stress created by frustration and other problems.* Management programs on stress reduction and attendance at professional conferences help achieve these purposes. Talking to people from other organizations at conferences and trade fairs is often emotionally soothing. It helps establish the fact that people working for other employers also face significant job challenges.

Step 5.   *Reduce the anxiety in the system.* Anxiety can be an effective motivator, but too much of it leads to worrisome attitudes that become self-defeating. Anxiety can be reduced by clarifying goals and being honest about upcoming changes such as budget cuts and layoffs.

Step 6.   *Help people at every job level prevent obsolescence by telling them what they need to know and offering them training.* Some people sabotage their careers by becoming technically and professionally obsolete. If they were aware of their knowledge and skill deficiencies and of how to improve them, they could prevent career self-sabotage.[6] A sales representative puts it this way: "I was headed toward self-destruction just because I never thought to catch up with the new way of doing things. I was hanging on to a used-car salesman approach in an environment that demanded more professionalism. My manager saw what was happening, and urged me to change. He showed me the way and helped me salvage my career."

12

A Master Plan for Removing Hidden Barriers

*M*any suggestions have been offered so far for overcoming the hidden barriers to your success. Pick and choose among them to fit your particular circumstances and personal style. But keep in mind that overcoming self-defeating behavior requires hard work and patience. A few sporadic moments of determined action will not eliminate career self-sabotage.

In addition to the suggestions you may already have begun to implement, or contemplate implementing, study the master plan in this chapter. It is an overall strategy, based on sensible principles of human behavior, to help people overcome career self-sabotage. The master plan has nine widely applicable components. Not all of them will be relevant to your circumstances. Only you can know what will work best for you, so choose accordingly:

1. Examine your script and make the necessary changes.
2. Stop blaming others for your problems.
3. Solicit feedback on the actions you take.
4. Stop denying the existence of problems.
5. Make positive changes in your life.
6. Modify or leave relationships that divert you from your career goals.
7. Get appropriate help from your organization.

8. Visualize self-enhancing behavior.
9. Make happiness your goal.

Examine Your Script and Make the Necessary Changes

Much importance has been attached to the influence of early-life programming in determining whether a person is predisposed to self-defeat. Note carefully the word *predisposed*. A person may be predisposed to snatch defeat from the jaws of victory, but that doesn't mean the predisposition makes defeat inevitable. It does mean that that person will have to work harder to overcome a tendency toward self-sabotage.

A script is much like a set point with respect to body weight. A woman whose natural body weight (her set point) is 145 pounds will experience difficulty getting down to 125 pounds and staying at that weight. Her body will fight her in such ways as slowing down her metabolism when she begins to decrease her food intake. Despite having set points of 145 pounds, many women who weigh in that neighborhood do nevertheless maintain a diet and exercise regimen that keeps them at a much lower weight. It may be a lifelong struggle, but it can be done.

The set point analogy applied to self-defeating scripts means that you can identify them and modify them. After asking yourself a series of penetrating questions, you can exercise conscious control over changing the script. An effective way of identifying your script, in addition to answering the ten questions posed at the end of Chapter 2, is to look for patterns in your setbacks.

Did you show up late for several key appointments with upper management or important customers? Did you blow up at people who have the authority to make administrative decisions about your future? Did you get so tense during your last few command performances that you were unable to function effectively? Marcel, a vending machine sales representative, successfully engaged in script analysis by identifying his pattern of mistakes. He explains:

"Three times in my career I have screwed up badly on an important sales opportunity. One time I brought a demonstration machine to a large office building. Two helpers from the company came along with me. We installed the vending machine in time for a demonstration to the building manager. When she inserted money to see if the machine could really vend decent pizza, the machine jammed. Nothing happened. I smiled and said that we may have jammed the machine in transit. I opened the machine, but I couldn't detect the problem.

"It dawned on me that I had failed to run a final inspection at the factory. If I had discovered a problem there, a technician could have bailed me out. The building manager bade me good-bye, and wasn't interested in setting another date for me to return. The embarrassment was even more painful than the lost sale.

"The second time I screwed up, I was at a vending machine trade show, in Niagara Falls, New York, demonstrating our product. I hadn't thought of the obvious fact that many of the potential customers would be from nearby Ontario, Canada. I lost a few prospective customers because the machine was not set for Canadian currency. The size of their coins is not identical with those of the United States. If I had planned ahead, we would have had two demonstration machines, one for each currency. Or better yet, one machine that took both U.S. and Canadian currency.

"My third blooper was to bring a potential big customer into our factory to demonstrate a fresh-fruit vending machine. The purchasing manager represented a major hospital. He inserted two quarters in the machine, then let out a howl and jumped back two feet at the same time. The poor guy had received an electric shock.

"Here's what happened: Because of a roof leak, rain water had dripped onto the machine all during the night. Enough water got into the controls to create a short circuit that directed electrical current to the outside of the machine. When the purchasing manager touched the machine, electricity ran through his body. He wasn't hurt, but I lost a potentially large account.

"My analysis revealed a pattern to the trouble I brought on myself. I messed up by not double-checking everything. In the excitement of a prospective big sale, I wasn't composed enough to be extra-thorough. I now keep a checklist of potential mistakes with me at every sale. My career is going fine, and I haven't made another agonizing blooper."

Stop Blaming Others for Your Problems

Blaming others for our problems contributes to self-defeating behavior and career self-sabotage. Projecting blame onto others is self-defeating because doing so relieves you of most of the responsibility for your setback and failure. Consider this example:

If someone blames the office backstabbers for not receiving a promotion, he or she won't have to worry about becoming a stronger candidate for future promotions. Not to improve one's suitability for promotion is self-sabotaging. If you accept most of the blame for not being promoted, you are more likely to make the changes necessary to qualify in the future.

An underlying theme in several components of the master plan is that we all need to engage in thoughts and actions that increase our personal control. This is precisely the reason that blaming others for our problems is self-sabotaging. By turning over control of your fate to forces outside yourself—to superiors, subordinates, co-workers, parents, children, teachers, and government policy makers—you are holding them responsible for your problems.

Suppose, you argue, that others *are* responsible for some of your problems. What about the ravages caused by a paranoid boss, a career-choking spouse, or a recession in your industry? Admittedly, these are all formidable factors that interfere with career momentum. Yet it is your responsibility to exert some control over these forces the best you can. Try to change bosses, take the initiative in working things out with your spouse, or do an outstanding job of servicing the customers the recession has not taken away.

Solicit Feedback on the Actions You Take

Throughout this book I have emphasized the importance of obtaining feedback on your actions and words so that you can monitor whether you are sabotaging yourself. A starting point is to listen carefully to any direct or indirect comments from your superiors, subordinates, and co-workers about how you are coming across to them.

Bill, a technical writer, heard three people in one week make comments about his appearance. It started innocently with, "Here, let me fix your collar." Next, an office assistant said, "Bill, are you coming down with something?" The third comment was, "You look pretty tired today. Have you been working extra-hard?" Bill processed this feedback carefully. He used it as a signal that his steady late-night drinking episodes were adversely affecting his image. He then cut back his drinking enough to revert to his normal healthy appearance.

An assertive and thick-skinned person might try another technique: Approach a sampling of people both on and off the job with this line of questioning: "I'm trying to develop myself personally. Can you think of anything I do or say that creates a bad impression in any way? Do not be afraid of offending me. Only people who know me can provide me with this kind of information."

Take notes to show how serious you are about the feedback. When someone provides any feedback at all, say, "Please continue, this is very useful." Try not to react defensively when you hear something negative. You asked for it, and the person is truly doing you a favor.

Stop Denying the Existence of Problems

Many people sabotage their careers because they deny the existence of a problem and therefore do not take appropriate action. Denial takes place as a defensive maneuver against a painful reality. Much denial takes place in the context of mergers, acquisitions, and hostile takeovers. Some people do not start looking for jobs until it is too late. Robert Bell, who has extensively studied the problem of takeovers, suggests:

> Talk to any consultant who has advised on the staffing issues in takeovers and any manager who has lived through a takeover, and one term will inevitably come up: *denial*. This is the belief that the next person will get fired, not you. This occurs despite the overwhelming evidence that your company, division, unit or you are on the scrap heap. So you stay until it is too late.[1]

Another self-sabotaging form of denial is to ignore the importance of upgrading one's credentials despite overwhelming evidence that it is necessary. Some people never quite complete a degree program that has become an informal qualification for promotion. Consequently they sabotage their chances of receiving a promotion for which they are otherwise qualified. For the self-employed, treating the importance of full credentials with denial can result in a serious business decline.

Katrina was a massage therapist with a large enough clientele to earn a good living. She had studied massage in both Europe and the United States. In the third year of her practice, her state passed a law making it mandatory for massage therapists to obtain a license. The paperwork and documentation involved in getting a license, however, are enormous. In addition, an examination is usually required. Katrina scoffed at the idea that the licensing law would have any teeth. She denied that there would be any negative consequences for her practice from not having a license.

Several years later, Katrina made an attempt to place her annual ad in the classified telephone directory. The telephone company explained that if she wanted to be listed as a "licensed massage therapist" or "licensed masseuse," she would have to produce her license number. Because Katrina could not advertise as a licensed practitioner, she had to list herself among the health spas.

Many of her clients soon began to inquire if Katrina were a "real masseuse" or a self-taught one. She also began to receive more calls from men who had interpreted her listing as being a "massage parlor." Katrina did not lose all of her clientele, but her practice declined to the point that it was no longer profitable. She now faced the dilemma of working for a health spa as a "body rub expert" or attempting to become licensed. Katrina's period of denial was at last over, and she began to take constructive action toward dealing with her insufficient credentials.

Make Positive Changes in Your Life

There is something almost mystical about making positive changes in your life as a way of overcoming self-sabotage. Although the changes you make may not have anything directly to do with self-defeating behavior, they do help you to achieve greater control over your life. For example, if you have always relied on others to prepare your income tax returns, and you now do it yourself, you have mastered one more part of your environment. You thus feel more in control of your world than you were in the past.

Sometimes the simplest changes can start a chain reaction of self-control. Some people who have never before pumped their own gas are delighted when they master this simple routine that perhaps 85 percent of other drivers can do. Preparing one's own income tax or pumping one's own gas alone will not conquer career self-sabotage. But suppose that you add to the list learning a foreign language, learning a new dance, developing two new friends, becoming a big brother or big sister to a disadvantaged child, giving an overcoat to a homeless person, and starting a recycling campaign in your house. You will feel a lot more in control of your life than you did before you acquired these new skills or did these good deeds.

Feeling in control of one's life—and therefore being more in control—is precisely the discipline the self-sabotaging person needs. People are sometimes propelled into counterproductive routines because they feel that they are being dragged along by external forces. Their experience is much like that of a compact car being pushed to the side of the road by the draft from a ten-wheeled truck passing on the left.

The person who consumes three drinks at lunch might say: "I don't know why I did it. I couldn't resist the temptation. Other people were paying for the drinks." If you are in control, you can decline the two drinks you don't really need—and that are sure to lead to an impression-damaging wooziness back at the office. The securities broker in control of her life can therefore avoid engaging in self-sabotaging stock manipulations. She can resist the one-time temptation offered by a gluttonous colleague.

Modify or Leave Relationships That Divert You From Your Career Goals

People sometimes blame their career setbacks on a spouse or a domestic partner who doesn't understand the importance of their work. A typical case is Ned, a field auditor who explained that he was doing a mediocre job because his wife complained so much about his traveling. He therefore cut back on his travel to please her. His boss, however, was displeased with his low productivity.

In the boss's eyes, an effective field auditor belonged in the field. Ned's wife, however, thought that being home more frequently to do his share of parenting and housekeeping was more important than being well-received by the company.

People who blame their spouses or partners for encouraging them to engage in self-defeating career actions are partially correct. A partner who doesn't share your career goals and dreams is a liability. To overcome this problem, and escape handicapping, your career, you definitely have to work things out with this "significant other."

Pam, a product manager, often worked much later at night than her husband, Corey, found acceptable. He claimed that when they married she had never mentioned that she would be spending so much time at the office. Pam could feel the tension whenever she prepared to leave for work, and she could sense a coolness in Corey's voice when she called home to say she would be late. Pam suggested that the two of them together should visit a relationship counselor.

The counseling sessions revealed that Corey felt insecure about Pam's devotion to business. He admitted to being concerned that her career was becoming more important to her than their relationship. Pam reassured Corey that her marriage and her career were both very important, and that Corey did not have to be jealous of her career. She also worked out a plan whereby she would rely more on her home computer in order to cut down on overtime spent at work. Pam now felt that she had more of the energy she needed to move forward in her career, without sacrificing her relationship with Corey.

Pam was able to modify her relationship with Corey. At other times a relationship may be incompatible with one's career because the partner does not share the same goals and values and refuses to change. Goal incompatibility of this kind can lead to career self-sabotaging behaviors. These include preoccupation with marital problems and withdrawing from heavy involvement in one's career because it leads to conflict at home. In such extreme cases, the person must choose between *this partner* and an unfettered career. Trying to arrive at a workable compromise before a heavy commitment or marriage takes place is obviously the preferred solution.

Get Appropriate Help From Your Organization

So far, I have not seen a box on any organization chart labeled Department of Self-Sabotage. Nevertheless, it is worth considering seeking assistance from within your organization when you are damaging your own career. The very fact that you are seeking help suggests that the process of overcoming self-sabotaging behavior has begun. Three sources of help are ordinarily available in large organizations: feedback and advice from a superior; an employee assistance program; and human resource professionals. The smallest of organizations can offer you only the first source of help, while medium-size organizations can usually offer you the first two.

Solicit Feedback and Advice From a Superior

Asking for feedback is a basic tactic for overcoming career self-sabotage. Aside from the valid information feedback may provide, it usually leads also to advice and suggestions. A supportive boss is likely to ask how he or she can help when a subordinate comes for advice.

Alex, a financial analyst, was troubled by the fact that when making a presentation to management he became so nervous that he would incorrectly state facts. Consequently, he was worried about being regarded as a mediocre financial analyst. The analyst asked his boss, who was experienced at presentations, if he had noticed this problem. The boss said that he had noticed a few instances in which Alex had flubbed his facts, but not to an unusual extent.

Alex then asked his boss what he could do about the problem. The boss volunteered to set aside time to listen to Alex conduct a dress rehearsal of his next two presentations. Alex took the boss up on the offer, and it did help him overcome his presentation anxiety.

The rehearsals themselves benefited Alex, but the support and encouragement shown by his boss were equally valuable. Donald Cole's research has shown that emotionally supportive managers are effective antidotes to career homicide.[2]

Make Use of Employee Assistance Programs

A major purpose of an EAP is to help employees overcome personal problems that interfere with their productivity. In the most typical arrangement, the employee assistance program coordinator refers the troubled employee to a treatment facility outside the organization. The same facility is used by employees from many companies. Some larger organizations have their own treatment facility located on or off company premises. The program is confidential, sometimes to the extent that the company does not even know which employees have referred themselves for help.

Many of the problems dealt with by EAPs involve self-defeating behavior, including substance abuse, cigarette addiction, compulsive gambling, financial problems, and the physical abuse of family members. A company employee is also eligible to spend one or two sessions with an EAP counselor to talk about self-sabotaging problems in general. If the counselor thinks multiple treatment sessions are required, an appropriate referral would be made.

Seeking help from an EAP rather than going to a mental health practitioner on one's own has an important advantage. Employee assistance counselors work regularly with people whose personal problems are negatively affecting job performance. Also, the company usually pays the entire fee.

Confer With a Human Resources Professional

Another organizational resource that may help in dealing with self-sabotaging tendencies is a human resources professional who specializes in career problems. Among these professionals are counseling psychologists, industrial psychologists, and career development specialists.

Lorie, a budget analyst, requested an appointment with a career development specialist to discuss career planning. During the second session it became apparent that "career planning" was a euphemism for "interpersonal problem." As Lorie explained it, she often entered into disputes with people she was supposed to be helping, especially managers from outside her department. Her role was to help people from other departments prepare their budgets. She bickered with operating people so often that several times they requested to work with another budget analyst.

In discussing her problems with the career counselor, it became apparent to Lorie that the root of her self-defeating behavior was a strong need to challenge authority. At the same time, she had a strong need not to be challenged herself. She also came to realize that budget preparation always involved negotiation. Therefore, when she did not agree entirely with the figures presented to her, it was not a signal to challenge their authority. Similarly, when people did not immediately agree with her analysis, it did not mean that they were attempting to challenge her authority.

The insights Lorie gained in the several sessions with the career counselor helped her greatly to improve her ability to engage in give-and-take over budgets without assuming an attack posture.

Visualize Self-Enhancing Behavior

Visualization is a primary method for achieving many different types of self-improvement. It is therefore an essential component of a master plan for removing hidden barriers to success. To apply visualization, program yourself to overcome self-sabotaging actions and thoughts. Imagine yourself engaging in self-enhancing, winning actions and thoughts. Picture yourself achieving peak performance when good results count the most.

A starting point in learning to use visualization for overcoming career self-sabotage is to identify the next job situation you will be facing that is similar to ones you have flubbed in the past. You then imagine yourself mentally and physically projected into that situation. Imagine what the room looks like, who will be there, and the confident expression you will have on your face. Visualization is rather like watching a video of yourself doing something right. An example:

Matt, an actuary in a life insurance company, has an upcoming meeting with top management to discuss his analysis of how insurance rates should be changed to factor in the impact of AIDS on mortality rates. Based on past experience, Matt knows that he becomes flustered and acquiescent in high-level meetings about controversial topics (such as rate increases). Matt also knows that to behave in this way is self-defeating.

As he prepares for the meeting, he visualizes himself calmly listening to challenges to his analysis. In response, he does not back off from his position, but smiles and presents his findings in more detail. Matt visualizes the people who challenged him changing their attitudes as he knowledgeably explains his case. By the end of the meeting Matt is warmly thanked for his recommendations on making rate changes to meet the incidence of AIDS in the population. The president congratulates him on how well he stood up to the challenges to his forecasts.

Make Happiness Your Goal

An inevitable consequence of career self-sabotage is that it makes people unhappy. The self-defeating person is typically a chronic complainer, moaning and groaning about bad breaks and bad luck. "Why does something like this always happen to me?" asks the self-saboteur. The answer is that the self-saboteur has actively contributed to his or her own problems.

Making happiness a goal can help overcome career self-sabotage because it helps you to become predisposed to feeling good. You develop a routine of squeezing positive experiences out of potentially negative situations. You become mentally ready to create conditions that contribute to happiness. At the same time, you learn to automatically ward off many sources of self-defeat and unhappiness. For example, if you are predisposed to happiness, you will most likely not misplace your car keys on the way to a crucial meeting. You will plan in hundreds of little and big ways to avoid mistakes that can ruin a day, a year, or a career.

Planning for happiness is possible because the evidence suggests that it is somewhat under people's control. Unhappiness, by contrast, seems to be more predetermined by heredity.[3] Nevertheless, if you have a predisposition toward unhappiness, achieving a substantial amount of happiness can outweigh your unhappiness. For example, even if being melancholy runs in your family, you may be able to feel happy 75 percent of the time.

The keys to happiness[4] presented next will help you to create the positive frame of mind that combats self-sabotage. They also serve as a convenient checklist for leading a better life in general.

1. *Give high priority to the pursuit of happiness*. Discover what makes you happy and create the time to pursue those activities. Spending time doing what you enjoy, on and off the job, contributes directly to your happiness.

2. *Experience love and friendship*. A happy person is successful in personal relationships, and exchanges caring and concern with loved ones. Happy people are able to love and be loved, and they also reach out to co-workers.

3. *Develop a sense of self-esteem*. Self-love must precede loving others. High-esteem enables you to love and be loved. Self-esteem can sometimes be increased by reflecting on all the good things you have accomplished so far in your career.

4. *Work hard at what you enjoy*. Love may be the most important contributor to happiness. Staying involved in work you enjoy is second. Find a job that fits your interests to help prevent engaging in self-sabotaging behavior.

5. *Seek accomplishments and the ability to enjoy them*. A fundamental secret of happiness is accomplishing things and savoring what you have accomplished. A major contributor to unhappiness is comparing one's successes, or lack of them, to those of other people. To be happy, you must be happy with what you achieve.

6. *Develop an attitude of openness and trust*. Trusting other people leads to happiness, but distrusting others leads to unhappiness. Happy people have open, warm, and friendly attitudes.

7. *Appreciate the joys of day-to-day living*. Live in the present without worrying unduly about the future or dwelling on past mistakes. Guard against becoming so preoccupied with planning your life that you neglect to enjoy the happiness of the moment. The essence of being a happy person is to savor what you have right now.

8. *Learn to cope with anxiety, stress, grief, and disappointment*. To be happy you must learn how to face problems without being overburdened by them or running away from them. After coping with problems you will be better able to appreciate the joys of day-to-day life.

9. *Energize yourself through physical fitness*. Whether it is the

endorphins released by exercise or just the relaxed muscles, physical fitness fosters happiness.

10. *Strive for a balanced emotional response to positive and negative experiences.* Emotional intensity can be costly. People who reach the highest highs also tend to reach the lowest lows.

11. *Develop a philosophy or system of belief.* Another key contributor to happiness is to believe in something besides yourself. Happy people have some system of belief—whether it be a religion, a philosophy, or science—that comforts them and gives them a reason for living.

12. *Have fun.* A happy life is characterized by fun, zest, joy, and delight. When you create time for fun, you add immensely to your personal happiness. However, if you devote too much time to play, you will lose out on the fun of accomplishing work. And that could be self-sabotaging.

If your master plan for removing the hidden barriers to your success is properly executed, you will have achieved a major milestone in your career. The only impediments to achieving success and happiness will lie outside yourself, and self-defeating behavior will no longer be your enemy.

References

Chapter 1

　　1. The statements in the Self-Sabotage Questionnaire are based on the behaviors and symptoms of people who engage in self-sabotage. The sources for many of these behaviors and symptoms are (a) the Appendix to the *Diagnostic and Statistical Manual of Mental Disorders*, 3rd ed. (New York: American Psychiatric Association, 1987) and (b) "How to Avoid Sabotaging Your Own Career," *Personal Report for the Executive*, October 15, 1989, p. 4.

Chapter 2

　　1. Dudley Bennett, *TA and the Manager* (New York: AMACOM 1976), p. 160.
　　2. Ibid.
　　3. Case researched by Katherine Werther.
　　4. Case researched by Bob Wilcox.
　　5. John Wareham, *Wareham's Way: Escaping the Judas Trap* (New York: Atheneum, 1983), p. 107.
　　6. Ibid., p. 106.
　　7. Case researched by Sheri Stanton-Follett.
　　8. Case researched by John Simmons.
　　9. Wareham, *Wareham's Way*, pp. 103–115. The questions are reproduced or paraphrased, but the examples and explanations are original.

Chapter 3

　　1. Thomas A. Widiger and Allen J. Frances, "Controversies Concerning the Self-Defeating Personality Disorder," in Rebecca C. Curtis (ed.), *Self-Defeating Behaviors* (New York: Plenum Press, 1989), p. 304.

2. Adapted from Kenneth M. Golden, "Dealing with The Problem Manager," *Personnel*, August 1989, pp. 56–57.

3. Seth Allcorn, "The Narcissistic Manager," *Supervisory Management*, December 1989, pp. 29–32.

4. Howard Figler, "Help for the Obnoxious, Meek, and Ugly," *Managing Your Career* (published by *The Wall Street Journal*), Fall 1987, p. 39.

5. Morgan P. Slusher and Craig A. Anderson, "Belief Perseverance and Self-Defeating Behavior," in Curtis (ed.), *Self-Defeating Behaviors*, pp. 12–13.

6. Case researched by Stephen D. O'Malley.

7. Case researched by Allen H. Bauxbaum.

8. Case adapted from Michael E. Cavanagh, "Personalities at Work," *Personnel Journal*, March 1985, p. 56.

9. Case researched by Dean S. Blodgett.

10. Pauline Rose Clance, *The Imposter Phenomenon* (Atlanta: Peachtree Publishers, Ltd., 1985); Joan C. Harvey, *If I'm So Successful, Why Do I Feel Like Such a Fake?* (New York: St. Martin's Press, 1985).

11. Janice Castro, "Fearing the Mask May Slip," *Time*, August 12, 1985, p. 60.

Chapter 4

1. Theodore Kurtz, "Ten Reasons Why People Procrastinate," *Supervisory Management*, April 1990, pp. 1–2.

2. "Don't Procrastinate," *Practical Supervision*, January 1989, p. 3.

3. Neil Fiore, "How to Get Procrastinators Up to Speed," *Working Woman*, March 1989, p. 32.

4. Case researched by Terry Hill.

5. Case researched by Diana Baker.

6. Karen S. Peterson, "Holding Grudges Can Hold You Back," *USA Weekend*, October 18–20, 1985, p. 29.

7. Morgan W. McCall, Jr., and Michael M. Lombardo, "What Makes a Top Executive?" *Psychology Today*, February 1983, p. 28.

8. Case researched by Scott C. Gill.

Chapter 5

1. "The Downfall of a CEO," *Business Week*, February 16, 1987, pp. 77–79.

2. Ibid., p. 78.

3. Jay T. Knippen and Thad B. Green, "Building Self-Confidence," *Supervisory Management*, August 1989, pp. 22–27.

4. Wolf J. Rinke, "Maximizing Management Potential by Building Self-Esteem," *Management Solutions*, March 1988, p. 6.

5. Donnah Canavan, "Fear of Success," in Rebecca C. Curtis (ed.), *Self-Defeating Behaviors* (New York: Plenum Press, 1989), p. 166.

6. Case researched by Patricia L. Schofield.

7. Based on Carole Hyatt and Linda Gottlieb, *When Smart People Fail: Rebuilding Yourself for Success* (New York: Penguin Books, 1988), pp. 185–87.

8. Adapted from Raymond L. Higgins and C. R. Snyder, "Excuses Gone Awry: An Analysis of Self-Defeating Excuses," in Curtis (ed.), *Self-Defeating Behaviors*, pp. 99–100.

9. Ibid., p. 101.

10. Howard Raiffa, *The Art and Science of Negotiation* (Cambridge, Mass.: Harvard University Press, 1983).

11. Case researched by Kathleen Peart.

12. Albert J. Bernstein and Sydney Craft Rozen, *Dinosaur Brains: Dealing with All Those Impossible People at Work* (New York: John Wiley, 1989).

13. Case researched by John K. James.

14. Bernstein and Rozen, *Dinosaur Brains*, pp. 89–94.

15. Case researched by Marla C. Cwynar.

16. Case researched by Robert Moore.

Chapter 6

1. Manfred F. R. Kets de Vries, "Leaders Who Self-Destruct: The Causes and Cures," *Organizational Dynamics*, Spring 1989, pp. 6–9.

2. Ibid., pp. 10–11.

3. Case researched by Jeffrey H. Clark.

4. Quotation from Carole Hyatt and Linda Gottlieb, *When Smart People Fail: Rebuilding Yourself for Success* (New York: Penguin Books, 1988), p. 125.

5. Case researched by Sheryl D. Towne.

6. Eric G. Flamholtz and Yvonne Randle, *The Inner Game of Management: How to Make the Transition to a Managerial Role* (New York: AMACOM, 1987), pp. 117–18.

7. Ibid., pp. 131–32. This and the next two sections borrow heavily from Flamholtz and Randle, *The Inner Game.*

8. Ibid., pp. 56–70.

9. Ibid., p. 67.

10. Ibid., p. 102.

Chapter 7

1. Case researched by Wilma E. Wandersleben.
2. Stuart M. Schmidt and David Kipnis, "The Perils of Persistence," *Psychology Today*, November 1987, pp. 32–34.
3. Case researched by Jean M. Scholl.
4. Case researched by Donald C. Buffum, Jr.
5. "Snap Back from a Blunder," *Executive Strategies*, February 6, 1990, p. 1.

Chapter 8

1. This section of the chapter follows quite closely Post's "Self-Sabotage Among Successful Women," *Psychotherapy in Private Practice* 6, no. 3 (1988): 192–94.
2. Ibid., 199–204.
3. Facts as reported in, and paraphrased from, Jim Schater, "Daddy Dearest," *Los Angeles Times* syndicated story, October 28, 1989.
4. Case researched by Christine B. Long.
5. Case researched by Roberta Fulton.

Chapter 9

1. Reported by Lori Ioannou, "Kick the Failure Habit," *Success*, April 1990, p. 46.
2. Michael E. Cavanagh, "Myths Surrounding Alcoholism," *Personnel Journal*, February 1990, p. 112.
3. Quoted by Jeffrey Lynn Speller, *Executive in Crisis* (New York: John Wiley, 1989), p. 4.
4. Cavanagh, "Myths Surrounding Alcoholism," p. 118.
5. Based on information in Andrew J. DuBrin and R. Duane Ireland, *Management and Organization* (Cincinnati: South-Western Publishing Co., 1989), p. 430.
6. Michael E. Cavanagh, "The Dilemma of Legal Drug Abuse," *Personnel Journal*, March 1990, p. 124.
7. Based on the facts from two cases presented in Cavanagh, "Dilemma of Legal Drug Abuse."
8. Constance Holden, "Against All Odds," *Psychology Today*, December 1985, p. 33.
9. Analysis by Henry Lesieur, cited in "The 'Pete Rose Syndrome': Managing a Compulsive Gambler," *Personal Report for the Executive*, September 15, 1989, p. 2.
10. Alexander P. Blaszczynski, "A Winning Bet: Treatment for Compulsive Gambling," *Psychology Today*, December 1985, p. 42.
11. Case researched by Renée Rhodey.

Chapter 10

1. Case researched by Coleen M. Dugan.
2. Case researched by Geoffrey Reynolds.
3. Case researched by Kimberly A. Conti.
4. Case researched by Anne Gravenstede.
5. Case researched by Thomas G. Strauss.
6. Case researched by Daniel M. O'Connell.
7. Many of these guidelines are from Gloria Welles, "Love in the Office," *USA Weekend*, April 24–26, 1987, p. 10.
8. David E. Terpstra, "Who Gets Sexually Harrassed?" *Personnel Administrator*, March 1989, p. 85.

Chapter 11

1. Don Cole, *Professional Suicide or Organizational Murder?* 2d ed. (Cleveland, OH: The Organization Development Institute, 1989), p. xi.
2. Ibid.
3. Adapted from Cole, p. 76.
4. Adapted from Don Cole, "Professional Suicide or Organizational Murder?" Unpublished article, 1989.
5. Larry A. Pace and Stanley J. Smits, "When Managers Are Substance Abusers," *Personnel Journal*, July 1989, p. 70.
6. Based on Cole, *Professional Suicide*, pp. 140–47.

Chapter 12

1. Robert Bell, *Surviving the 10 Ordeals of the Takeover* (New York: AMACOM, 1988), p. 123.
2. Donald W. Cole, *Professional Suicide or Organizational Murder?*, 2d ed. (Cleveland, OH: The Organization Development Institute, 1989), p. 142.
3. Diane Swanbrow, "The Paradox of Happiness," *Psychology Today*, July/August 1989, p. 38.
4. This material is based on Maury M. Breecher, "C'mon Smile!" *Los Angeles Times*, October 3, 1982; and Swanbrow, "The Paradox of Happiness."

Index